POLY LAND

MY BRUTALLY HONEST ADVENTURES IN POLYAMORY

POLY LAND

MY BRUTALLY HONEST ADVENTURES
IN POLYAMORY

PAGE TURNER

Braided Studios, LLC
PO Box 770670
Lakewood, OH 44107
https://braided.studio

Published By: Braided Studios, LLC

ISBN: 978-1-947296-00-8

Thanks to those who read this book early:

Elan

Elizabeth

Matt

Tom

-

A special thanks to our Patreons

Jeff & Elan

This is a work of creative non-fiction. Significant liberties have been taken to protect the innocent and the filthy. I put the story first, and recommend you do too.

Polyamory (n.) –

the practice of participating simultaneously in more than one serious romantic or sexual relationship with the knowledge and consent of all partners.

THE PARTY

I t's amazing how quickly things change. Or how a single piece of information can make such a difference, even when essentially nothing's really changed at all.

After years of working crappy jobs for crappy pay, my husband Seth and I were finally starting to gain some traction. We took turns going back to school. I went first and earned an associate's degree and now had a good job that paid well.

After two years of taking gen eds at community college, Seth had cleaned up his grades enough to qualify for admission to the University of Maine. The only obstacle was the 40-minute drive each way.

In good weather, it was a minor annoyance, but in blizzard conditions, an inevitability with Maine winters, exacerbated further by Seth's gun shy attitude towards bad roads, such a commute would certainly mean absences and, by extension, failure. To deal with this preemptively, he and I moved to an apartment near the university.

We wanted to make the new place feel as much like home as possible, so we threw a party. It was impromptu, last minute, so only John, Megan, and Tara could make it, but a gathering of five would make for a good time. Not a full-on rager or anything, but more booze for the rest of us.

And drink we did. Seth had always been a heavyweight when it came to alcohol tolerance, but the other four of us were anything but, and before long, we'd all loosened up considerably, and as the conversation ebbed and flowed, it seemed the right time to address with Megan something I'd been rolling around in my head for a while. I had noticed that her husband, Pete, was acting strangely with a female coworker and started to suspect he was having an affair.

As I began to voice my concerns about some of Pete's behavior, she started to laugh and stopped me.

"He's seeing her," Megan said. "But he has my permission. One hundred percent."

She explained that they had a polyamorous relationship and that their marriage had been open for over a year. Because of childcare issues and her work obligations, their schedule really only allowed Pete to have relationships, but she assured me that she was happy for her husband and that his seeing other people had added a lot of passion to their relationship.

I was riveted, floored by the revelation. Megan and Pete had been our friends for years.

It wasn't that the idea of ethical non-monogamy as a format for long-term relationships had never occurred to me. I'd run into it a few times in my travels.

At 17, attending summer jazz workshops, I made friends with a hippie gentleman in his late 50's (a jazz violinist) who had an open marriage and informed me that if I'd been 18, he would have liked to date me.

A few years later, I had a boyfriend who had formerly been in a 2-year relationship with two women, the three of them committed and living together as a unit. I was also quite familiar with swingers, no strings attached one-night stands, and drunken party orgies.

What was mind boggling was how invisible the nontraditional arrangement had been, low drama and harmonious to the point that this had been going on for a while, and I'd never known or sensed that there was "any trouble in paradise."

And if anything, Megan and Pete had seemed *more* conservative than Seth and me. Like Barbie had married GI Joe and had 2 kids from a cereal commercial.

This was shocking.

I'd like to say I was extremely mature, open minded, and instantly accepting of her open marriage.

That, however, would be a lie.

It was the first time I'd even heard the word "polyamory." This was 2009. In rural Maine.

I was pretty skeptical.

We poured more drinks, chatted a bit more. Already low inhibitions limboed even lower as the liquor flowed.

"I've always wondered what it'd be like to kiss another girl," Megan said to me. "You're always talking about your ex-girlfriends, and I get so jealous."

"Oh? You've never kissed a girl?" I said. "It's... nice. It's different than kissing guys but the same. I know, helpful, right?"

"Oh my fucking God already!" Seth said. "You two should *totally* kiss."

"Yes," John agreed. "For... science."

"For totally hot science," Seth added.

"Well, I'm all for education, but..." I hesitated. But? But why? Why was I so nervous? What was my problem? Seth didn't have a problem with it. He was actively encouraging me. And I'd had a crush on Megan for ages. Still, I floundered.

For one, I've never been a fan of girl-on-girl action as a performance to turn men on. To me, it's unwelcome objectification that demeans the authenticity of the physical connection that I've felt with other women by turning it into some kind of show. Not only that, but I still had serious reservations about being non-exclusive, even casually, recreationally, in a party setting.

Then Megan made it easy for me. "Honestly, I'd rather kiss Tara," Megan said. "No offense, Page."

"It's fine," I said. "We all have our preferences."

I was hardly surprised. Tara was young and beautiful, tall and lean with curves in all the right places prancing around in heels and hot pants with legs that went on forever.

But even though I wasn't surprised, it still hurt.

After years of telecommuting from home at a desk job, I'd packed on the pounds and was a rather large woman. I wore a size 26. I was jovial and friendly, to be sure, but hardly a picture of the sexual ideal, waddling around in sweat pants and sneakers with the laces untied. Most people in Megan's situation would have preferred Tara.

But before I knew what happened, I was pounced, and it was Tara that was kissing me, her arms locked around me, her tongue exploring my mouth. It was surreal but glorious. She was drunk and forceful, but her passion was evident, and I melted into the first kiss I'd shared with a woman in over 8 years. I don't know how long it lasted. It felt like forever and yet ended much too soon. When it was over, I kissed her on the forehead and said, "Wow. Thank you."

"Now you two kiss," John said, gesturing to Tara and Megan. They did. I watched them, still reeling with desire from kissing Tara. Megan's hands traveled all over Tara's body, feeling her shape as Tara moaned into her mouth. It was amazingly erotic.

"And you two," John said, connecting Megan and me.

I felt my heart leap up into my throat in anticipation. My face burned with desire. The first kiss with Tara, a friend that I'd always held in a more sisterly light, had been amazing. The prospect of kissing Megan, who was my long-time crush, someone I'd fantasized about on occasion, was exquisite.

We kissed. And it was absolutely awful.

I excused myself after the kiss to get another drink.

John decided at that point he wanted to get home to his girlfriend, that the festivities were making it very difficult to not misbehave. Seth dragged me off to the bedroom, where he proceeded to tackle me.

As we were getting down to business, we heard Tara and Megan having quite a good time themselves in the living room, which only fueled our fire.

It wasn't quite an orgy but not too far from it.

COMPLICATIONS

Nothing like that had ever happened at one of our parties. That night became an instant legend. Which is not to say that things didn't become complicated in the days and weeks following.

Megan reached out to Tara afterwards to see if she'd like to continue a physical relationship, but Tara was mortified when she sobered up. She was straight, totally not into girls, didn't know what had come over her.

Once a regular at our get-togethers, Tara started avoiding hanging out at our place for poker or game nights.

I couldn't say I blamed her. As news of Megan and Pete's open marriage spread through our group of friends, that night was a topic of constant conversation.

"We should all become swingers!" Dan said. He wished he'd been there that night.

John proposed an adult slumber party, a free-for-all, where we'd set up a space to explore one another, establish some ground rules about what activities were acceptable and which ones weren't, and just go to town.

Dan was gung ho.

While I thought it could be fun for sure, I had reservations about the wisdom of such a venture, the possible ramifications to all of our friendships. There was already fall out from what little had happened at the first party as Tara was obviously upset and uncomfortable.

With more people on board, the risk of people getting hurt or things becoming awkward increased exponentially. I wasn't alone in this. Seth and Megan agreed that as much as fun as a sleepover sounded in theory, it was likely to end badly.

It soon became little more than an intellectual exercise when John's girlfriend vetoed the whole thing.

It started to seem like things were more or less back to normal since that wild night. Really, the only things that had changed were that Tara had started laying low, and Megan and I became closer friends. Relieved at finally not having to hide that she and Pete were open, Megan and I talked frequently, discussing some of the challenges and frustrations involved with her job and lonely nights spent taking care of the kids while Peter was out with his girlfriend.

Threesome talks aside, after being together for so long on our own and strictly monogamous, Seth and I privately rushed to judgment of their relationship. We pretty much took the attitude of "How could he do that to her?" and were passive aggressively angry at Pete and felt bad for Megan.

After all, she *did* seem really lonely. We took her out to dinner, had her over to watch movies with us, and would spend long nights until the sun came up talking to her about everything.

Through getting to know Megan better, we realized that their situation worked for them and that she was actually happy – and we were both falling for her. I'd of course had a crush on her for quite a while, but other than that awkward kiss the night of the party, I hadn't acted on it or even said that much about my feelings for her.

It was an even bigger shift for Seth, who though knowing her for years had not thought of her that way. Then all of a sudden, Seth and I were having discussions about whether he and I wanted to bring up the idea of a relationship with Megan.

There were a number of reasons why it wasn't an easy decision to approach Megan with the idea of dating Seth and me.

For starters, I was heavier than I'd ever been in my whole life. I was riddled with intense pain so crippling that I couldn't walk across a room without wincing, cringing, grunting in pain, and sitting down quickly for an extended rest. I would sprain my ankle routinely in my normal daily routine. At 5 feet 6 inches, I weighed well over 300 pounds.

I've never been a terribly visual person with regard to other people and have struggled with some degree of body dysmorphia my whole life. Self-love and body acceptance were things I'd worked extensively on – to the point where I'd completely tuned out the weight gain. Before I realized what had happened, this pseudo-zen disconnect from my weight coupled with my penchant for amazing servings of Hamburger Helper and Doritos had made me in a prisoner in my own body.

One day, I couldn't take it anymore. As I worked as a medical transcriptionist and often transcribed notes for a bariatric medicine group as part of my job, I knew a lot about gastric bypass surgery. However, instead of beginning that process, I wanted to give diet and exercise a full-fledged effort. I figured if that alone didn't work, then I would enroll in the bariatric surgery program.

Contrary to what I hear a lot of people say, I don't view gastric bypass as the "easy way" out. It's a multistep process, and actually quite a lot of work goes into it on the part of the patient. It was more that I've never had surgery and didn't want to start now unless I absolutely had to – that and the commitment to permanent anatomical changes in my digestive tract made me nervous.

Still I wanted to give it extreme effort – so I wanted a very strict diet that would be safe for someone of my size. I took the diet that the nutritionists put gastric bypass patients on in the months leading up to the surgery and modified it to be lower carb and higher in healthy fats but still with very controlled calories and portions. I also bought myself an exercise bike and started to only let myself watch TV shows while I was riding it.

I'd started this process about a month before and had already lost 20 pounds and was starting to feel good, but I was still extremely overweight and far from feeling my most attractive.

There was also the issue of my battles with jealousy and insecurity. It's tough to know from where exactly these feelings stem. I'm sure the fact that I was one of four children and therefore always had to share and compete for my parents' attention didn't help. Part of what I loved about having a romantic partner was that feeling of unlimited access, that I always had someone to talk to when I needed or to go to dinner or simple things like that.

And it didn't help that my mother clearly had serious issues with jealousy and insecurity.

My mother was an incredibly beautiful woman, but she never felt confident about it or secure. Instead, she was so defensive that she saw threats everywhere and would attack them at the slightest provocation. Mom frequently insulted other women's appearances. "Look at her, what a slob." Women who she thought looked attractive were called "airheads" or "sluts."

She worried incessantly that my father (a rather quiet, unassuming man much more interested in machines than in people) had cheated on her or was about to.

She didn't allow my father to view pornography or even racier R-rated movies. If any nudity came on the screen (like the strip club scenes in dad's beloved buddy cop movies), she would get up and cover it with her hand so he couldn't see.

And I still remember the time Mom found a Hooters receipt in my dad's jacket. He'd gone there with coworkers for dinner on a work trip. But she didn't care. To her, it signaled betrayal. That he was ogling other women.

My parents were normally the kind of people whose anger was quiet and cold. But when she found that Hooters receipt, she screamed at him and disappeared for two days, without telling any of us where she was going. When Mom did come back, she punished him with the silent treatment and barred him from their bed for weeks.

Growing up, I'd had this kind of behavior modeled for me again and again.

I'd also been privy to the weird rivalries that can spring up between women. I'd experience it with ex-girlfriends who'd complain about the discrepancies between the sizes of our breasts or hips or with female friends who would turn on me at the drop of a hat due to some perceived threat.

I tried to explain this to Seth, how many women were competitive with other women and would play these games of invisible power struggle, but he told me he'd never seen such a thing and that I was clearly paranoid and imagining it, but then again he hadn't grown up as a woman, or with two older sisters. It gives you a distinctly different perspective.

But polyamory, ethical non-monogamy, appealed to me in a way that the idea of having purely physical threesomes or extramarital sex just didn't. For me, I found sex the most enjoyable when I could be vulnerable with partners and build intimacy and really bond. I'd learned early on that trust could easily be abused in casual hook-ups.

I'll never forget that night. November 1999, my first semester of college.

I had gone to a party hosted by the music frat. I knew a lot of people there because I played in the jazz ensemble and orchestra, even though I wasn't in any Greek groups. I was there with Jay, this beautiful genderqueer boy I had met through the atheist group on campus (having become quite enamored with secular ethics), a dear friend with benefits. We'd had a few wine coolers back in Jay's dorm after making out, discussing philosophy and scripture and cuddling and then walked across campus. I genuinely enjoyed Jay's company. He was funny and handsome, and I wasn't quite sure where all we were going, but it was very exciting not knowing.

By the time we got to the party, everyone was way more blazed than we were. There's a kind of laughter that gives a party away. We got there just in time to see a trumpet player

I knew emerging from his bedroom to loud cheers from the crowd. "I banged that skank," he yelled pointing into his room.

I saw a vocal major push past him to leave, clutching her clothes around her. "Fuck you," she said. At least I think that's what she said. She was crying, and it happened really fast. Once she was gone, there was laughter. A few of the other guys gave the trumpet player high fives. The group of them proceeded to bad mouth the vocalist.

Before I knew it, my world was spinning, and I was profoundly nauseated. It was odd. I hadn't had much to drink. I gripped the couch, laid my head down. Jay and a friend of his (this gorgeous blond actress we both had the hots for) coaxed me outside to smoke with them. I didn't know it then, but that was my first clearcut anxiety attack. And the stimulus was disrespect.

Genuine disrespect. Not play humiliation: "Oh, dirty whore, you like it up the ass, don't you? You're filthy. You have to beg me to fuck you," yadda yadda, kinkster foreplay. But, "I'm going to lure you in, make you trust me, and then betray you." OR "I'm going to hurt you, and then I'm going to harm you. And it'll be the world's biggest fucking joke."

I remember how difficult it was later that night to focus when Jay and I were naked, how I kept returning to the disgust and the shame on the vocalist's face, the genuine cruelty on the trumpet player's. And yet, no one else had seemed the slightest bit affected by what they had seen.

In a lot of ways, Jay was my first poly relationship, though neither of us called it that – or called it anything, really. It was a warm, loving connection with no expectations of exclusivity – we acted as each other's confidants and sounding boards. I held him as he talked about the girl he'd left back home, who'd broke up with him when he went away to school. I sorted through the guilt I had from recently breaking up with my fiance. We went to hockey games together, went out for pizza, hit on some of the same girls – with varied rates of success.

Jay was happy for me when I went to a talent show with a great girl who was covering it for the campus newspaper. And Jay was happy for me again when that date went well, so well in fact that the girl I'd gone out with invited me to write alongside her at the campus paper.

And I was happy when he had good dates, good encounters, supported him as he explored the varied facets of his sexuality.

He took it in stride when a cast party for a show I'd written got steamy, and I'd had quite a group adventure – all of which he'd missed, home for the weekend visiting his parents. We were loving and supportive – but pretty damn casual about it. No games. No dishonesty. And always respect.

He and I eventually drifted apart. We were still friends but found ourselves physically intimate less and less. We moved on to other partners, other lives. To be quite honest, I had a lot friends in college and lost track of Jay altogether. I'm not even sure where he ended up, but I still think highly of him to this day.

I guess that's what I liked about poly. The respect. I found a lack of that in random hook-ups, the drunken one-night stands. I didn't think relationships always needed to be serious – but I wanted them to be respectful.

Our decision to have a relationship with Megan was almost sabotaged when one evening, tired from a long day at work and wearied from my conflicting emotions towards our desire to bring a relationship with Megan into the picture, jealousy, insecurity, excitement, and attraction, I decided I didn't want to make the trip with Seth out to watch movies at Megan and Pete's house (a 40-minute car ride).

Seth was excited to see her and still wanted to go. I was torn. I needed time to re-energize, but I didn't necessarily want to be alone in the apartment all night, and I worried about it causing me to stew all night, growing jealous, resentful, and bitter, feeling replaced.

I tried to explain this to Seth, that I didn't want to be alone. He asked me what I was afraid of, but I couldn't tell him. So much of it I simply couldn't put my finger on, and the rest I could barely admit to myself, let alone him.

To make matters worse, Seth had always been a low-jealousy individual and didn't understand the torment involved with the worry, the blind terror that I wasn't good enough, Megan was better, and that at the first opportunity he'd leave me.

As irrational as it may have sounded to him, or just about anybody else who knew us, it was 100% real to me and my emotional reality. I felt like I was gambling my happiness, the one thing that really mattered to me, trying to win a prize that only he cared about. Ultimately, I cared about it only by association, by virtue of my caring for him and consequently caring deeply about what he cared about.

At the same time, I was fighting a fierce internal battle against my core values. My picture of romantic love was intense, complicated, and exclusive. The exclusivity was key. It added to the sense that such connections were "special." I worried by sharing that with more than one person that it would dilute those feelings, make the connections less intense and more impersonal. Or worse yet, Seth would realize that what he thought was love for me was a mere infatuation and, with his newfound perspective, leave me.

I got my first taste of it that night, when after a heated back and forth with Seth escalated to the point where he stormed out of the apartment, angry, his final words, "Well, fine! I'm just going to go off and fuck Megan then!"

I was stunned, collapsed to my knees, crying, trying to figure out what had gone wrong, what I'd said that set him off, but I was in too much pain to think. It was only 6:00, but I didn't want to be awake any longer. I'd had enough of this day, and it had been a long week in general, and an early night in could do me some good. I brewed myself some Valerian root tea to drink and took some Benadryl and lay down to sleep.

A bit later, I came to, in the middle of a conversation I was having with Seth on my cell phone. Stuck between sleep and waking, I wasn't even sure what we were talking about, only that it was him. I felt myself drifting off again and then was shaken awake by Seth.

He said I'd dialed him while I was asleep, and concerned by the strange things I was saying, he'd turned the car around and came home. I was groggy but explained the best I could what I'd taken, how much, and when. Safe doses, but apparently the substances were interacting with each other, causing an altered mental status.

Seth got me some coffee. With the caffeine in my system, I still felt fuzzy and "off" but definitely more with it. Seth apologized for the way he'd left, and in that haze, my mind working in slow motion, I was finally able to articulate what I'd been trying to say when we'd gotten into our fight.

Serendipitously, Megan texted Seth, let us know she was running late, one of her staff had called off, and she had to stay but that she'd be home in another hour.

"What do you think?" Seth said. "You game?"

"Sure," I said. And we went out to Megan's house that night together.

With so many reservations, that surely would have been the end of it for a lot of people.

The trouble was, as worried as I was, I didn't have any actual experience with polyamorous relationships, so any concerns I had were theoretical, unsubstantiated.

I was afraid. That much was true. I was terrified of losing the only stable relationship I'd ever had. It would have been easy to surrender to the fear, to say "it won't work, and it'll ruin our marriage," but cutting through the bullshit and being brutally honest with myself, I was able to realize that it was largely fear of the unknown.

It was a lot like my fear of snakes.

I cannot remember a time that I wasn't terrified of snakes. One of my earliest memories is of the summer my family lived in Buffalo in company housing, technically an efficiency, but for our family of six, it served as little more than a glorified hotel room.

I was three years old, so much of that time is represented by singular images taken out of context, flashes, an abstract collage of miscellany I connect with but without explanation as to why, but one memory is very clear, intense: A black snake has infiltrated our home. My sisters, eight and nine, are screaming at the top of their lungs. I jump up onto the bed. My mother grabs a broom to sweep it towards the door. She is screaming, too. I curl up into a ball on the bed and cover my head, overcome with sheer terror. And the memory cuts out.

To this day, when a snake emerges, I jump up, let out a blood curdling scream, and run as far away as I possibly can. It is a completely irrational response, visceral, instant, reflexive. Zero thought goes into this intense fear. I spent my formative years in Central Maine, a climate in which only the garter snake, usually of modest size, can live. They are completely non-lethal to humans, and if anything, they're largely helpful for gardening because they eat insects and rats and other pests.

But the fear doesn't negotiate. It just exists, grips me, throws me into a state where I have no control.

For years, I tried desperately to minimize my exposure to snakes. Back in the day, I purchased a trailer with a beautiful garden. I was thrilled to get the opportunity to try my hand at maintaining the plot – that was until the night I met the baby garter snake who was living there.

I was seized with terror; I gave up on rifling around in there, let the weeds set in, tried to walk at a quick pace past the garden and avert my eyes to not risk catching even a glimpse of the snake.

I never walked barefoot on my property again.

It's natural to avoid the things we fear.

Seeking out what terrifies me seems insane on a certain level, but more and more, the longer I'm alive, I find myself drawn to my most intense feelings, both good and bad. It seems that they are screaming out to me for a reason and that I have to know what they're trying to say.

Some of my biggest rushes in life have come from having buttons pushed that took me well beyond the limits of comfort, skating off into the unknown.

And much of my personal growth over the last few years has come from making the life decisions that made the most sense to me regardless of how much anxiety they provoked.

I suppose fear should be an instructive reaction, a helpful instinctive way of knowing that danger is near, that I ought to modify my behavior to match the situation, and yet, the more I challenge it, the more I discover that often it's a false alarm, a paralytic, an emotional immune system gone into overdrive, cannibalizing my happiness.

I reached the point where I decided no more of this: I do not belong to fear; I refuse to be its slave.

I've often had nightmares about snakes. Usually, a lawn is crawling with snakes of all colors, like a tropical rainbow of the fake ones you get at the dollar store, huge jungle serpents completely saturating the mowed grass. I have to get from the street to the house, get indoors, and I am barefoot. I leap across the lawn, landing on my toes, springing from point to point, my brain grappling to wrestle lucid control of the scenario and warp me onto the steps.

Sometimes they bite me; the poison weakens me; I collapse on the lawn and pass out, ostensibly to be devoured.

Sometimes I make it across the lawn, bitten up, but my feet are hopelessly damaged, and I worry I'll never walk again.

On the rare occasion, I wake up before anything bad happens, or I manage to intervene on my dream and warp myself onto the porch, unscathed.

They were dreams I've dreaded, that cast bitterness over days that should start out as neutral.

I wasn't going to dread them anymore. I welcomed the challenge, hoped I'd dream of the snakes.

The next time, I'd lie down with them as they slithered harmlessly over me, barely registering my presence, feeling the grass in my fingers and my own breath moving through me.

I was terrified of opening my marriage to outside influence. Because it was the center of my life and meant more than anything.

But as I thought through my fears, I realized something: Testing that bond was a win-win scenario.

Best case, we would weather the challenges, and I would have a wealth of experiences and emotional bonds with others that could complement my life.

Worst case, I was wrong about the strength of what Seth and I had together, and it would tear us apart.

But if what we had were that easily ruined, was it really all that great in the first place?

And wouldn't I want to know now, 4 years into the marriage, rather than another 20 or 30 years down the road?

And with that, I was on board, ready to leap in the unknown. Or at least ready to have a very awkward conversation.

But how to start?

"Excuse me, ma'am. I know we've been acquainted for 4 years, and every time the prospect of swinging and open relationships has come up in conversation, I've weighed in as staunchly monogamous. I see that you don't seem at all physically attracted to me, and we've shared an awkward kiss we'd probably both just soon forget, and you and my husband have even less of a connection, but how would you like to be our girlfriend?"

Yeah, not so much.

Even after coming to a consensus that we wanted to attempt a relationship with Megan, it was tough to know how to proceed. After being friends for so many years and sharing many mutual friends, the last thing I wanted was for things to get awkward, so I thought a more subtle approach would be best.

New to ethical non-monogamy, I was out of my depth as to how a person (or a couple, in our case) "wooed" a potential partner or made their romantic interest known within this other framework, this new relationship paradigm, so I simply went with what I knew. I tried to signal my interest through actions and observed how Megan responded.

These days, I probably would just tell her, but back then, I had far more lessons to learn about open, honest communication in relationships.

No, instead we came over late and cooked her stir-fries and played racing games with her on the Wii, like always, but this time, I tried putting my legs next to hers on the couch and gauging her reaction. She didn't flinch, didn't move, and if anything, I felt like she enjoyed the closeness.

However, I knew nothing for sure. The tension was intense and the results I got back from my little experiments frustrating and ambiguous.

Finally, we just broke down and told her. She was reluctant, admitted that while she valued our friendship that she didn't feel much for physical attraction towards either of us.

She also expressed concern that being it was our first experience dating a third party that there were bound to be bumps in the road and that she couldn't bear to be the cause of any problems in our marriage.

Seth and I set her mind at ease, said worst case scenario she might have to attend a few sessions of marriage counseling with us should things go horribly awry.

Megan said she was comfortable with that level of risk and was willing to keep an open mind about the possibility of physical attraction developing as things progressed.

And with that, the triad was formed.

The first time we all got together after that, things were subtly different. Megan dropped by our apartment noticeably more dolled up than I was used to her seeing.

We ordered in some Thai food, ate our curries and chatted politely, but the tension was palpable. The elephant in the room was making it impossible to focus.

Seth put on a movie, one his favorites, Ingmar Berman's *The Seventh Seal*. As the movie progressed, Megan and I gradually came together, cuddling on the couch. By the time the movie had ended, she was sitting between my legs, and I was holding her from behind, massaging her shoulders.

I'd been resisting kissing her neck for quite a while and, in a distracted moment, simply forgot to resist. Before I knew it, my hands had wandered up her shirt, undoing her bra, caressing her breasts.

I looked up to see that Seth was watching up, completely rapt and clearly aroused. I could clearly see he wanted to join in but had no idea how to proceed.

"You two should kiss," I said. Immediately, I felt a bolt of adrenaline. What had I just said? Watch my husband kiss another girl in front of me? What if I freaked out? I had worked it out intellectually in my head and was okay with it in theory, but what if I had a violent gut reaction? What would I do then?

But it was too late. Seth and Megan were kissing.

And much to my surprise, it was wonderful. Two people I cared about were sharing a passionate moment. I couldn't take my eyes off them. Not only was it sexy but heartwarming. I was right when I thought that watching them kiss would stir up strong feelings within me – but they were strong *positive* feelings.

I had just experienced compersion for the very first time.

POLY SIGNPOST #1: COMPERSION

O ver the course of this book, I'll occasionally stop at signposts to take a break from the story and talk about certain subjects in more detail.

Compersion is so fantastic and ever-present for me that it gets to go first in these signposts.

I've included a basic definition below (quick, rough definition of compersion is "the opposite of jealousy"):

> "Compersion is a state of empathetic happiness and joy experienced when an individual's current or former romantic partner experiences happiness and joy through an outside source, including, but not limited to, another romantic interest. This can be experienced as any form of erotic or emotional empathy, depending on the person experiencing the emotion"

> "Compersion." *Wikipedia*: The Free Encyclopedia. Wikimedia Foundation, Inc. 27 July 2012. Web. 6 Aug. 2012.

There's another, much older word for this specific feeling in Buddhism, *mudita*, the Sanskrit word for unselfish joy, delight at the happiness of others, but "compersion" is generally the word poly people use to describe it when communicating with one another.

Compersion is awesome.

The warm glow I felt in my chest the first time I saw Seth kiss Megan took me completely off-guard, but it was unmistakable. Or when later I'd come home from a night out with friends and see them snuggled up on the couch watching *Dexter*. They were adorable, and I was happy for them.

I had no cultural models for this and before experiencing it had never even heard of compersion. But once I was actually *in* the situation, I found I liked seeing Megan and Seth together. A lot.

I liked seeing people around me happy, even if I wasn't the direct cause of it.

And as I continued to explore ethical non-monogamy, I would feel compersion in a dizzying array of situations (some of which are in this book).

But even as the surroundings changed, one thing remained the same: Compersion? Pretty damn awesome.

Cultivating compersion successfully can lead to genuinely feeling happy for your loves' successes in non-romantic/ non-sexual situations.

Lover gets that job they wanted? Warm bubbly feeling. Finishes their degree? Warm bubbly feeling. Has a good nap? Warm bubbly feeling. You name it.

It's not all about just hanky panky. Being able to celebrate in a loved one's joy is a powerful and wonderful thing, and I find it does wonders for the relationships I'm in, regardless of the number of them going on simultaneously.

Cultivating compersion successfully can lead to genuinely feeling happy for people who are not your partners (be they friends, acquaintances, or even strangers) in non-romantic/ non-sexual situations.

I find myself cheering when I hear good things are happening to my friends.

I jumped up and down when a friend bought his first house.

I glow for days when a friend gets a new job they like.

Feeling happy for other people results in feeling happiness frequently and being more happy in general. I feel this every day.

The change within me has been remarkable. I used to be a very zero-sum thinker. Before when good things happened to other people, I'd be envious, feel like it was just another bit of evidence to underscore my relative failure.

I came to realize that sort of bitterness is just arrogance. Other people's happiness is not an attack on me. It's a triumph for them.

That alone is a huge blessing, that alone is worth so much of the work that poly relationships took, the fantastic journey I went on.

SETH

I met my future husband Seth at a weird time in my life, having reluctantly moved back in with my parents after my last relationship exploded spectacularly.

The whole thing had started out as a joke. Seth was frustrated with his love life, sick of being single, watching everybody around him go out on dates and fall in love while he spent his days working tech support at a call center and his nights on *EverQuest* raids.

"That's it," Seth announced one day. "I'm going to need to form a committee to get me laid."

And so The Committee to Get Seth Laid was born.

The committee immediately declared I was a prime candidate (I've never known whether to be flattered or insulted by this). I hear they warned him that I was a bit of a wild child, sexually liberated.

After a stint in rehab, I was mostly dried up but only mostly, though I seemed to be on the upswing, on my way to a sober life. Talking with me, they made sure it was okay with me that he was a bit chubby. At that point, I was dating mostly gaunt stoners with messiah complexes.

I told them I didn't really have a type as far as body types go and that the boys I dated in high school were bigger guys. We were good to go.

It was an incredibly awkward meeting.

It didn't help that it was the very first blind date I had ever been on, and while first dates are bad enough, blind dates are inherently nerve-wracking affairs. I had virtually no information about Seth, other than a few stories our friends had told me and a photograph I'd been shown.

To make matters worse, we were introduced in a haphazard way, in which our friends basically just invited us both over at the same time in one of their dorm rooms, and we all hung out together. The expectation that we were being set up hung awkwardly in the air. Everyone knew it. No one acknowledged it.

Seth and I feigned ignoring each other for the first hour or so, avoiding eye contact, speaking to others, but each trying to discreetly listen in while the other was talking to another friend. It was hellish.

Eventually, we were getting hungry, so the gang piled into Seth's car to ride to the grocery store to get stuff to make pizza in the dorm's basement kitchen.

Seth and I barely spoke during the shopping trip or while cooking or eating. I'd consciously been trying to initiate more eye contact with him, engaged him in conversation but kept on floundering. It's hard enough to get to know someone one on one; surrounded by 6 mutual friends watching your every move with great interest like you're on reality TV, the difficulty level climbs a bit.

Usually an outgoing person, my nerves crescendoed, and I shut down. Shyness overtook me. Weary of the experience and its challenges, I sat at the basement piano and played a few of my compositions.

"What are you playing?" Seth asked me.

"Just some stuff I wrote," I replied, all too aware of everyone's eyes on us.

"She's self-taught!" one of my friends piped in.

I got up, shrugged, embarrassed. "Kind of," I said. I pulled on my coat and walked towards the stairs.

"Where are you going?" Another of my friends asked.

"To take a walk," I said. "It's too hot in here. I need to think."

"That sounds like a great idea," Seth said, to my surprise. "Mind if I join you?"

We walked all over campus that night under the stars, talking about our friends, our interests, our lives.

"I have very few deal breakers," I told him.

"Oh?"

"How do you feel about gay rights?" I asked.

He was for them. Virtually all of my friends were, so this wasn't a huge surprise, but I'd wanted to make sure before I got emotionally invested.

I explained that it was a key issue of mine, being supportive and accepting of alternative sexuality. I was bisexual, and my oldest sister, who I loved dearly, was gay, and I simply wouldn't tolerate bigotry on the basis of sexual orientation.

He got that familiar gleam I had seen in the past at the mention of "bisexual," and I added, "I'm totally monogamous though. One person at a time. It wouldn't really affect our relationship you and I would have."

By the time we got back to the dorm, about an hour later, I was much more relaxed and really starting to like him. We made plans to hang out with our friends together the next day.

And that following night, as everyone around us had fallen asleep, the two of us kissed while watching *American Beauty* on the world's flimsiest futon.

And like that, The Committee to Get Seth Laid disbanded, the motion tabled until further notice.

Seth and I started to date regularly, seeing each other nearly every day. It seemed the next logical step, partnering up, becoming exclusive. All my friends were pairing up with each other, breaking off into couples. Group gatherings were becoming less and less frequent, and my friends prioritized their romantic relationships much more highly than the friendships I had with them.

Before I met Seth, I'd been forced to spend more and more time alone when friends would ditch me last minute to spend time with their boyfriends. I wanted my own companion, someone I could count on.

Not only that, but I was sick of living with my parents and couldn't afford a place on my own with the entry level jobs I could get as a student. I decided my partying days were behind me, and it was time to start building a reliable support system, and I saw that potential with Seth.

He was a lot different than the guys (or girls) I usually dated, but I took this as a good sign. After all, my dating resume had a glaring number of abusive or unhealthy relationships. It was clearly time to try something different.

Sure, I got frustrated on our third date when I came over to his place with the expectation of going out to dinner with him, like we planned, and instead spent 4 hours lying on his bed talking to him while he played *EverQuest*, his Plane of Hate raid going into unanticipated overtime. But I'd been through worse with partners. When it was over, it was too late to go to dinner, so we cooked food there and made out.

When he blew me off again for an in-game commitment, I took what I thought the most reasonable course of action: I started playing the game with him.

In those days, Seth had long hair and a fuzzy beard and was never without his herringbone cabbie hat. He had a quiet confidence that drew me to him. The most apt word would for it would be "certain," where I felt anything but certain about life and the nature of people at that point. I was totally attracted to this certainty.

Despite my frank assertion that I wanted monogamy and was through with the recreational sex and partying of high school and my first year of college and was really looking to settle down, about 3 weeks into our relationship, Seth started asking me about threesomes.

To be fair to him, he didn't bring up the issue out of the blue. A friend was very attracted to me, and she offered, wanted to give it a go. She was cute, funny, and had a dark sultry laugh that made my face burn. I seriously considered it, knowing it'd be fun, but stuck to my earlier decision, much to Seth's dismay.

Seth's most intensely gratifying sexual experience at that point in his life was a 3-person makeout session in high school with his ex-girlfriend and a female friend of hers. The girls eventually started hooking up on their own without telling him and eventually formed a triad with another guy, shutting Seth out completely. Even given how badly it ended, the initial experience had been so sexually intense that it had left him craving more.

Seth and I had many tense moments when he would allude playfully to bringing another girl into our bed. I'd mutter, feel inadequate, get resentful. It didn't help that many of my female friends were flirtatious with me, something I had otherwise welcomed, but which only served to bring up the issue time and time again.

I was accommodating to Seth in every other way imaginable. I'd often wait on him hand and foot, budget our expenses so that the majority of our free funds went to things he wanted to buy. He wanted to know why if I loved him and trusted him would I deny him this. Why wouldn't I be open to threesomes?

I tried to tell him that it was that I didn't trust myself and even more so that I didn't trust other women.

That things got muddy and confusing when feelings got involved.

That women are often culturally programmed to be competitive, insecure, and vindictive with one another, a fact that had ruined more than one relationship with an ex-girlfriend.

That I was afraid of how much damage a third party could do to our relationship through insinuation and games.

That I was afraid of losing the one stable relationship I'd ever had.

Having a few friends in the sex industry, I considered hiring an escort to indulge him without all the emotional baggage and heartache. He was not thrilled about that option, especially the stigma involved.

After 4 years of dating, we married and continued on our own for another 4 years of marriage.

And then about 8 years into our exclusive relationship, the planets aligned.

MEGAN

The first time I met Megan, I was convinced she hated me. I'd met her at my friend John's birthday party, at a Mexican restaurant. She and her husband Pete were John's "other friends." John had met her on the psych ward where they both worked.

I've always had a thing for blonds, a preference I can track at least back to a much loved ex-girlfriend and ever further back to an elementary school teacher who always wore skirt suits with satin slips that'd peek out and shimmer past my face whenever she'd walk by me as I played on the classroom floor.

Megan caught my eye immediately, her pale skin, almost translucent. Delicate features like a porcelain doll.

She was breathtaking. Unfortunately, she seemed to wince after I said anything.

Huh, I thought. *Guess she thinks I'm obnoxious.*

It was much later, after she and Pete started coming to more of our group's regular gatherings that it came out that Megan was just uncomfortable around new people, and as I was one of the more extroverted and gregarious of the bunch, I overwhelmed her more than most.

Once we cut through the awkwardness, I found she was quite funny and, as a social worker, had a wealth of interesting stories. Between this and her ethereal beauty, I found myself gravitating towards her at gatherings, chatting her up at every opportunity.

Oh shit, I realized. *I have a crush on her.*

It was one of those stupid little crushes, like in elementary school. I'd feel shaky around her, and everything would feel vaguely surreal in her presence. I'd see her and get drunk on the adrenaline, comb my mind for something charming to say.

As much as I was drawn to her, it wasn't the first time my heart ached for someone other than my spouse, and as usual, I discounted the feelings and behaved myself.

I didn't even mention it to anyone else until one night when Seth and I were talking before bed, engaged in a conversation about which friends we found most attractive, one of those hypothetical exercises for entertainment.

He mentioned Tara, the gorgeous leggy younger sister of one of his long-time buddies. Tara was a good egg, running organs around in her car all summer for one of the local pathology firms. She'd recently started coming to our poker parties, tolerating our drunken antics. She even played *EverQuest*.

"And you?" Seth asked me. "John, right?"

After all, John and I talked about everything, the more disgusting and lewd the better. It was him who first turned me on to She Hulk and the "Horrors of Porn." Recently John and I had made a sport of exchanging emails with x-rays of people with bizarre rectal foreign bodies. John was frank about his nihilism to a refreshing extent, and I found him fascinating.

"Well, yeah," I said. "And Megan," I added sheepishly.

"Megan?" Seth asked. "Huh. Really? I never would have thought."

"She's beautiful," I said.

"Eh," he shrugged. "She's okay."

And yet, years later, we somehow all ended up in love. Or lust at least. How's that for okay?

THE TRIAD

For the uninitiated, a triad is a relationship that involves three people who are all involved with one another (in a way, a triad is to three people as a couple is to two people). That was how Seth and I structured our romantic involvement with Megan.

Starting out dating other people, Seth and I had the rule that we were a "package deal" and that we would only date people together. The prospect of either of us dating alone and all the unknowns triggered too much insecurity and jealousy, especially for me. In addition, as a result of the debacle on the night where Seth had left angry and I'd sleep dialed him, we set the rule that neither of us would see Megan alone, that all dates would involve both of us.

Furthermore, the number one rule was that our marriage would come first and be the highest priority above anything that happened with Megan.

In polyamorous circles, our marriage is what is typically known as a "primary" relationship. This can mean any number of things to different polyamorous people. Sometimes, "primary" is used to denote shared responsibilities like cohabitation, intermingled finances, or childrearing.

In our particular situation, it meant all those things (well, except for childrearing; Seth and I had no kids), and in addition, it had the additional meaning that our relationship would come first and be prioritized above our relationship with Megan, which we considered a "secondary relationship."

If anything that happened in the secondary relationship emotionally or practically threatened the health or longevity of the primary relationship, then the secondary relationship with Megan would be over.

This a particularly strict hierarchical form of polyamory, and for many extramarital partners, this would have been simply too much to agree to. It's hard enough to form authentic connections with people, even harder while dealing with time constraints and grappling with jealousy and layers of feelings, and even harder still to be vulnerable knowing that at any second the relationship could be over – at the first sign of turbulence.

However, Megan had a primary relationship of her own with Pete in addition to her professional and parental responsibilities and preferred things to remain open-ended and casual as she was exploring things with us and considered us her secondary partners as well.

So everyone could walk away at any time if they felt like what we had together was interfering with our primary relationships.

Another point that was stressed early on by Megan was the importance of open, honest communication. The more I've talked to other polyamorous people, the more it's become evident that this is as close to a universal value as polyamory has, that things should be discussed frankly and shared with partners, even difficult topics, *especially* difficult topics. Communication is crucial to the health of any relationship. This becomes even more evident as additional partners are added into the picture.

In a way, Seth and I were wading into polyamory with baby steps. With so many restrictions, I joked that our marriage wasn't really open, but slightly ajar.

But the rules really did make me feel a great deal more secure starting out.

And start out we did. We made out for the entire first two seasons of *Dexter*, hands roaming until the sexual tension was unbearable and our bodies would intertwine, and clothes would come off.

There were definite boundaries established on Megan's side. Pete had banned her from having vaginal sex with others as Pete wanted to keep that particular act something Megan would only do with him. Megan, for her own part, was refraining from oral sex with either of us while her attraction for us was so low level and her romantic feelings for us ambivalent.

That said, there were many sexy things we could do even within these limits, and it seemed like there being strict rules drove us to be kinky and creative. Necessity is the mother of invention, after all!

Megan was on her own weight loss program as she had maybe 30 pounds to lose, one which entailed a cup of black coffee as a meal replacement once or twice a day. We'd drink flavored coffee together at highly inappropriate times, chatting about our dieting strategies until the sun came up.

The group energy and the make outs were a lot of fun, to be sure, especially at the beginning, but the shiny newness wore off for me after a couple of weeks, and our conversations were what I looked forward to.

I suppose it didn't help that, despite my best efforts to talk things through with Megan and figure out precisely what the technical issues were, our kissing styles were still incompatible, and I found myself avoiding it, preferring more to kiss her neck, her shoulders, her breasts. She likewise seemed to avoid kissing and focus more on other contact.

Seth and Megan, on the other hand, had crazy chemistry, in all facets, including kissing.

Their spark was a bit unnerving as Seth as well had never liked my kissing style, saying I was too aggressive for his taste. This was a criticism I'd never received prior to dating him, and now it seemed that Megan wasn't a fan of how I kissed either.

Conversely, Seth loved the way Megan kissed, even though I found it frustrating and passionless. I started to wonder if there was actually something wrong with the way I kissed. Maybe I was just a bad kisser.

I found myself more and more withdrawing early from the make-outs to the couch on the other side of the living room and opting instead to watch Seth and Megan make out while I solved *Picross* picture puzzles.

Virtually all the novelty had worn off for me, and I wasn't feeling physically connected or sexually engaged when participating and was more turned on by watching them than getting action. I was in a difficult spot. With the sexual disconnect and without a strong emotional connection, a romantic component, I was starting to get a bit bored.

Megan and Seth seemed so happy though that I didn't want to throw in the towel. Instead I turned my focus on investigating polyamory. I've always been a research junkie. Pete shot me a few URLs to get me started, and I was on my way.

From what I could gather, there were a much larger number of people identifying as polyamorous than I ever would have guessed. Not only that, but they were dealing with the same issues I was: Jealousy, rules, boundary setting, time management, communication. And here I was, trying to reinvent the wheel.

I remember later down the road when I finally came out and told my mom about my open marriage that her response was, "Polyamory? That sounds made up. Is that something from the Internet?"

She wasn't so far off base.

It was a word coined in the 90's from a combination of Greek and Latin roots (*poly* meaning "many" in Greek and *amor* being Latin for "love") for something people had been doing long before that, some said for decades, some for centuries, some for millennia.

Giving polyamory a name had given it a sense of community with shared values, beliefs, concerns. It was an exciting movement, a revolution in the way people could think about and structure romantic relationships.

Though there were few to no hard and fast rules about how a polyamorous person should be, I noticed quickly that there was a strong contingent of geeks and artists within the subculture. Not surprisingly, polyamorists were largely socially liberal and far more likely to be bisexual than the general population.

Megan and Pete themselves had been introduced to polyamory by their friend Fox, a scrawny geek and gun nut with long hair and an offbeat charisma who frequented anime cons.

The legend goes that one evening Fox and his girlfriend were hanging out with Megan and Pete when Fox's girlfriend started hitting on Megan.

Megan was mortified and outraged and left that evening angry, but the experience sparked a conversation between Megan and Pete where Megan confessed she'd always felt bad that she'd settled down and married before fully exploring her sexual attraction to women. Even though she really wasn't Megan's cup of tea, the door had been opened, and apparently Pete went on to have some furious, if awkward make outs, with Fox's girlfriend. Sound familiar?

I finally got to meet Fox at the state fair. He was lanky and awkward but charming. "Page," he greeted me. "I've heard so much about you. Megan seems positively smitten."

"Oh really?" I asked, incredulous. This was news to me. If anything, Megan was coming off as a cold fish to my advances and overtures.

"She lights up whenever she talks about you," he said. It was nice to hear.

Megan blushed, pulling me aside to get a sausage and peppers at the bratwurst stand. "Be careful with Fox," she warned me as we waited for our orders. "He's a collector."

"A collector?"

"He tries to have as many relationships going on at the same time as possible. It's a sport to him, feeds his ego."

I thought I heard insecurity in her voice and wanted to reassure her. "You have nothing to worry about. I have a full plate right now with you and Seth."

"It's not that I'm jealous," she said. "Not to slut shame or anything, but he *really* gets around. I just don't want to see you get hurt."

We returned to the group with our food. I chatted with Fox some more, who told me he'd had a trying day. His girlfriend, who was his primary partner, had kicked him out of their apartment earlier in the day. She was tired of polyamory, gave him an ultimatum: Break up with your other partners or lose me.

"It was 5 versus 1," Fox said. "I love her, but was it worth losing my other loves? Absolutely not." He seemed to be doing pretty well, considering.

"Do you have somewhere to go?" I asked.

He nodded. "I'm moving in with these other two girls I'm dating. They live together already. Have for a while, actually. I'm psyched. It should be exciting."

Though there were certainly pain and frustration on his face as he discussed the dysfunctional situation with his newly ex-girlfriend, I was impressed by his optimism, his resilience.

"We've been fighting for a while," Fox added. "It's almost a relief to be putting it behind me."

In a way, I really admired him.

Megan wanted to go on a few of the fair rides. For the most part, the friends present really weren't ride people, but she wanted company, and I wanted to impress her.

I went on the Scrambler strapped in with her and her husband Pete, spinning around in a little cart, Pete and I screaming our heads off, much to Megan's amusement.

After that little experience, Pete decided he'd had enough. Megan had her eye on a ride that spun so fast that it pinned the riders with centripetal forces to the walls. It was like the original Gravitron I'd ridden as a kid but a much more hardcore version with safety harnesses for being strapped in. It went up high in the air and because of its more open design treated the riders with terrifying views.

As I waited in line, I felt raw fear I typically reserve for local fair rides, where I know it's entirely possible someone could die a few states away on the same machine, and no one would even know about it.

The fear did not abate as I was strapped in, and the engine came alive.

The ride began to spin, and I surrendered to the situation, aware that I had absolutely no control over what was about to happen.

"Megan," I said, realizing we were alone, and that she was my captive audience. "I love you."

She laughed. "You're crazy!" she replied.

The world passed by in a blur. I listened to the other riders' screams. My own fear had been supplanted by confusion.

Why had I said that? At all? Why now? And what did her laughter mean?

My sexual education was rudimentary at best, a combination of what they'd put us through in health class, mostly menstruation facts and the gruesome reality of childbirth videos. I was raised in a sheltered Catholic home in a rural area outside of the town I went to school in. We had no cable television until I was in college, and the Internet was pretty much restricted to the local BBS scene as well.

When the whole Lorena Bobbitt crime happened, I called up my best friend who lived in town and had cable and asked her what "anal sex" was as this was cited as the reason for Ms. Bobbitt lopping off her husband's penis. My friend knew; it was the first time I'd heard of such a thing.

In elementary school on the bus, it had been explained to me that "gay," was a slur that referred to grown men who had sex with young boys (a friend later thankfully corrected this misinformation). The next time I meaningfully encountered homosexuality was in the context of my 18-year-old sister coming out when I was 11, and then it was a different word, "lesbian." I accepted her pronouncement easily and was happy for her. My sister was androgynous and never had boyfriends, so in my stereotypical and simple young mind, everything was consistent.

In fact, lesbian or gay when applied to women to me was an adjective that meant "not attracted to men." This sort of thinking is what led me to believe for some time after I began even having oral sex with other girls that I was "straight." My misconceptions weren't dented by the fact that I was giving girls orgasms.

I thought of things as a binary – you were either straight or gay, and if you liked the opposite sex, there was no way you could be gay.

I remember authoritatively pronouncing to my best friend at 15 (as she was at that point exploring her sexuality and attending meetings at a collegiate group for GLBT youth in the area) that I supported her regardless of her sexual orientation but that I was "extremely straight."

Six months after that pronouncement, I had my first official "girlfriend." I was 16. She was 14. Very smart, extremely cute. I wasn't overly tall, but I towered over her by a good 4 inches. The whole thing took me by surprise. I had never connected with a girl in this way. It was powerful, intense, and meaningful. She made me melt.

There were a few others, but I kept things under wraps, hidden from all but my closest friends – and sometimes I didn't even tell them anything because I didn't know how to explain the confusion I felt.

It felt sometimes as I was two different people sexually, that reality had become unglued. I did all sorts of crazy things to try cope with my confusion. Even when I did start officially in high school seeing women, I simply stopped calling myself straight. I didn't call myself gay either. And I didn't use that "B" word.

When I got to college, though, I felt the need to identify. I was dating rather vigorously, and it seemed important to identify whether I was looking for men or for women to date. My college friends still recall with smirks on their faces how I'd proudly pronounce one week, having developed a crush on a man, that I was straight – and the next week that I was gay, starting to chase some women.

Finally, one of them interrupted me and said, "You're obviously bi, silly." To which I responded, "What's that?"

In retrospect, I may have heard the word "bisexual" once or twice in passing but dismissed it as meaning "hermaphroditic."

And suddenly everything made sense.

Transitioning from a monogamous marriage into a polyamorous one, I became close to a lot more self-identifying bisexual women than I ever had before (really, most of the women I've had sex with up until recently considered themselves straight) and had many more female friends who identified as bisexual.

One theme I noticed was an abundance of women involved with and committed to men who primarily fantasized about being with other women usually through exposure to girl on girl porn and with the encouragement of their male partners, who found these latent desires profoundly arousing.

When they spoke of their bisexuality, they were lighthearted and optimistic, and I didn't detect the weight of experience, the sum of years, the reality of the fact (in my opinion) that all interaction is work, all meaning has some sort of cost.

I envied them to a certain extent. Female bisexuality has been fetishized extensively as of late, and it's now standard for straight girls to make out to attract males, an act unthinkable in the years of my early and late adolescence.

As I set out dating outside of my marriage, I longed to find someone who had an experience similar to mine, a dysfunctional relationship with their own sexuality, to discuss it with. I wanted to talk to someone who understood because she lived it – because they struggled with the reality that she was attracted to people regardless of what they possessed for genitalia and was profoundly confused because she lacked the words for what she was going through. I wanted to know on some level that I was never really alone.

Whatever we were together, I had come to realize that Megan wasn't going to be that person.

As the shiny newness wore off, Seth frequently expressed frustration with the physical limits of the arrangement.

I did what I could to think of kinky work-arounds, like giving him blow jobs while the two of them made out, but he remained focused on the acts that were off limits, that she wouldn't go down on either of us, let us go down on her, or have vaginal sex with him.

"Why won't she open up?" he'd ask me.

"You'd have to ask her," I'd reply.

But time and time again, opportunities would arise to ask her about it, and he'd remain silent.

Finally, I could stand it no more.

"Where is all of this going?" I asked her one night as the three of us hung out at her house.

"Going?" Megan asked.

I sighed. "Well, I've had a lot of fun, but without things progressing deeper, either emotionally or physically, I hate to say it, but I'm getting bored. It's a big time commitment."

I knew it sounded harsh, but 3 or 4 nights a week, I'd get off work and we'd make the 40-minute drive to and from Megan's where we'd spend all night, not getting home until 2:00 in the morning and having to be at work at 9.

Every few weeks, Megan could get away for a weekend night at our place, but those evenings were few and far between.

I knew it was a lot for Megan, too, as she worked full time and had kids.

"It's not so bad," Seth said.

Of course he wasn't feeling the time crunch. It was summer. He was a student and, despite my urging that it would take financial pressure off me for him to get a job over breaks, hadn't worked since returning to school.

"The thing is," Megan said, "I've been really trying to keep my feelings for the two of you as close as I could, to treat you as one unit, but it's really hard."

I nodded.

"Honestly," she said. "My feelings for Seth are much stronger than my feelings for you, Page."

Ouch. Like a bolt to the chest. Tears welled up in my eyes.

"I'm sorry."

"You can't help how you feel," I replied.

I was embarrassed. How had I gotten so confused, not realized that the connection I felt was one-sided? I'd put myself out there, told her that I loved her – and Seth, who seemed more focused on the way he was getting his rocks off than anyone's feelings or inner life, was the one she was falling for. Shit.

I needed to be alone. Normally a tiny house, at that moment Megan's place felt even smaller. I went outside and sat on the lawn to cry in peace and collect my thoughts. I was numb.

Eventually, Megan and Seth came out to check on me.

"Are you okay, Page?" Seth asked.

"I'll be okay," I said. "I just don't think I can do this anymore."

"I understand," Megan said. "It's probably for the best."

We called it an early night. Seth drove us home in stony silence.

When Seth finally did talk, he was far from pleased.

"What the fuck did you do that for?"

"I just wasn't feeling it," I replied.

"Things were going fine," he said. "Slow, but fine. Life isn't like some romance novel or movie, Page. Well-adjusted people don't fall that fast."

"What's that supposed to mean?"

"You're melodramatic about love," he continued. "Always looking for the big romance, your soulmate. What did you call it?"

"The Great Love," I grumbled.

"Whatever. You've gone and ruined something good."

"I was unhappy," I said.

"For now," he replied. "Your moods change like the weather. You didn't even give the relationship a chance."

"I don't really think there was much there to build on, Seth."

"How do you know?" he asked me.

"She seemed relieved when I brought up breaking things off. She didn't question it at all, didn't fight it."

He frowned. "You're just jealous, threatened by the fact that she's into me more."

"Maybe I am, but that's the not my only reason for wanting to end things."

"You're ridiculous," he said. "Just own up to it. You're jealous."

We fought well into the night, chasing each other around in logical circles until the sun came up, and we were both exhausted.

Knowing I had to be up for work in a few hours, I apologized for everything, took all the blame, conceded to his points, desperate to end the argument.

"I know you're placating me, but I'm exhausted. We'll pick this up tomorrow."

The fight continued. The more we discussed his frustrations, the more I felt my reserve fade, and before too long, I was actually in his corner, agreeing with him not out of a desire for peace but genuinely regretting severing things with Megan.

I had made a rookie mistake. I thought I was riding the relationship escalator.

Once you move away from the standard template of what romantic relationships are supposed to be, how things are supposed to progress from stage to stage, the relationship escalator, there's a dizzying variety to the types of connections we can actually forge with people.

I was no different than a lot of people new to polyamory. It's always remarkable to watch them come to this conclusion. Some of them have a very hard time accepting it. They may reach a certain place with a partner where things are comfortable but not "progressing" to a more serious entanglement, and it confuses them. Further complicating the picture for some is that they don't necessarily mind that things are "stuck."

But they aren't necessarily stuck. Rather than products stamped out on an assembly line, relationships are custom jobs.

However, we're raised to believe that they all follow a particular pattern. When you start a relationship, you step on an escalator and magically progress to the top. It's clear-cut, straightforward, uniform.

And in my assumption that there was something wrong with not progressing "to the next level" (whatever that meant), I'd messed things up with Megan.

It was time for a grand gesture.

On the third day, we asked Megan if we could come over to talk. We brought a full complement of Chinese take-out that included all her favorites.

After we'd eaten dinner, she asked us, "So what did you want to talk about?"

"We made a mistake, Megan," I said.

"You think so?" she asked.

"I let jealousy get the better of me. I acted before thinking. Yeah, things are moving slowly, but this is a secondary relationship. Putting the same level of expectations that I would put on a serious monogamous one was foolish. I'm so sorry. Polyamory's new to me."

"It's okay," she said. "You don't have to be sorry."

"I guess what Page is getting at," Seth said, "is we'd like to try again. We want to get back together."

"Ah," Megan said, cracking open a fortune cookie. "Your wish will come true," she read, flipping around the fortune to show us.

Seth smiled. "So what do you say? Give us another chance."

Megan sighed. "This is all extremely flattering, and I appreciate dinner, but I have to say that I think Page made the right call. The three of us don't really work."

"I'm sorry you feel that way," Seth said.

"And besides," she added. "After being with you and Page and seeing how intense and hot things got for the two of you with a third person there, I really think I'd like that for me and Pete, for us to have a girlfriend. "

PICKING UP THE PIECES

To say Seth was disappointed by this turn of events was an understatement. He was crushed. I had never seen anything affect him like this. He moped like I'd never seen him mope. It was all he talked about.

"I can't believe she said no. What are we supposed to do now?"

"We move on," I replied.

"That's easy for you to say," he said. "It's not like you just lost your fantasy."

"Here's the thing, Seth. You were always complaining about her, even when we were with her, how frustrated you were with the lack of chemistry, how slowly things were moving. Megan wasn't your fantasy. A triad was. And that's not something you necessarily need Megan for."

He perked up. "It's hard to meet people."

"Maybe so," I agreed, "but it's not impossible, and if you really want it, you should get back out there. Try again. Either that, or accept that it's just us for now and be open to an opportunity if someone else with potential comes along."

Seth sighed. "I don't want to give up."

I pulled out my laptop and started to search. Before long, I'd identified a handful of dating sites.

An avid photography buff, Seth transformed our living room into a photo studio to take flattering pictures for our profiles. I was thrilled at the results.

I'd lost 60 pounds over the summer going from a size 26 to a size 18 by cutting back on carbs and playing as much Dance Dance Revolution as I could. My dieting efforts were haphazard, but I worked hard to carve out a program that was realistic – with strategies that reflected my life. In the past, I'd strictly followed the Atkins plan. I paid no mind at all to calories and instead grew fixated on hidden sugars and starches to the point where I was unwilling to eat something unless I'd prepared it myself. I had great weight loss results but found I couldn't stick to the plan. I was too social to put those kinds of restrictions on my eating, always out to dinner with friends, either at their homes or at restaurants.

This time around, I was still very carb conscious but kept an eye on portion size to give myself a little wiggle room. Going out for Thai, I'd get curry and skip the rice. At the Chinese buffet, I'd eat chicken wings and egg drop soup. Dating Megan, the three of us went out to eat frequently, and the weight nonetheless peeled off me. Sure, I was still plus sized, but my shape had started to emerge. The difference was dramatic.

Pleased with the improvement in my appearance, I uploaded the photos and filled out a profile, Seth following suit. We crossed our fingers and hoped for the best.

I struck up conversations with a few people who seemed interesting. The first thing I noticed about the small handful of possibilities that were within a 20-minute drive, who identified as polyamorous or at least expressed a willingness to have open relationships, were references on their profiles about an interest in BDSM and/or kink.

BDSM stands for Bondage and Discipline, Dominance and Submission, and Sadism and Masochism. Yeah, it should really be BDDSSM, but BDSM looks less like a cat sitting on a keyboard, so they went with that.

Kinky folks taken as a group are interested in a wide variety of sexual experimentation and physical and mental play. There's huge diversity among kink communities as to what exactly play entails. Some very common activities involve restraints, power exchange (one person having control over another), and inflicting pain for gratification.

As I perused dating profiles, sometimes a potential poly partner's interest in BDSM and kink was blatant, and other times more subtle, but there seemed to be a huge overlap between poly and kink, one that held up even as I widened my search radius.

I was initially very irritated by this.

First off, I had the misfortune of the first few kinksters from the Maine scene that I corresponded with being really not my cup of tea for a number of reasons.

They were paradoxically more socially conservative than would have been my taste and anti-intellectual to boot, and I found the mere way I expressed myself seemed to offend. I'm a nerd, and in particular, I'm a word nerd, and it was off-putting.

Not only that, but I tended to ask questions about the lifestyle from an academic standpoint, which I now know would have been tedious to all but the geekiest kinkster.

I probably came off as judgmental, like I was a lawyer cross-examining a witness. So things went pretty

badly, and I started to develop a distaste for the BDSM/
polyamory crossover.

Media portrayals of BDSM sadly are often very cartoonish
and silly (e.g., the *Reno 911* episode "Wiegel's New Boyfriend"), and I just didn't get it. In actuality, I had a strong
kinky streak in me, felt passionately and carnally about sex,
but thought the leather costumes, the dungeon, the chains,
etc, were all a little unnecessary and comical.

Thankfully, through talking to poly kinksters, I was managing
to pick up a lot of knowledge and insight about BDSM, kink,
energy work, and their specialized jargon. All of this would
serve me well if I did end up meeting someone I clicked with
a little better on "the scene." Even if I hadn't met someone to
explore these new ideas with, I found myself growing more
intrigued even as Seth remained confused about and disdain-
ful of my newfound curiosity.

I thoroughly enjoyed many of my initial correspondences
with people on OkCupid, even if I wasn't forming any romantic connections. Seth, however, quickly grew frustrated with
the lack of results.

Oddly enough, the following conversation took place while
we were strolling through the mall, of all places. I wanted a
new outfit to wear as most of my wardrobe was getting comi-
cally huge with the large change in size.

"We'll never meet someone this way," he complained.

"Never's an awfully long time," I said.

He scowled at me.

"Okay, that wasn't helpful," I conceded.

"You know," he said. "I think I know what the problem is."

"Oh?"

"It's the whole 'package deal' thing," Seth said.

"I suppose you do have a point. It does make it a great deal more difficult, finding someone who'd be into both of us. It's just... I don't know. Just thinking about dating alone makes me feel..." I searched for the word. I couldn't find it. Anywhere.

"It makes you feel how?" he asked.

"I don't know how to explain it," I said. "Oh! Okay. I guess I don't need someone who'd be willing to be with both of us. I think I'd be okay as long as they were okay doing things with you even if I were in the room."

"What?" he said. "What are you talking about?"

"Like, you know, if I came home, and you two were on the couch together doing something physical that she wouldn't leap up mortified or want to leave or something. I'd want her to be comfortable fooling around with you in front of me. Not that it'd have to happen at all and certainly not with any frequency, but you know... like I wouldn't want her to be ashamed about it or feel like she had to hide her physical relationship with you from me."

"That's fucking weird," Seth said. "You can't expect that from a sane person."

"I guess I just want to know she accepts me or something. That she's not ashamed of what she's doing. For some reason, I'd feel rejected if she felt uncomfortable being physical with you around me."

I was having trouble pinpointing why, and I was well aware of how odd a sentiment I was expressing, but it rang true to me as I said it.

"I don't know why you're so weird about this," Seth said. "Megan has no problem with Pete dating on his own."

I stopped to admire a mannequin, not sure how to respond to this.

"And here I thought I had the 'cool wife,'" he added bitterly.

I frowned.

"I was joking," he said.

"It's hard to hear, even as a joke," I replied.

"Well, you have to admit, you are quite a bit behind Megan in the jealousy department."

I felt that familiar sting, like a slap in the face, of being told that I was more jealous and insecure than Megan and Seth, an unfortunate theme in conversations we had as a triad, with the connotation being that I was somehow less emotionally evolved because of it.

Again I said nothing. My feelings were complicated and conflicting. I worried I might burst into tears in front of the other shoppers.

Finally, Seth said, "There's this girl in my poetry class."

MARY

" I like Mary. There's something about her," Seth said. "She's so... approachable. And she says the best things in class."

His face lit up when he talked about her, in a way it never did when he'd talked about Megan. It was endearing and gave me an instant wave of compersion. It seemed like he really liked Mary.

"You should ask her out to coffee or something."

"What?" Seth looked confused. "You were just saying..."

"It's coffee, not sex, not necessarily even a date, *per se*. If you like her, you should get to know her."

"What's the point?" he said. "It's not as if I could date her, even if she did like me since you wouldn't let me date on my own."

"I don't know about that," I said.

"Huh?"

"I'm uncomfortable, but that doesn't mean that I couldn't adjust or work towards it. Just because I'm uncomfortable doesn't make it the wrong call or something I'm completely unwilling to try."

He looked at me like I was speaking a foreign language. "Sometimes I think you're the weirdest person I've ever met."

"Thank you," I replied.

"How'd it go?" I asked Seth, after he'd returned from having coffee with Mary.

He laughed. "Apparently my cruising radar is completely broken. She's chaste."

"Chaste?" I said. "You mean, like, modest?"

"No chaste," he said. "You know, chaste."

"Ohhhh," I said. "Celibate."

"Yes, but more than that. She's Baha'i. She doesn't even kiss or drink or anything."

"Oh, the Baha'i!" I said.

"You've heard of it?"

"I met a family of Baha'i at UMass when I was playing at a mall. I'd run out of money, and they fed me. Really nice people, actually. Definitely some conservative rules, but I always liked their concept of all religions containing spiritual truth," I explained. "I suppose this means there wasn't a love connection."

"Of course not," he said. "Though we had an *amazing* conversation. She was really polite and, if anything, intrigued by polyamory. She asked a lot of questions about it, and I had a lot of questions about chastity and her faith. If anything, our conversation made me like her more."

"That's great!" I said.

"Not really, no."

"Huh? It sounds like you had a good time."

"Maybe," he said, "But I'm falling for someone who I have zero chance with."

"She sounds like she's going to be an awesome friend at the very least."

"It makes me think we just should have stayed with Megan. You should have never broken up with her," he said.

At Seth's urging, I revisited my attempts at online dating. "You need to initiate more first contacts, be more active. If I could do it myself, I would," he said, "but the fact that I'm a man makes me creepy."

After reading some excellent profiles, I worked on my own, fleshed it out, tried to get it to reflect who I was, my interests – to give anyone who read it a real sense of who I was. Over the many months I searched for partners online, I worked on it often, adding bits and pieces at a time as they struck me until my profile was practically epic.

MEGAN, REDUX

Though Seth continued to hang out with Mary after class, talking about history, philosophy, linguistics, and the typical humanities English majors become enamored with (I say this as a former English major myself), his frustration and dissatisfaction with the situation continued to grow.

He had confessed his attraction to Mary, and for the most part, she'd responded very well, said that she was flattered and thought he was a great guy but could in no way date a married man. Her religious beliefs did not condone such a practice, and she was staying chaste until her wedding day. Seeing as people in modern America aren't permitted to have multiple spouses, not legally (or yet) anyway, there was no chance of that happening without his divorcing me, something she was not at all interested in setting into motion.

Even though polyamory was a completely new concept to Mary, she wasn't offended by his interest, loved talking to Seth, and still wanted to hang out. I took this as a distinctly positive development. After all, she could have been creeped out by his affections and our nontraditional arrangements and run for the hills, never to be seen again. Instead, they were friends.

Seth continued to wish for more than friendship and was frustrated that things hadn't gone that way. I couldn't blame him. Mary was absolutely perfect for my husband to date. Well, except for the whole chastity thing.

I told him that I understood that it bothered him but that it was par for course when dating to have near misses and rejection before happening on something worthwhile, lasting. Seth was skeptical. He didn't have much dating or sexual experience, really none to speak of, as I was his second girl-friend, the other being a girl he saw in high school. We'd be-come exclusive when we he was 20 and married at 24. I knew he was upset, but I didn't see temporary setbacks as a big deal.

In his frustration with the situation and how unperturbed I was by it, he reached out to Megan to have another place to voice his frustrations about Mary being off limits.

Initially Megan and Seth spoke as friends, but as they talked, their feelings for one another reemerged. It had been a matter of weeks, no time at all. Megan herself was frustrated at how things were going with Pete and his new girlfriend, Trish, whom Pete and Megan had unsuccessfully tried to coax into a triad situation with them.

Trish was cute and sprightly, androgynous. I liked her instant-ly when she'd come to poker night with them. Identifying as a lesbian, she confided in me that Pete was the first man she'd ever developed feelings for, a development that had confused her considerably. She said polyamory was not something she had any experience with and not something she'd normally do, but her feelings were so strong for Pete that she wanted to at least give it a shot.

Trish had formed a good friendship with Megan, but there was no sexual or romantic chemistry to speak of. No click. Nothing was gelling, despite Megan's fervent hopes. Megan shared with me the memory of a particularly awkward night when she had sidled up to Trish on the couch, impeccably coiffed, shooting knowing glances at Trish, hoping that Trish would "make the first move."

I laughed at this because I'd done pretty much the same thing when trying to date Megan.

Frustrated when Trish didn't pick up on the signals, Megan came out and told Trish how she felt, what she hoped for. Trish, though flattered, wasn't interested. At the point, Megan ceased trying to start something with Trish and left Pete and Trish to do their own thing.

Unfortunately, Trish's confusion about being attracted to a man coupled with the fact that he had a wife was doing a number on her emotions, and even the relationship between Trish and Pete was becoming rocky.

As Megan and Seth's feelings for another grew, so did their regret that they had broken up. "I really took for granted the stability with you guys," Megan told us.

I wasn't surprised when Seth came to me and asked how I'd feel about his dating Megan again, on his own.

I know he was surprised when I told him I was okay with it. I worried because he'd been so heartbroken the first time things had ended, when the triad dissolved, and I was starting to see how badly he took break-ups and rejection. Not that I took them terribly well myself, but to see those things affect him was a phenomenon that blind-sided us both; he'd spoken rather authoritatively about how much easier he thought polyamory would be for him because of his naturally lower propensity for jealousy.

I knew there was a definite possibility that this new relationship would end up hurting him when it ended. Even though Seth and Megan had a great connection and true feelings for one another, in her absence, he complained about her frequently, both when we were in a relationship with her and after we'd broken up.

It seemed like there were quite a few issues there that troubled him. Nothing that couldn't be worked through, but still, it concerned me.

I told him all these things, shared my concerns (this open, honest communication thing was rubbing off on me!), and then told him he had my blessing, that I wanted him to be happy.

"But you were just saying..."

"I can have concerns and still be okay with it. There's a difference between saying, 'I'm uncomfortable,' and 'Uh uh, no way. Don't do it.'"

He looked at me like I was speaking Martian. We launched into a 2-hour conversation in which he tried to make sure my agreeing to the relationship wasn't a devious and passive-aggressive trap designed to test his love for me.

"It's just that you were so nervous before about dating on our own," he said.

"Getting myself mentally prepared for you dating Mary helped a ton," I said. "Even though it didn't pan out, it laid the groundwork in my head. I know Megan really well. I trust her. Hell, I was in love with her. There's no reason why you two shouldn't be able to date each other without me, even if it didn't work out between me and her."

"I guess that makes sense."

"Besides, if we are going to date people on our own, this would probably be the gentlest way to start, with you independent but with someone really familiar to me. It's less scary than someone who is a complete unknown."

Seth nodded. "And you can still date on your own. I still want a triad, but who knows? Maybe *you'll* meet someone who could date us. "

I shrugged. "I appreciate the thought, but I need friends more than anything. I'm pretty satisfied with just you. I don't *need* a lot."

"Well, just don't rule it out," he said. "You never know."

Even when I'd given the okay, Megan had some difficulty accepting that it was really okay to proceed one on one with Seth. I started by chatting about it with her online:

> **page:** I'm trying to send out the message, "I'm happy, so you guys be happy!!"
>
> **page:** I disappeared on purpose the other night when Pete fell asleep so you and Seth could get it on
>
> **megan:** I'm just being super sensitive about stuff
>
> **megan:** the reason I didn't say anything is because I knew I was being stupid
>
> **page:** also – you and Seth should see each other more and I will do just about anything I can to help you guys out in that regard

Megan and I ended up going to dinner together at the local pizza joint where I told her in no uncertain terms that she had my blessing and that I wasn't being bitchy and practicing some form of medieval reverse psychology. I was starting to grow rather worried at the impression they both had of me with how hard I had to work to convince them of this. Thankfully, that night they *finally* accepted my willingness for them to move forward.

All told, it took about 3 weeks of IM chats and 3 separate in-person communications, the third belabored and emphatic for my part, to drive home the point that yes, it *really* was okay.

Which is not to say that the reality of it was easy or that I was sunshine and rainbows 100% of the time. The first few nights alone were difficult. I tried to make plans with other friends, but it wasn't always possible, especially since Seth and I shared a car.

One notable hiccup occurred when Seth went out and bought new clothes to wear specifically to impress Megan. Seth hated shopping, and generally didn't give much thought to his appearance. Even when he and I were first dating, he wore whatever he had handy.

The reality that he was clearly trying so much harder in that department with Megan than he ever had with me hit me. Hard. *Does he like her more?* I tried to separate out all the different potential fallacies in my inductive reasoning to quiet my panic, but as hard as I tried, a trace of insecurity lingered, refusing to be snuffed out by logic.

To make matters worse, I didn't feel like I could go to Seth and talk about my insecurities, chiefly because it had been so difficult to convince the two of them that I was *really* okay with them having a relationship in the first place. I was frightened that I would be labeled, to borrow the *Wayne's World* term, a "jealous hose beast."

Consequently, I bit my tongue and tried to process on my own, reading more books and poly forums on my own, sharing my troubles with a few trusted (monogamous) friends.

As my internal distress grew, I became increasingly conflicted and afraid to share my feelings with anyone. I didn't even write much about the experience and my emotional state *privately* while it was happening (completely uncharacteristic of me), but when looking through my writings from that time, preparing to write this book, I did find the following:

> In the evenings my husband's visiting his girlfriend, I watch a lot of reality TV while going full speed on my bike. Long hot showers. Tuna Helper made with fresh ingredients. I spend a lot of time trying to make healthy food that tastes like it should kill me. I do. These evenings I'm almost happy. If only he could be happy, then everything would be okay. But he's never happy. He feels like she won't open up to him. Asks me what I think, what I would do. I give him the best advice I can, but it still doesn't work.

Thinking back now at how much I was struggling in silence, and suffering for it (needlessly!), I wish I'd really understood the difference between new relationship energy and old relationship energy.

POLY SIGNPOST #2: DON'T FIGHT THE MOONLIGHT

I've seen it over and over again. Two people meet and form a new polyamorous relationship, become absolutely cracked out on love for each other and consumed by the flames of passion – while their older, more established partners twitch in their respective corners, feeling ignored and insecure.

And many times, this is precisely when things go terribly wrong in otherwise seemingly stable long-term relationships.

I've been on both sides of this equation and played the role of ignored partner and cracked out love junkie. Despite what one might think, the neglected partner has a lot of the control regarding how things play out and whether the older relationship can weather the storm that can come with adding a new person to your poly web.

A web is a term for the interconnected relationships and often sets of relationships shared between a group of poly folk who are actively involved with multiple people. Charting it out can look rather complicated and very much visually like a spider's web.

Realize that your partner is under the influence of some pretty serious chemicals.

Falling in love is a wildly emotional and irrational experience. I had the experience of starting two new poly relationships within a few months of each other, and I was so excited and happy that I spent most days feeling like my heart would actually burst with joy. My libido soared. I spun around in a manic haze. And a few months later, the intensity faded, and I had my wits back about me.

Was I crazy? If so, not for that reason anyway. The phenomenon I experienced has a name and happens to lots of perfectly sane people.

Limerence, more commonly known in polyamorous circles as New Relationship Energy or simply NRE, is a physiologic state many love birds find themselves in when a relationship is bright and shiny and new. All sorts of outrageous chemicals flood your body, causing you to form emotional attachment with your partner, pushing you to mate, and causing you to overlook many of their flaws.

So if your partner seems loopy over someone new in a way you haven't seen them be about you in a long while, it's not necessarily a warning sign or something that should make you terribly insecure. That's actually fairly normal. Old relationships have a very different character than new ones. And it's a good thing, too! While falling in love is extremely fun, it's not something we're necessarily meant to perpetually do. Under the influence of NRE, people have been known to neglect important responsibilities at work, make poor financial decisions, and skimp on sleep and other self-care.

Don't lecture them.

They are basically high on love.

Keeping that in mind, the last thing someone in NRE wants to hear is a reminder of how irrational they are being, how they are infatuated, etc, so it's best to keep that sort of criticism to yourself or at least be tactful when discussing your frustrations. In time, they'll regain their senses, and then you'll have a much more productive discussion. They'll come back to earth eventually.

When you make yourself tough to juggle, you raise your chances of getting dropped.

When I see a lot of trouble as a result of the addition of a new partner to an existing web, especially with groups newer to polyamory, it is usually because one partner is off gallivanting and being generally inconsiderate under the spell of NRE, and the ignored partner starts making ultimatums and escalating demands, and an angry spiral ensues, hurtful things are said by both parties, and even formerly serious relationships (ones where partners share finances, live together, and/or are married) end in extremely nasty breakups, ones that end up damaging everyone involved, even the ancillary relationship.

Instead, I propose that you support your partner the best you can, cultivate compersion, try to help them with any neglected daily tasks that need doing, be a good friend and listener when and if they need it. Even if they don't acknowledge or appreciate your efforts while they are wrapped up in their new relationship or relationships, such behavior makes it infinitely more likely that they will be grateful once the dust has settled rather than bitter, resentful, or in many cases – completely gone!

Now this isn't to say that there aren't some valid reasons for calling out someone in the throes of NRE. There are. Sometimes rules and boundaries are violated that must be addressed when they happen, NRE or no NRE. But it's folly to fight every battle. If you do, you risk making your lover your sworn enemy, and there are a great many times when it's simply better to wait until everyone has returned to their senses.

For good measure, I've written you a limerence limerick.

There once was a young man named Wally
who set off on adventures in poly
he was too busy humping
to notice his dumping
but found himself nonetheless jolly.

NATHAN

I wasn't on my own for very long.

Not too long after Mary and Seth's fateful coffee meeting, I got to meet her as well. One of the requirements for the poetry class that Seth and Mary were both in was to attend readings being hosted at the college by established poets visiting the school. I'm a poet myself, so Seth invited me to come listen. Mary was dying to meet me.

Seth and I arrived early and got prime seats. We tried to save a third for Mary, but the lecture hall got progressively more crowded, and out of pure civility, we had to surrender our extra seat to someone in need.

By the time Mary arrived, all that was left was space on the floor, and she joined the others sitting there. I could tell, even from a distance, that she was awkward but in a way that was endearing, and though only 22, she carried herself with an elegance that at once signaled to me that she was an old soul.

After the reading was over, we went out for pizza, grabbed a bite to eat. Mary and I hit it off, chatting easily about literary topics, art, places we'd traveled. I shared with her the positive experience I'd had with a Baha'i family and my impressions of the faith.

Pizza became coffee. Coffee became chatting in the student lounge until the janitor locked up the building at 1 a.m., not so subtly glaring at us as we reluctantly shuffled out the exit doors, still chatting, exchanging ideas. Seth had checked out of the conversation hours ago, but Mary and I were still going strong.

We eventually forced ourselves to say our goodbyes as we both had to be up early in the morning.

As I got to know Mary better, I found that she was, for all intents and purposes, universally liked – or at least as close to being universally liked as a person can get.

She introduced both Seth and me to the lounge for commuters and nontraditional students where she and her many friends hung out, though the vast majority of them lived on campus and were of traditional college age. But who was I to complain? I wasn't even a student.

One evening I was chatting with an acquaintance about how romantic I found some of the tenets of physics, particularly observer effect, when a slender unassuming man wearing a hockey jersey chimed in, gently correcting some of my lay mistakes.

I quickly conceded I was a mere enthusiast with only a casual introduction to the phenomena I was describing. As I was gushing about the vastness of the universe (I was on quite the Carl Sagan's *Cosmos* kick), he talked about his work with crystals and the tiny worlds they were, extrapolating their intricacies and miniature vastness abstractly to the macrocosmic whole.

Okay, wow.

His eyes were shining. He was so intense. I was riveted.

I'm sure we were obnoxious and pretentious sounding and probably annoying everyone else in the room, but I was so present with him in that conversation. Like Mary, the conversation was easy, and the words flowed. With him, there was not only a give and take, but I instantly felt his emotions and amplified them, which he would then reciprocate.

"I'm Page," I finally said, realizing we'd been talking for nearly an hour and that I hadn't gone through this simple step.

"Nathan," he replied. "I'm a friend of Mary's. I think I saw you with her once or twice. I heard you talking about poetry earlier in here. I write poetry myself."

We started to discuss poetry, poetics, linguistics, my views on meaning, meta-meaning, obscurantism, and accessibility – my field. This time, I was the "expert," and the exchange was just as meaningful.

He was 24, getting his master's in chemistry, his focus on crystal morphology. He was brilliant and sensitive, and I could not stop looking at him. He captivated my attention.

After Nathan had left, Seth, who had been working on one of the computers, turned to me and said, "You like him."

"Yeah, he's nice," I said.

"No," Seth said. "You *like* him."

"Oh. Oh? Oh! No. What? No."

"You totally do," he said.

"Seriously? Do I?" I wasn't being coy. The whole thing had me flustered and off guard.

"Oh yeah. You have it *bad*."

"Well, shit," I said. "That's... unexpected."

Nathan and I quickly became inseparable, chatting frequently in the lounge and online. The next time Seth and Mary went to a poetry reading for their class, I invited Nathan. We sat together, stealing natural gaps in the performance to commiserate like schoolchildren, giddy, giggling. The four of us went to the pizza place afterwards, and it felt like the world's strangest sexless double date.

Nathan invited me to his birthday party at an Indian restaurant. I wrapped up my favorite book of poems, the best anthology I've ever owned. It was in pristine condition because it was precious to me, so I'd cared after it over the years. Seth was furious. Much like my strong response to his buying new clothes to date Megan, he found it triggered powerful emotions and that I was, in his words, "giving away something of mine to someone you barely know."

I told Seth that the book was actually mine, that I'd purchased it and enjoyed it, that he hadn't even read it.

"Everything that's yours is half mine, so that book is mine, too," he said. "And I've always meant to read it."

I sighed. "I'm only giving my copy away because I just thought of it today based on something he said, and I don't have time to get a new copy shipped to me. I'm going to order another." I promptly ordered a replacement.

"I know it's a stupid little thing," Seth said. "But... wow, that really bothered me."

"Oh, I know," I said. "In poly, it's the stupid little things that'll get to you."

We made up, joined the party. It was a great dinner in a cool little restaurant. Nathan and I spent all dinner talking with each other, which again was probably obnoxious to everybody else but felt incredible to me. (Megan remarked one time that even talking about Nathan without him around or simply having his name brought up by someone else during this time period, regardless of what I'd been doing or talking about just prior, my mood would radically change, and I'd drift away into a lovesick haze).

As we had the biggest place, Seth and I invited everyone back to our apartment to hang out after dinner. Seth put on some Mel Brooks movies, and for the first time, Nathan and I found ourselves cuddling.

What is going on here? I wondered. *I never would have wanted this, but here he is.*

Nathan knew Seth and I were polyamorous, had asked me plenty of questions about our arrangement, what it meant to us. He also knew Fox (Megan's polyamorous friend I'd met at the fair) through a few degrees of separation, having dated someone who'd dated Fox, though Nathan and the girl were monogamous at the time.

I had no clue if Nathan wanted to be more than friends, and my feelings for him grew so quickly that by the time I really wanted to ask, I was terrified of the answer.

First off, the friendship was amazing. Spectacular. It was like a drug just talking with him and being near him. I didn't want to lose him as a friend. Not only that, I go into romantic situations skeptical, expecting rejection, but the hope of something more happening between us, the fantasy of things working on was something I also didn't want to lose if he said he wasn't willing or able to... to...

To what?

To be my boyfriend?

No, that wasn't quite it. It was much worse than that.

To be everything I thought he could be to me.

I longed for him, out of control and terrified.

Having been fully incorporated into Mary's circle of friends, Seth and I decided to throw a huge party for Halloween.

We went all out. It was a 3-bedroom place. One spare bedroom was being used as a computer room/den, and the other was the office that I used to work from home. Since my workstation took up a small portion of the room, we decided to transform my office into an opium den for the party. Not that we were going smoke anything illicit, though we did purchase a hookah and 100% legal shisha, a 4-foot black light, and a half dozen large Oriental patterned pillows for people to sit on the floor (originally intended as beds for large dogs, but they were comfortable).

I went as the Japanese goddess Izanami because I wanted to wear my kimono but had been a geisha too many years in a row.

Though our apartment normally felt pretty large, with over 20 guests in it, chaos ensued. But, oh what beautiful chaos!

An incredible portion of the attendees got completely trashed. One of the girls in the belly dancing troupe (Mary's roommate was a belly dancer) decided that spin the bottle would be a fabulous idea, and about half of the people there joined in. Fortuitously, the bottle really liked me. I ended up kissing most of the people playing.

It was super interesting to experience how each (rather new) friend kissed, even when it was a bad fit and awkward, kind of like opening someone else's gifts. Even when it wasn't something you wanted, it was exciting guessing what was inside.

The very last spin of the bottle was mine. I spun, and it pointed right at Nathan. I leaned towards him, and he literally lunged at me, rolling me over on my back, knocking me on the floor. We proceeded to make out for a good minute in front of everyone. It was rough, intense. His kisses were deep, invasive, and incredibly passionate. I didn't care that he'd smacked my arm against the wall in the process. I was really, really, *really* turned on.

When he and I finally came up for air, the consensus was that spin the bottle was over. Somebody mentioned Denny's, and a head count was made, scrambling to make a plan to cart people as efficiently as possible with the number of sober designated drivers and vehicles that remained.

Mary drove our car with Seth riding up front. Nathan and I piled in the back, where he snuggled with me. "I think we should be cuddle buddies. Will you be my cuddle buddy?" he said. It was half slurred. My heart rose in my chest.

"Oh yes, I would love that," I replied.

Nathan and I continued to cuddle and snuggle at Denny's, holding hands.

It seemed like things were absolutely stellar with Nathan. I could talk with him about anything, and he'd be interested and engaged. He was very hard to offend, which was a relief as Seth was a great deal more prone to irritation and frustration, which could lead to anger.

Nathan was often very silly, sometimes humorously and harmlessly, where he'd randomly say something ridiculous and *non sequitur* that would make us both laugh by simply how bizarre it was. Other times, he'd take a completely irrational view and defend it for no good reason even though he didn't really believe it or care about it and would give up with the exercise as soon as it bored him, something I could quickly identify and found very amusing but which drove Seth crazy.

"Sometimes I think Nathan is absolutely insane," Seth said.

"He might well be. But if he is, he's the kind of insane I like."

Nathan had a weird mix of comfort and discomfort with polyamory. His relationship and boundaries with me were governed by what seemed like a complex inner logic that whenever I try to convey it to other people always sounds ridiculous to them. I suppose that's Nathan for you. Part of what I always liked about him. I got him when most other people didn't, and I don't think he was at all used to being understood.

Nathan and I frequently told each other "I love you," sent each other love poems, spoke in flowery grandiose terms of our love for one another. He'd often come over and hang out in the apartment with me when Seth was over at Megan's for the night.

Soon after we became friends, we discovered that we actually lived in the same apartment complex, so Nathan would often drive me for groceries or go out to eat at the Thai restaurant with me (Dutch), and even though I was strictly dieting, and had gotten down to a size 16 at this point, he even managed to convince me to get a banana cream pie blizzard with him at Dairy Queen. Twice.

We'd cuddle constantly but rarely made out. In fact, that was the odd part. Nathan would only make out with me when he was drunk. He was explicit about this fact. When I inquired as to why, his response was, "I don't know how I'd explain it to my future wife that I fooled around with a married woman unless I was drinking at the time."

Classic Nathan.

And that statement and all it reflected was our undoing. He wanted the wife, the picket fence, the house, the dream. Who could blame him? I certainly hadn't aspired towards an open marriage at his age.

Eventually, our intense connection became a more traditional friendship when he fell in love with another girl and started a monogamous relationship with her. He met her through a friend that had attended high school with her, spoke to her online, decided she was his soulmate, and went so far as to travel to visit her in Croatia, where she was from. Though they had a wonderful time together on his trip and continued the relationship long distance for a short while thereafter, he became absorbed in his Ph.D. program, and the two of them drifted apart.

I remember one time Seth was pointing out Nathan's myriad flaws to me, and I replied that Seth was correct. The negative things he was saying about Nathan were true.

Seth looked stunned. "What?"

"I've never loved Nathan because he was perfect. I love him because he's interesting."

SLUT MONKEY

I met Mark through Mary. And then I met Mark through Megan. And then I met Mark through Fox. And then I met Mark through Nathan.

It seemed I couldn't stop meeting Mark.

He was on his sixth (penultimate) year trying to earn his bachelor's degree in English, spending summer breaks doing heavy labor on a fishing boat in the Atlantic, carving his normally chubby build into rows of muscles.

"I like to eat. I'm a good Italian boy that way," he'd say, rubbing his belly and smirking with his usual mix of modesty and confidence. He said his dream was to work as a high school teacher during the school year and a ship captain over the summer, writing short stories in whatever free time was left over.

I felt instant chemistry. He had such an air of mischief about him. Roguish and cheeky, he had a way of making the most innocent statements seem filthy.

I first started seeing Mark on a regular basis when he joined in for poker nights at Megan and Pete's house. Pete, Megan, and Seth were also there, as well as one of Pete's girlfriends. I made six.

Mark and I fell quickly into a heated rivalry when it came to cards. Showdown after showdown, we were the last two standing, playfully trash talking one another.

"Read 'em and weep, Slut Monkey," I said, laying down my cards.

"Slut Monkey?" he laughed, lightly shoving me.

I pushed him back.

"Get a room, you two," Pete said.

Huh?

After all, despite the obvious sexual tension, to my thinking, Mark and I were clearly friends, nothing more. We'd talk about his past relationships, the girls he was currently dating, his own observations about my open marriage. He'd been friends with Fox for quite some time, even had a fling with Fox's girlfriend. It was a good time, he said, though awkward.

"Awkward how?"

He laughed. "You try waiting for a girl to call her boyfriend to ask if you have permission to fuck while you're lying there naked in their bed."

Mark hated the whole concept of permission. I understood his point. It wasn't terribly romantic even to my thinking, and I could see how it would be even less so to someone without a primary partner. The trouble was that a free-for-all, sexual anarchy, was terrifying to contemplate in long-term non-monogamy. While some could embrace an "anything goes" relationship style, I felt it carried an unacceptable level of risk. In a world without STIs or the threat of unintended pregnancy, things would certainly be simpler.

"Well, for what it's worth," he said. "You and Seth seem to have the healthiest poly relationship I've seen."

"I don't know whether that's a good thing for us or a bad thing for poly," I replied.

He smirked, poured another shot of peppermint schnapps.

We played another round of crazy 8's with the XXX playing cards he'd brought with him.

"What about that hot doctor lady you were scoping out on OkCupid? You should message her," he said.

"Oh, her?" I said. "She's out of my league."

"Seriously, Page. That's lame."

"She's thinner than I am," I tried to explain. "And a doctor."

"I repeat, lame."

I sighed. "I guess the thing is, Mark, I really *like* her."

"So you're telling me you'd rather put effort into messaging people online that you're only partly interested in than reaching out to someone you really like?"

"Uh yeah?" I replied.

"Lame," he said.

"What if she doesn't like me? It's easier to be rejected by someone if I'm not all that interested in to begin with."

"Still lame," he said, taking another shot of peppermint schnapps. "If you like her, you should at least say hello."

"I don't know."

"Oh c'mon. You're great. And from the sound of her profile, at the very least, the two of you would end up friends."

He had a point.

I took the leap, sent her a message, meticulously crafted. I tried to mention specific things from her profile so that she knew that I had read it (my usual *modus operandi*) and wasn't just sending out a bunch of impersonal e-mails to people with cute profile pictures, a practice an alarming number of folks seem to employ in online dating. I'd gotten quite a few generic messages myself and rarely responded to them.

She had mentioned polyamory in her profile, so I knew that it was likely she had polyamorous friends or had been exposed to polyamory in one way or another, and something about the way she wrote about it made me think that she was receptive to the idea of open relationships, if not currently involved in one.

Even though things weren't always a walk in the park, I tried to give things a positive spin and communicate my own relationship status to her in the most idealistic terms I could while still being honest. This was both to be a good advocate for polyamory (a responsibility that I viewed as larger than the confines of my own romantic relationships) and to not shoot myself in the foot with too much negativity before I figured out if she would be a good match for me, Seth, or potentially both of us.

This is what I came up:

> **I really liked your profile**
>
> Hello,
>
> I was looking through profiles, and yours caught my eye — limbic, subcortical, and cerebral. :) And then of course you mentioned Munchkin,

```
Roborally, and Carcasonne, and I was floored.
It's always a good feeling to know you share
quirks with someone else.

You mentioned on your profile that you were in-
trigued by polyamory. My husband and I have a
polyamorous marriage, and it has enriched our
life together and our bond in a way I nev-
er knew it would. The one downside is that
most of our friends have been less than to-
tally supportive. They say they're okay with
the change that we've gone through but deftly
change the subject every time we bring up the
topic - which is sad because it's been a real-
ly big deal for me and something I feel I need
to discuss.

So if you have any questions at all about poly-
amory or how it works for us, seriously any
questions at all, feel free to ask.

-Page
```

After a bit of a slow start, spending so much time with both Mark and Nathan meant I had suddenly become a busy, busy girl. Often I chatted with Mark about my issues with Nathan. One day I'd get a banana cream pie blizzard with Nathan at Dairy Queen before retiring to his apartment where I'd cuddle with him while he played *Batman: Arkham Asylum* on his Playstation 3. The next I'd go for sushi with Mark, commiserating over sake.

One fateful poker night at Megan and Pete's, someone got the bright idea of passing around a bottle of coconut rum while the five of us (Megan, Pete, Seth, Mark, and me) formed a giant cuddle pile on the couch to take in a movie. Roving hands were everywhere, and Pete, professedly quite a straight individual (a reality he rued as horribly inconvenient), joked that Mark's stray hand on his thigh had bumped his score on the Kinsey scale by a point.

I was sprawled across Mark's lap, our usual physical chemistry crescendoing. I swiveled my body around, ran my hands through his hair, meeting his gaze. "Hi," I said, looking straight into his eyes.

"Hi," he answered, back more softly.

"Hi," I replied, feeling something stir in me.

"Hi," he said, his tone reading more sexual.

We traded dozens of intense exchanges of simply "hi" before breaking eye contact, and I rested my head on his shoulder.

"What the hell," Megan said. "That was... special."

The other three laughed at us, but the moment was far from ruined for me. I was feeling hazy, swooning, the heat from Mark's body intense.

Seth stepped out to smoke. Megan followed, and Pete joined them a handful of seconds later. I couldn't blame him. After the weird back and forth, few people would have wanted to be left alone with us.

As soon as the door closed, Mark and I melted into a kiss. An amazing kiss. It was feral and powerful and raw.

"Woah, easy there, Voltron," Mark said.

"Voltron?"

"You make out like a robot lion."

I punched him in the arm. He sniggered at me.

"But seriously," he added. "Chill out the tongue action a bit. You're like a kitten with a saucer of milk."

My heart sunk in my chest. It was difficult to hear but good to know. I struggled to regain my composure. "Okay." I leaned in for another kiss, taking his advice.

He sighed happily. "Much better."

DRUNK AND ERIC

At the same time I was building a friendship and ambiguous "something more" with Mark, Seth and I also started hanging out with Dan (and his group of friends) more.

I'd personally known Dan for the length of my relationship with Seth (8 years), and Seth had known him for a few years longer still. Dan was in Seth's Dungeons and Dragons group, and we regularly extended him invites him to our parties, though he accepted very few. As a result, we had known Dan for an awfully long time and had spent a lot of time with him but didn't know him terribly well.

This was partly due to the fact that Dan had another group of friends that he partied with. Partied hard.

"I'm not an alcoholic. Alcoholics go to meetings. I'm a drunk. We go to parties," Dan said.

These friends called themselves DRUNK (Drinking Renders Us Ninja Kings). The legend goes that the day after he'd gotten his gallbladder out that Dan got together with DRUNK and got wasted, that the party stopped for nothing, no one. They took their right – no, their *responsibility* – to party seriously!

We'd been invited a few times to hang with DRUNK but had never gone, apprehensive about being at a party where we knew almost no one.

Not too long after Seth and I had opened up, Dan's wife had gotten a boyfriend herself, someone from work. Dan hadn't started seeing anyone himself but was open to the idea and had grown progressively more supportive of our open marriage as the months went on. Not only that, but word had it that other members of DRUNK were looking towards non-monogamy, even if it were more akin to swinging than polyamory.

Seth had become frustrated with Megan, having once again reached an emotional and sexual dead end with her.

"Maybe we should go to a DRUNK party, meet Dan's friends," I suggested.

"Really?" Seth said. "I don't know."

"Yeah, we should get out there. Meet new people. Especially since it sounds like they've been having open relationships. Even if nothing comes out of it, a change of scenery could really help."

So the next time Dan invited us to one of their parties, we accepted.

Not too long after the festivities began and the first shots had been swallowed, I found myself chatting in the kitchen with a man who I felt watching me intently since I'd first arrived. His name was Eric, a long-time friend of Dan's. I'd heard bits and pieces about him over the years, but we'd never officially met. Eric was a handsome devil indeed, dark and introverted and vaguely haunted by something – in short, a classic type that I am virtually defenseless against.

I'd had a shot and a wine cooler, so the exact path we took to get there is hazy, but before I knew it, the two of us were making out, between breaths discussing his experiences studying art history when he went to school for film making, Dutch painters. Feeling his hands on me, tracing the outline of my hips, my mind wandered to the reality that here I was completely absorbed in the kiss, fantasizing about what it'd be like to fuck Eric, and I didn't even know his last name.

We kissed for a long time, in the kitchen, in front of everyone. It was so good though that I simply didn't care. It was like no one else was even there.

At one point, a girl came over and interrupted us. "Excuse me." Her words were polite enough, but it was the kind of "excuse me" that always sounds incredibly rude and forceful.

We stopped kissing. "Yes?" Eric said, breathless, looking a bit dazed.

"No, I'm talking to you," the girl said, poking my arm.

"What is it?" I asked.

"Is that your husband over there?" she asked, pointing to Seth, who was doing some shots with Dan and laughing and seemed to be having a generally good time.

"Sure is," I replied, kissing Eric again.

"Hey!" she shouted in my face.

"What?" I snapped.

"How can you *do* this to him?"

"Look, I don't know you at all, but he and I have an open marriage. I have his permission to do this."

It was true. Having been inspired by Mark's story about how awkward it had been to wait in Fox's bed while his girlfriend phoned Fox for permission to do the deed, Seth and I had discussed what we'd do in such a situation, venturing out to a party, some general guidelines of what was acceptable and what wasn't.

Making out was an A-OK, full speed ahead, preapproved activity.

Really, oral, anal, and vaginal sex were the acts that needed some discussion because of their higher risk profile for sexually transmitted infections. Sucking face though? That was considered relatively harmless, good clean fun. Same for hand jobs and other assorted low-risk sexy mischief.

The heckler girl continued to carry on. Eric learned in for another kiss.

"Look, if you have a problem with it, go talk to him," I said, pointing to Seth.

Eric put his arm around me. "Maybe we need some privacy," he said. I laughed as he led me up the stairs.

We holed up in the bathroom, still making out. His face had a day or two of growth on it, and it chafed me like a Brillo pad, but instead of recoiling against the roughness, I found it excited me, stoked animal lust within me. I licked and bit and sucked his ear. His hands traveled up my shirt.

We moaned and groaned into each other's mouths, grinding. He pressed his erection against me as we vertically dry humped against the bathroom wall. It's comical to think about in hindsight, definitely dirty (stranded somewhere in that no man's land between the gross and hot kind of dirty), but in the moment, it was maddeningly hot.

He unzipped my fly, put his hands in my jeans, fingered me while he took off his jeans and underwear. I stroked his erection, moaning against his hand on my clit.

"Please, please," he said. "I need you. I need to be inside of you."

"I can only go so far," I replied.

He kissed me, moaned. "You're so hot," he said. "And gorgeous. You're so fucking gorgeous."

I felt a thrill go through me. Gorgeous? That was new. I was stranded somewhere between size 14 and 16, down a good 100 pounds but still overweight, not a thin girl. But his eyes told a different story. He was really into me, painfully aroused, totally attracted. It wasn't just the booze. There was just too much intensity.

I'm not terribly sure what I said next, only that it was a badly worded joke about him not raping me, that he later told me made him really uncomfortable. I know not soon after that my stomach turned sour, and I vomited, though fortuitously I was in the bathroom, and so there wasn't much of a mess.

Even after I got sick, Eric immediately resumed making out with me (a fact that makes me uneasy and turns my stomach to think of it now) and then started to beg. "I just want to bend you over this sink and have my way with you," he said.

"I'm sorry, Eric. We don't know each other well enough."

Eric pulled out a condom. "I'm prepared."

"Honey," I said to him, clasping his hand in mine. "You don't know me well enough. For all you know, I could have *AIDS*."

Someone started to pound on the bathroom door, angry that we were monopolizing a precious resource.

He sighed and hiked up his pants.

That could have been the end of it. But it wasn't.

I saw Eric again a few weeks later on St. Patrick's Day. DRUNK was having another get-together, and both Seth and I had such a blast at the first one, drinking, playing Rock Band, and swimming in sheer hedonism that we jumped at the opportunity to go to another gathering.

Dubious details aside, I was pretty taken with Eric. He'd made quite the impression.

I put on a black tank top that showed off my neck and shoulders while offering some pretty impressive cleavage, a pair of jeans that hugged my ass just how I liked, and a pair of 4-inch stiletto black patent oxford booties that managed to be hard and soft looking at the same time. I topped it off with a green lace choker, and I was off.

Things were a bit awkward at first with Eric. His normal shyness seemed to have intensified in my presence since our last encounter. Still, I worked my way towards him as the night went on, finally striking up a conversation.

"I had such a great time with you last party," I said. "You left me reeling."

"Me too," he replied, a warm smile creeping onto his face.

"You're a really good kisser," I added.

Though we were surrounded by people, amongst the whole DRUNK crowd, he casually let his hand fall behind me and felt up my hips, my butt. "Very nice," he whispered.

I blushed.

"Follow me," he said, leading me to... where else?

A bathroom. Seriously?

It was a different house and therefore a different bathroom, but even in the moment, the irony wasn't lost on me. I started to complain, and he grabbed my face between his hands and kissed me aggressively, like an exquisite attack. I sunk my nails into his back. He worked his hands up my shirt, freeing my breasts from my bra, starting to work my nipples.

And then someone knocked on the door. Scarcely any time had passed. Served us right for trying to get in on in the bathroom again, I suppose, what with all the DRUNK drunks around.

"Oh shit," he gasped. "Just a minute!" he yelled at the door, giving me a knowing look and gesturing to the other door (this bathroom conveniently had 2 doors). I scrambled outside, a bit frustrated that we'd been cut off so abruptly but at the same time highly amused that we were spacing out our exits. It seemed so Scooby Doo.

Perhaps 30 seconds later, I heard the toilet flush inside, and Eric left the house through another door.

"Let's go for a walk, Page," he said.

I was more than game.

It was a cold night, as nights in mid-March in Maine often are. I wasn't dressed for the weather – not for the cold certainly in my tank top – or the road conditions as the street was icy and the shoes I was wearing treacherous. Still, the one drink I'd had helped to keep me warm enough, and I was so aroused and otherwise excited by my adventure with Eric that I barely felt any discomfort. For his part, Eric held my hand and steadied me as I navigated the slippery sidewalks.

Though we were in a more populated area of Bangor, the streets were completely empty, the lights shut off. The city seemed motionless, completely dead. In that moment, I felt like Eric and I were truly the only two people in the world. That somehow the city had decided to sleep just for us so we could have it to ourselves. On a street corner, he stopped and kissed me for what seemed like an eternity.

"This is amazing." I gasped. "This moment... it's perfect."

Normally quite a reserved person, and very private even to his closest friends, Eric opened up to me about how he grew into atheism over the course of his life, the difficulties of being raised by Pentecostal parents. He talked a bit about the war in the Middle East that he was in and how difficult it was to come home night after night from a job that he hated to an empty apartment.

And before I knew it, I was opening up to him as well, telling him about what I had found the hardest part of being monogamous for 8 years with my husband: The fact that I'd meet great people who were lonely and that I felt like I could emotionally help but that my hands were tied. I could only go so far in my connections. I couldn't save them from their loneliness, what I really wanted to do. That was the best part of opening my marriage in the Spring of 2009. My hands were no longer tied.

I did everything but say, "I want to save you from your loneliness."

But it hung in the air between us.

We made our way back to the party. Eric led me around to Dan's back yard, where we made out for a bit, leaning up against the side of the house by moonlight. He lowered me to the ground, slid off my pants and fingered me again, this time trying to go down on me.

"Hey," I said. "Don't do that."

"What? Why?" he asked.

"Eric, I don't know you well enough yet. Not yet."

He seemed frustrated but respected the boundary. We kissed for a while longer until he helped me up, I pulled myself together, and we went inside.

I was extremely excited when we exchanged phone numbers later and made tentative plans for a date.

"I'll cook you dinner, and we can watch the film I made," he said. "What do you like to eat?"

"I dunno. I like lots of things. Right now, I'm on a mushroom kick," I replied.

"Something with mushrooms then."

In the days leading up to my big date with Eric, I was ecstatic. I went out and bought a cobalt blue sweater that showcased my curves in just the right way. I set aside a beloved pair of black chunky heeled Mary Janes I had been saving for a special occasion.

I'd only started wearing heels about 6 months prior, in the fall, when I'd lost my first 80 pounds or so. I was excited about my weight loss and wanted to celebrate by buying some new clothes, but Seth had dissuaded me, reminding me I'd only shrink out of them. He recommended fancy shoes instead as I'd always been a sneakers and Keds kind of person, and he loved heels, thought they were very sexy.

The first few months that I wore heels were comical. I endured incredible amounts of pain struggling with barely suitable shoes that I'd worn on days when I'd end up walking far more than I'd anticipate. I took one memorable spill in the parking lot of my apartment complex that resulted in a broken 4-pack of energy drinks and the loss of most of the skin on my right knee and my promise to myself, "No more wedges."

One time, having gotten totally stranded trying to cut across a snowy field in a pair of sky-high pumps, what escaped my mouth was, "Fuck my balls with Jesus!"

A real date! After all the weird back and forth with Nathan (who I had decided was the king of mixed signals), I was excited to have such a strong connection with Eric – and so soon! And very excited to be doing something relatively normal, traditional, even given my nontraditional arrangement.

And then I got the news via text.

I'm gonna have to cancel. My friend needs me.

I immediately felt stick to my stomach. *I understand.* I texted back.

I know it's short notice, he replied. *I'll explain when I can.*

I was crestfallen. I didn't know what to think. Had he just been fucking with me? Had he gotten frustrated with my repeated requests that I needed more time to go further physically, decided I was too much of a tease, had second thoughts? Was there actually some kind of emergency? And, would he reschedule?

I cried and moped and carried on, completely sick with disappointment. I scolded myself for having been so excited, so optimistic about things with Eric going somewhere.

The next day news filtered in through other members of DRUNK that Eric's best friend had left his wife and moved in with Eric, that a divorce was underway. Oh. Well, then. That was completely in line with what Eric had told me. A spark of hope was lit once again.

I saw Eric on Facebook a few days later and messaged him, told him I'd heard his friend had moved in, asked if he wanted to reschedule our date.

Ah, he typed. There was a long hesitation. *I've had some time to think, and I don't think I can do this.*

He told me he couldn't see me anymore. That he was starting to have feelings for me, and it scared him, that he couldn't see a happy ending for us, that he'd eventually lose me to my husband. He said he understood polyamory in theory but just couldn't wrap his mind around it – let alone his heart. Besides, he'd been on a good first date with a girl from OkCupid and wanted to give things with her the best shot he could. He felt bad enough that he'd made out with me at the second party after starting things up with her.

It was a good thing the conversation was online because I completely broke down, sobbing. I put on a good show on Facebook chat, told him I understood, all the while trying to withdraw from the conversation as gracefully as I could. It was pretty easy because Eric seemed happy just to let me have my space.

Well, fuck. I closed Facebook, ran my hands through my hair.

It was at just that moment that my phone rang.

"Hello."

"Page?"

"Yes," I replied.

"Hi Page, this is Tina."

Tina, the girl I had finally worked up the courage to message, with Mark's help. The doctor who I'd said was out of my league. We'd been trading emails back and forth, had even a couple of good conversations over Google chat, and though she and her husband lived an hour south of us, I'd given her my number and told her to let me know if she wanted to meet up the next time they were in the area.

"Oh hey, great to hear from you!"

"Don and I are going to be in the area today looking for a new car, thought maybe we could meet up."

I smiled. My eyes were puffy from crying over Eric. Seconds before, it had felt like my world was ending, and now my long-time online dating crush was asking to meet up with me. We worked out the details. They were already in the car, heading our way. Coffee in a half hour at a bookstore. I splashed water on my face, changed into something pretty, and Seth and I were off.

I knew we were a good match when Tina confessed to Googling me. This was something I'd done in the past recreationally, Googling people I knew in real life, everybody, really, friends, co-workers, exes, friends' exes, etc. It was fascinating to see what would pop up, though on occasion I'd discover something I really wished I hadn't.

The trouble was, once you've read something, it is impossible to unread it. So I decided that I'd do things a little differently with Tina and go into the meeting with an open mind. No MacGyver-style background check this time.

When Tina confessed she had Googled me and then went on to ask me a few questions about what she'd found, the poetry zine I used to edit, etc, I knew we had potential. Our quirks were lining up.

Don as well was very funny, in an understated way, and the conversation flowed easily. Coffee quickly became dinner, and we headed to my favorite sushi place, which was practically across the street.

Seth seemed a little detached, but Don and Tina had a lot of geeky interests like board gaming and sci fi shows that Seth shared. Seth had more in common with them, it seemed, though Tina and I were both quite interested in medicine and could have chatted all night about various ailments.

It was a great first meeting. They seemed like really nice people who I knew at the very least they had the potential to become good friends.

As dinner was ending, Seth got a call from the DRUNK crew. They were having an impromptu party, and Seth wanted to go. We said our goodbyes to Don and Tina, and we were off.

Part of me wanted to see Eric, and part of me didn't. Since all of me was about to, I unwisely decided to ease the process by drinking as much as I could as quickly as I could. My memory of the night isn't clear, but I do have the email I sent him the following day:

> subject: the aftermath - it's cool like school, etc.
>
> Hi Eric,
>
> That was quite a surprise for me that I'd run into you last night. Seth got the call last minute as we were eating dinner and really wanted to go hang out, so though I was nervous, I came, too.

First off, that was some sad drunkenness I displayed - and yes, I was the proverbial hot mess. Truth be told, the disappointment pertaining to you was in the mix, but I really have had a rotten week, and there were many things (such as the death of my family dog, which I'm sure I whined about; having to comfort a friend who was dumped; my dad's ongoing illness; and some really stupid nonsense with an ex-girlfriend who I think just likes to torture me) just coalescing in order to fuck my week the shit up. Last week was a really terrible week - like one of the worst in a long time - but really I think disappointment, longing, or weirdness with you was probably 10% to 25% of the picture. And unfortunately when I'm a sad drunk, I'm a really fucking sad drunk. One of my greatest failings as a human being actually, but so it goes.

I've thought about what we discussed on Facebook, and what you said (or typed) makes a lot of sense. It's easy for me with the security and stability of a solid committed relationship to take for granted the benefits of a traditional long-term relationship. A year ago, Seth and I were exclusive, and I didn't even allow him to have close female friends. When we found out close friends of ours were polyamorous (and had been for some time), we were outraged, thought he was a pig, and felt sorry for her. I am absolutely amazed by the turn my life has taken. Amazed and delighted.

But there are as many ways to be happy as there are people. And I do mean what I said to you one of those exciting gallivanting evenings, I do think you deserve to be happy.

Hope you're doing well today and not too tired at work.

-Page

P.S. I don't regret it, and I'm glad those 2
nights happened. It was easy to be fond of you,
and you did make me feel beautiful and sexy,
and when you see yourself through someone's
eyes, it's not something you "un-see." So thank
you for that.

The family dog? Oh man. Ten to twenty-five percent? I wince
to read this now, though I suppose it was tough to be honest
with him when I could barely be honest with myself about the
depth of my disappointment.

I had been on an incredible rollercoaster, from being dumped
by someone I felt like I was building something really special
with to having a promising first date with a long-time crush in
a space of hours. And then topping the whole thing off with a
drunken meltdown.

If there was one thing poly life was not, it was boring.

POLY SIGNPOST #3: MORE

Though the literal translation amounts to "many loves," I tend to think of polyamory as translating into "more love."

More is not better or worse; it is just different.

On good days, this led to my announcing, "I'm a walking emotional erection." On bad days, this translated to my soberly explaining, "Mo' lovers, mo' problems."

More love means more first dates.

This has to be one of my biggest gripes with polyamory. More love inevitably equals more first dates.

When I date, I date a lot. I give most people a chance but let very few into my heart. Think of it like trying on clothes before you buy them. It takes out the guesswork. Why commit before you're ready? And ideally you end up having to make fewer returns. Of course there are those awkward moments when you're standing in unfamiliar light in front of a questionably shaped mirror squinting at your torso and thinking to yourself "Do I have a bra somewhere that'll make this thing work? Could I get one?"

That brings me back to first dates.

There was a relatively small pool of poly/nonmonogamy friendly people in my area when I first began dating (in Eastern Maine), so I couldn't just rely on one strategy. I formed friendships that happened naturally and came out to those who were already friends as poly. And I politely and frankly expressing romantic interest in those I thought had potential, whether they were an old friend or a new one.

And online dating was mostly something I used to make new friends. New friends who may or may not blossom into something more.

It should have been a little less awkward than a typical blind date because we'd corresponded virtually and had read each other's' profiles so at least have some kind of starting point for conversation. It should have been less awkward, and maybe it was (having not been on too many blind dates), but it was still darn awkward. As of this writing, I've only had 2 meetings that I felt in my gut went well, and only one of them resulted in another meeting. It's just really hard to tell.

Nevertheless, online dating was an excellent resource, one that would eventually lead me to places I never would have anticipated.

More love does not necessarily mean more sex.

It can.

I've wanted to have sex but been completely unable to – due to my own sex bureaucracy. It was out of necessity of protecting my partners from disease risks bound by a number of rules upon which we had mutually agreed. Being bound by those rules and being unable to satisfy every carnal urge was the price of being protected by them. Basically a microcosm of the social contract, petri-dish style.

More sex does not necessarily mean better sex or a better sex life.

Quantity does not mean quality. I've had the worst sex and the best sex of my life when in open relationships.

When I was monogamous, I pined after Megan for years, only to find when my marriage opened and I had the opportunity to make out with her, that kissing her was extremely unpleasant. Our styles weren't compatible, and she was unwilling to communicate about it or come to some kind of consensus. I ended up licking her teeth.

I've had sex "to make a good impression." It was an exciting but tense night in bed. I had sex with someone's wife because I found myself in the position that to do otherwise would offend them both. I knew technically I could say no, but I also knew all too well about the weird unspoken inter-couple dynamics, and I feared things would get weird if I said no.

I'd been with another couple without a spoken package deal, hit it off with the woman, fizzled with the man. And though it seemed like there was no problem, over the ensuing months, a rift developed. I think she felt guilty, though she never admitted to me, maybe never even admitted it to herself.

And I've had sex that was a real blast, presided over small orgies, steeped myself in another couple's energy. I've had earth-shattering orgasms. I discovered the rough landscape of my kink, was shocked to find masochism and submission so present and powerful.

More love can mean more break-ups.

It did for me. This was something I never considered when I opened my marriage. And despite what the uninitiated might think, it doesn't matter how many partners you have, when a relationship ends, it hurts just as much. Before I was poly, I never ran into a situation where I had to cope with more than one breakup at a time. But if you're non-monogamous and dating a lot, it can *happen*.

So that's the flipside. While you can be swimming in New Relationship Energy, and all the good things in your life are happening all at once, the converse is also true: All the bad shit can come down at the same moment.

This is especially true if you undergo radical personal change and find that you've formed relationships that don't suit the person you've become, and the parties involved (your part-ner{s} and you) cannot or will not come to a compromise. If your entire emotional landscape shifts drastically, then you can find yourself with a major cast change.

With so much data available from concurrent relationships, things can seemingly change overnight.

For me, to embrace polyamory was to embrace change, and though it wasn't all smooth sailing, I am happy to say I am better for it.

LAYERS

Even though at this point I had no formal poly "relationships" to speak of, I was still dealing with layers of feelings, juggling emotions in a way that I had no paradigm for.

Though Nathan and I had cooled off our romance a considerable amount and were no longer physical with each other because he'd started seeing someone else exclusively, he was visibly upset when he came to a Rock Band party at our apartment and witnessed Mark (who was essentially there as my date) cuddling and flirting with me.

I took him aside, asked him what was wrong, but Nathan was at a loss for words.

"It's nothing," Nathan said, his eye twitching.

"Are you sure?"

"Positive," he replied, pouring himself an amaretto on the rocks.

"Look, that's not the best amaretto, you sure you don't want anything to cut it?"

"Page," he said. "I'm *fine.*"

"Okay," I said. "I love you. You matter to me."

Nathan walked into the living room and beat some frustration out on the drums.

Through the course of the night, the rest of the guests left one by one, two by two until it was just the four of us: Seth, Nathan, Mark, and me. At about three in the morning, Seth finally announced that he was off to bed, and Nathan decided to trudge across the complex to get to his apartment across the way.

Mark, however, stayed with me. We sat on the couch, fingers interlaced. "Nathan was acting funny," Mark observed.

"I thought so."

"If I didn't know any better, I'd say he was jealous," he teased.

"That much was obvious," I said.

Mark was well versed in my strange more-than-friendship with Nathan, the seemingly arbitrary distinctions Nathan would make in order to make what we did together seem "right."

"It's curious though, that he'd be jealous," I added.

"Oh?"

"Well, what would he be jealous of? I don't even know what exactly is going on between us," I said.

"Me neither," Mark agreed. "And I like it that way."

He put his arm around me, told me a bit about his family, his childhood, his friends back home in Rhode Island.

I got into his lap, wrapped my legs around him, felt the tension of his body, the muscles in his arms as we pressed our bodies together. He was so sexy and warm, nearly irresistible. Full of desire. And yet, we only talked. We didn't even kiss. We talked until well after the sun came up, and he decided he should get home so he could get in a nap before his first class. He gave me one sweet kiss at the door, and we said our goodbyes.

Later it felt as though the whole thing had been a dream, a dream that I had no chance of meaningfully interpreting.

Though my love life was flourishing (with the sole exception of the flopped connection with Eric), Seth's was anything but. He and Megan had been dating for the better part of a year on their own, without me in the picture, and he was running into the familiar issues: Her unwillingness to go past a certain point with him physically, a lack of romantic or emotional connection, a feeling that things were stagnating.

Removing me from the picture hadn't changed things drastically between them. I knew that chiming in with an "I told you so" would be counterproductive (as much as the sentiment was burning in my brain), so I focused on possible solutions to his problem.

"You know what would be *fun*?" I said. "A double date with Mark and Megan."

It made perfect sense. Mark had been a regular at poker nights at Megan and Pete's house for quite some time, and though Megan and Mark didn't know each other terribly well, they'd been friendly acquaintances for years, with quite a bit of overlap between the social circles they were both in, so at the very least, they were really comfortable with each other.

And it gave me an excellent excuse to spend some more time with Mark.

"You know, that's not such a bad idea," Seth said.

"We could push back the couches, put all the cushions and pillows from the opium den on the floor, make it into a giant bed."

Seth grinned. "I like where you're going with this."

"And porn! We should watch porn!"

I didn't have to twist Seth's arm. When I ran the idea by Mark, he volunteered the use of his campy classic porn collection, including *Debbie Does Dallas* and *Alice in Wonderland: An X-Rated Musical Fantasy*.

Megan, typically more reserved, reluctantly agreed.

It seemed like the perfect night. The movies were great, funny and sexy both. The "floor bed" was comfortable and easily accommodating the four of us with an optimal view of the screen. After a few decently strong drinks, Mark and I had made it to third base, and my head was spinning.

Megan had brought *Across the Universe* with her as she'd been meaning to show it to Seth for a while. Somewhere along the way though, things suddenly took a turn for the worse.

I was stroking Mark's cock and nibbling on his ear when I heard Seth slam the sliding glass door behind him, much harder than normal. Megan was standing up, rubbing her face, crying.

"What's going on?" I asked Mark.

"Come get a drink with me," Mark said, practically dragging me off to the kitchen.

Our apartment had a fairly open layout with only a blanket hanging in the doorframe blocking the sound between the living room and kitchen. I heard Megan convince Seth to come back inside.

"I don't mean shit to you," Seth said.

"Look, it's not like that," Megan said.

"Like hell it's not."

"Mark's just very... convincing," she replied.

I shot a glance at Mark. "What?" I whispered at him.

Mark pressed a finger to his lips.

"I saw you two. I saw the way you were looking at him, the way he was touching you."

Megan sighed. "We were just having fun, fooling around. I had no idea it'd bother you so much."

"Neither did I," Seth said.

"It's not like I'm your one and only, or that I'll ever be."

"That doesn't mean that you aren't special to me. I love you. I think about you constantly. But to you, I'm just some guy. The thought that all this time I wasn't really special to you when I thought I was, it's..." Seth's voice was breaking up.

"I don't know what to tell you. I care about you. I love what we have, but you're right. I don't think we're at the same place."

The movie had ended, and the DVD menu music was looping over and over.

"Well, if that's how you feel, I think we should end it," Seth said.

"It's probably for the best."

They fell silent. I pulled back the blanket draped across the doorway, peering in at them. Seth was crying in her arms, his head over her shoulder. Megan was stroking his hair, her expression blank. When she noticed my gaze, she shot me a dirty look, and I let the blanket drop back into place.

I wrote in my journal the next morning: "He feels interchangeable. I can't blame him. I feel that way, too. I'm disappointed, rejected by all of them, but my feelings are inconsequential, inconvenient. I need to help him heal."

POLY SIGNPOST #4: THE HOSTAGE SITUATION

One of the best things about opening my life and my heart to loving multiple people at once was the sense of interconnectedness, especially when considering phenomena like compersion.

The downside is that the reality of being intimately linked with so many others is also a serious liability. Opening up to more love can entail opening up to more pain, frustration, and disappointment.

Never was this so clear to me as when one of my lovers, especially my husband Seth, was hurt by someone he loved. When a metamour (a word used in poly circles to denote a person your partner is seeing that you are not involved with) hurts someone you love, be it for any reason, the fallout can be devastating. The same qualities that can cause you to experience so much compersion, empathy, sensitivity, etc., also cause you to feel a partner's pain.

And the worst part is that it's very difficult to *do* anything about it, without risking making the situation significantly worse.

In the moment, it is often difficult, if not impossible, to discern the offending party's true intent – whether a slight is deliberate or incidental. The pain bursts forth, the explanation to come later, if at all. Additionally, even though intentionally offensive behavior is malicious and a great deal more troubling, it doesn't mean that unintended offenses don't do damage. This is further complicated by the fact that there are infinite degrees between the extremes of the completely benign oversight and the all-out attack.

To make matters worse, it's difficult to completely understand a relationship you are not a direct part of, so as much as a conflict might affect you and cause you stress and pain, you are probably only getting a very limited view of what is actually going on. In addition, even in situations where you have a wealth of information, your own insecurities and vested interests (such as the desire to have as much time with partners who are splitting their affections with others) can bias your perspective to the point where you become inordinately upset with the metamour, attributing most or all blame to them in the conflict, vilifying them and completely ignoring your partner's role.

This can cause additional problems if you mention these frustrations to your love, who may not be assigning any blame whatsoever to the other partner and may become highly offended that you're doing so. Push too hard, and you risk alienating your partner and may very well trigger an additional conflict of your own.

In these situations, many a poly person becomes frozen in terror, watching a partner and a metamour intently in rocky times, worrying and fretting with little recourse.

I call this emotional interplay the hostage situation.

In a hostage situation, you're watching what amounts to an emotional stand-off from a relatively short distance as a frustrated bystander, or perhaps you're acting as mediator for the parties trying to talk them out of whatever crisis they've ended up in. In either case, there's tension, and the stakes are high. In the first case, you're powerless, doomed to watch what happens without having a hand in the outcome. In the second, you carry the additional pressure of being part of the process, and consequently, part of the failure should things go terribly awry.

These are the times when polyamory simply is not fun.

DON AND TINA

Despite my growing feelings for Mark prior to our doomed double date, things became unbelievably awkward immediately following that night. Apparently, Mark had made some kind of move on Megan, and Seth had seen and flipped out. Completely focused on Mark, I was oblivious to what was happening with anyone else.

I brought it up to Mark in the days following, and he explained that he hadn't meant to encroach on anyone's territory or offend. Mark said that he was used to how things worked in Fox's poly circle, and in that group, everyone became physical with one another and linked in situations like that.

In that poly circle, to not make a move would have been considered rude, the only explanation being that he was not attracted to Megan, which simply was not the case.

I had gotten that vibe as well the times that I'd chatted with Fox about polyamory and that he employed a distinctly different strategy with love and dating than I did, one of the plethora of reasons that Fox and I weren't dating.

However, I didn't know what to think when I spoke with Megan. Mark and Megan had crashed on our couches to sober up and get some rest before heading home. She filled me in that the following morning when they woke up that Mark had made another pass at her. Megan said she'd fooled around with him just a bit but held her ground against things getting too serious.

"It wasn't easy to say no," Megan said. "He's very... persuasive."

"He is a good kisser," I said, my heart sinking.

"Oh yeah," she agreed. "But I don't know. He's kinda... meh."

"You think?" I asked, feeling even worse.

"He's kinda... sleazy or something. Not what I'm looking for at all."

So that was how it was going to be. Megan was too good for not one, but two men I was with, men I felt like I was always chasing (the struggle to win my husband's approval had been relationship-long), but who were instead focused on chasing her.

It felt like she viewed me as someone only fit to date her rejects.

Not only that, knowing what happened the next morning between Mark and Megan put Mark's explanation for his behavior in a completely different light.

It wasn't that I minded that Mark was interested in Megan. After all, I had pursued her myself for quite a while. It was that he'd misled me. While I figured what he'd said about Fox was technically true, it was far from the whole story.

With the semester ending soon and Mark heading out of state to work on a fishing boat for the summer, the matter was tabled for the foreseeable future, but I was no longer optimistic. My former excitement about Mark was gone.

As disappointing as that alone would be, I had bigger problems at home. As hard as breaking up with Megan had been for Seth the first time, the second time was even worse. "I hate that you were right about her," he said.

"Right about her?"

"That she wasn't capable of giving me what I want, that she wasn't as into me as I was into her."

"Eh, I say lots of things," I said. "When you talk as much as I do, some of what I say is bound to happen."

"Is that your pretentious, yet modest way of telling me 'I told you so?'"

I sighed. "I just want you to be happy."

"It's back to the drawing board," Seth said. "Any bright ideas?"

"Well, there's Don and Tina. I had a really good time at dinner with them the other night. And she is *really* cute."

"Eh," Seth said. "I dunno."

"That's what you said about Megan, too," I said.

"There you go again with your 'I told you so.'"

"Fair enough," I replied. "I just think you should give her a chance."

"They just read more as friends to me," he said.

"I get that. But you never know. They always say that the best relationships start out with being friends first."

"Yeah, but that's in monogamy."

"It's still dating. And like I said, you never know. I'd like to get to know them better."

Tina, for her part, continued to email me from a medical mission in Haiti every few days using the hotel connection. We'd kept up a vigorous correspondence over the months since I'd first messaged her, even when she was a busy resident. I'd get messages from her at 2 or 3 o'clock in the morning while she was taking a break from her ER rotation.

When I started writing her, I'd made sure to always end my emails with at least one question so that Tina always had a reason to respond, so we'd fallen into a regular format where we'd first answer the question the other had asked, share whatever else we felt like sharing, and then asked a new question. It worked well and over the months had exchanged more than 200 messages.

Though we'd only met in person the one time, I felt like I knew her better than most other people in my life. And what I knew, I liked. She'd been timid at first, but as I dug deeper, I found she was quirky and sweet, and though she presented as the perfect stereotype of the introverted geek, she could be quite bold and adventurous, and when I'd start her on about a subject she liked, it was hard to stop her. And just as importantly, I could listen to her (or read her) all day.

The fact that she was making such an effort to keep on writing to me (even while in a remote country) spoke volumes. It seemed I wasn't the only one who was invested. It didn't hurt that she didn't seem to mind my flirtations, while not responding as aggressively in kind. As time went on, she opened up to me more and more about her sexuality, her limited experience but healthy curiosity when it came to other women.

When she got back from Haiti, Seth and I continued to make the journey down to see Don and Tina. Sometimes we'd just visit their house to play board games and hang out. Another time, we joined them for a film festival. Don and Tina were quite the foodies, and Tina had taken it upon herself to cater for my low-carb diet, so I was met on each occasion with her newest recipe, black bean brownies, chicken paprikash without the spaetzle, lemongrass chicken wings, all delicious and perfect and more than I would have ever asked for.

We'd settled into a comfortable friendship with Don and Tina. Things were moving slowly on the romantic front, but I was having so much fun with them that I hardly noticed, and then one night on a lark, Tina pulled a new board game out of the closet, a naughty one, one of those silly XXX things sold at adult shops. A few hours later, all four of us were naked with our hands all over each other. Like that. After all that buildup, all it took was an elaborate game of truth or dare to push us out of the friend zone.

With the promise of an orgy looming on the horizon, I mustered up my courage and scheduled an appointment for STI testing. I figured it'd just be easier and set our minds at ease if we could be sure of things. It seemed the responsible thing to do. I thought it would be a cinch.

My regular provider was on vacation, so I went through the process with a different one, a nurse practitioner in her late 50s. She asked me a barrage of questions, spending an inordinate amount of energy typing a summary of the visit into Centricity.

At intervals, she would read back what she had written to me and ask if it was okay. Even if it wasn't exactly correct, it was really more effort than it was worth to fix the minor discrepancies, so I'd just agree.

For starters, she indicated in my history of present illness that I had "entered into an unexpected relationship," which is *technically* true.

After all, I couldn't predict the future and had no idea my great fortune would lead me to such wonderful new partners. But really the unexpectedness of the relationship had nothing to do with the STI test. It was the impending sexy time, really. I was being tested as a preventative measure, and her wording made it sound like I'd already done the deed and potentially been exposed.

But not liking lectures and knowing non-monogamy as a lifestyle choice might certainly provoke one, I settled on her misrepresentation.

She then asked me if I had sexual encounters with men or with women. When I hesitated, she asked, "With both?" and I said, "Yes, men and women." She typed a bit and then asked, "Would you consider yourself a bisexual?"

I winced. I wasn't sure what this had to do with getting a pelvic swab and a blood draw. It was jarring to hear "bisexual" in its noun form. I've always thought of it as an adjective that described my sexual habits and proclivities, not my definition. Not to mention, I don't think anyone had ever asked me my sexual orientation before. Usually, I'd tell them on my own time on my own terms when it seemed relevant to the situation, or they simply didn't ask.

"Yes, I would," I replied, feeling a little choked up. I didn't know why.

Maybe it was dreading what came next, the cold speculum, the wait for my results, the inevitable red tape and technical truths between me and paper copies of them.

Maybe it was the interrogation-grade lighting or the extra-large Tim Horton's iced coffee I'd downed in a hurry on the chance I'd have to provide a urine sample.

"You know," she said, "It's understandable that you're so uncomfortable. Our culture doesn't really address you."

I nodded.

"Would you like to talk to someone, a counselor? I know this one therapist who is a lesbian you could talk to. I could make a referral."

I shrugged. Really, I just wanted my lab tests, but she was being so nice, and I didn't want to hurt her feelings. I figured worst case scenario I didn't have to make the appointment. I could always cancel.

She started typing something into the computer. I didn't even realize I was crying until she handed me a paper towel. "Get the feelings out," she said.

How humiliating.

It said something that it was a relief when it was time for the pelvic exam. No more questions whose answers were easily misinterpreted. No more uncomfortable silence. This was familiar territory, robotic, automatic.

"It's all very complicated," she added to my chief complaint as a direct patient quote.

As a friend of mine told me when I recounted the story, it was mostly likely the trio of married, bisexual, and STI testing that prompted a counseling referral, but it was definitely not the way I had wanted things to go.

On the bright side, at least I got the testing done.

Tina underwent a battery of tests herself, and once we'd compared notes, we both came up completely negative, so it was a green light. Full speed ahead.

Even though I hadn't expected for anything to come up positive (after all, I'd spent the last 8 years mutually monogamous with Seth), I was the highest risk person in our little poly group. I'd lived a pretty wild life before settling down with Seth.

While I'd been tested a few times during my riskiest period and had been asymptomatic, I knew there was enough of a window between my latest series of tests and the end of my slut-tastic days that there was an outside chance that I could be carrying an infection that I didn't even know about.

I was extremely relieved when the official results came in. Relieved and excited.

With the preliminaries out of the way, the four of us burst into what amounted to an ongoing game of Sextris, most nights together ending (and on occasion, beginning) with everyone naked and sexually entangled with multiple others. I'm sure to a lot of people that sounds pretty wonderful, and it often was.

I remember fondly the time that, after hearing Tina boast about her awesome under the bed restraint system, I tore off my clothes, ran into their bedroom, and threw myself onto Don and Tina's bed, demanding to be handcuffed and leg cuffed. Not the most submissive move, to be sure, but it was a world of fun to be secured there, completely exposed, at the mercy of the others – though I have to say, at 5' 6" and stretched to my limits, being spread eagle on a king-sized bed is no joke!

It wasn't without its hiccups though. Not everything that happened came straight out of a porno. On one dreary night, Don completely shut down while I was giving him a hand job. Apparently he had an earache, completely understandable, but something that he didn't communicate to me (Tina was the one who told me, a few days after the fact when I mentioned that I was worried about Don, that he'd seemed distant during our last encounter).

I ended up withdrawing as he curled up into the fetal position and waiting awkwardly while Seth and Tina had fun on the other end of the giant bed we'd set up in the living room.

Earache or not, a pattern emerged where Don wasn't exactly rejecting my advances but didn't seem terribly enthusiastic about them either.

I'd try to talk to him about it, in person and through email, and he'd clam up. "He likes you," Tina said when I checked in with her about it, after not getting much of a response from him. "I'm not sure what the trouble is."

But Don's body language told a different story. It was closed off, unapproachable. Though I had plenty of chemistry with Tina and Seth, and the two of them seemed to be getting along, Don didn't seem like he was having fun, with me or anyone else. As time went on, the disconnect spread throughout the group, and Tina engaged less and less with Seth, preferring to connect only with me. I couldn't tell whether it was a conscious decision on her part or not, but in either case, it seemed like she was readjusting her physical relationship with Seth to be more symmetrical to the one I had been able to establish with Don. It certainly put a damper on things.

Frustrated, one night I left the orgy early, pulled out my laptop, and played *Fairway Solitaire*.

"That's how you know you're a group sex pro," I later joked. "You can switch gears instantly."

The truth was that I was getting burnt out. It wasn't fun anymore. It felt forced.

MATTHEW

Time and time again, I was learning that while physicality was fun, without a deeper emotional connection, the novelty would wear off, and I'd quickly grow bored. In Don and Tina's case, the fact that Don seemed so uncomfortable was overshadowing everything else, upsetting the group dynamics, ruining even the raw physical pleasure.

Serendipitously, I was at the same time building another connection on online dating, a polyamorous man in his 40's named Matthew, a British expatriate living in Canada. Matthew was quite the character. He had his own Wikipedia page and was a minor web celebrity. And in an extraordinary nod to his Dr. Who fandom, the guy actually owned a Dalek.

Matthew first found my dating profile in the spring, not too long after I started seeing Don and Tina, and wrote me one of the most adorable and thoughtful messages (if brief) I've ever received:

> **Shopping lists.**
>
> Awww, and here was me thinking that I was the only people who picked up old shopping lists.
>
> Have you ever tried shopping from them and working out what on earth you could make?

Truly. It was exactly the kind of thing I liked to be sent, basically found poetry. That coupled with the fact that he and I were a 98% match led me to message him in return though he was over a 7-hour drive (and an international border) away, even though I'd joined online dating with the express purpose of meeting people locally.

My first replies (yes, I wrote two):

> No, I haven't – but that would be amazing!
> Maybe throw together some kind of sculpture...
> hmmm... It does bring me back to the time when
> I was at the grocery store with 2 male friends,
> and we were buying baby oil, condoms, and a
> banana. Oddly enough, it really wasn't what it
> seemed like. I wanted to grab the cashier by
> the shoulders and say, "Baby oil damages la-
> tex! Do you really think I'm THAT stupid?!" But
> I digress...
>
> Sex in a Dalek? They look so small on TV – it
> doesn't seem possible. :) I suppose if you
> could manage it that you'd end up with a hell
> of a story – and many strange cuts and lumps,
> etc.
>
> Yes, I am quite taken with your profile, but you
> probably get that a lot.
>
> I might craft you a better, more thorough re-
> sponse later. I'm running off to a party (it
> will probably be a bit of a disappointing gath-
> ering, but I adore the girl throwing it and
> want to make sure she isn't all alone surround-
> ed by uneaten veggie trays), but I wanted to
> say that I'm happy you dropped me a line about
> the shopping lists and had a fantastic time
> reading your profile. Seriously – Profile. Envy.
>
> So message me and tell me not to bother within
> a soon-ish time frame if you wouldn't like an-
> other longer message because knowing me I will
> write one if you don't. :)
>
> -Page

P.S. I don't care what people say. You're way cuter than your cat. Don't tell your cat I said that though. :)

Message #2:

So here I am typing up a response early in the morning into notepad, which I will undoubtedly copy + paste into this message when I finish it and get the balls to do so. Ay! I had rotten anxiety dreams last night (a rarity) in which I was a failed entrepreneur and was mocked incessantly for it. I have no idea what it means. It might be because I have a bit of a road trip planned for later today. Honestly, I'm not at all sure.

I thought again of the strangeness of having sex in a Dalek when I was at that dreary "party" last night and realized another problem other than the cramped space. I would be far too tempted to keep saying "Exterminate. Exterminate. Exterminate," in that angry robot voice, so unless my partner had a bizarre angry homicidal robot fetish, it would ruin things. Of course, we would be having sex inside a Dalek, so I suppose the bizarre angry homicidal robot fetish probability would be at all-time high levels.

You are probably saying to yourself, "This woman's a creeper. I write her 2 sentences and get a novella." And of course you might be right. I indeed might be a creeper. The world is full of them, and I DID like your profile, which I understand might alarm you. :)

I'm also rather fond of polymaths myself. I try and fail miserably to be one.

Of course as I'm sitting here typing this up, it occurs to me that you are probably much too cool for me and won't write me back. Chances are. I will say that you are the person the furthest away that I have written a message to and that I really focus on local folks (which given the social environment of Maine is a pretty scanty offering), but the way you have presented yourself really spoke to me, and I felt compelled to write you (there I go with creeper language again). I do hope you write back though. Truly.

Hmm... How about a question? One other than the one I just asked of course. It will give you a reason to write back to me (if you so desire).

What embarrasses you?

-Page

P.S. My condolences on OkCupid rejecting your questions. They hated mine, too.

P.P.S. I love postscripts, though I guess they're a little precious.

We traded e-mail and IM info and started to correspond.

From the beginning, he pushed me out of my comfort zone. In general, I was a big e-mailer and preferred leaving static messages to IM when I was getting to know someone (though if you were someone I knew already and really liked, I was usually fine with chatting or texting). I liked to have time to think about what I wanted to say to new people. In any case, Matthew was very firm about not e-mailing and greatly preferred IM. Finding him fascinating, I capitulated and started spending more time on IM. It was actually kind of nice because I could chat with Matthew while I was talking with other friends and draft e-mails to Tina, Mark, or Nathan during the conversational downtime.

During the first few months, I had a GREAT time chatting with him.

> **page:** you there, Q type?
>
> **matthew:** Yes maam.
>
> **page:** so polite!
>
> **page:** you must have a good upbringing

Matthew was quirky and random, and we instantly formed private jokes.

> **page:** sooo... a personal question... how long have you been a non-monogamous person?
>
> **matthew:** Ummm... 15 years?
>
> **matthew:** Longer really.
>
> **page:** ahh I see
>
> **matthew:** You?
>
> **page:** 1-1/2 years
>
> **page:** I'm a baby, really

matthew: hehe awww.

matthew: But blame the giraffes.

page: oh yes, I do – every day

I felt like I had met a male version of myself. Seth commented that Matthew and I were "goofy in the same exact way." The fact that Matthew even existed brought me great joy. We discussed meeting enthusiastically trying to work out the logistics involved.

And then Matthew withdrew, became tough to reach. When he was online, he was always "hiding" (his word, not a status). Didn't want to talk. Described himself and his life as "broken." I was disappointed but gave him his distance save for one drunken night that I expressed how much I'd like to get to know him and how hard it was that it seemed like I wasn't going to.

Retracing the steps we'd taken, reading old chats and messages, I realized that as taken as I was with him that I'd put far more effort into our correspondence through the very act of trying harder to keep in touch and through the quality and quantity of what I said.

It occurred to me that I could have jumped the gun with my excitement, that I'd idealized him and fallen in love with a potential that wasn't there. At the very least, it had dawned on me that I was far more into him than he was into me.

So I phased Matthew out. Gave up. I figured if he came back, he came back. I half expected to never hear from him again. The winds had shifted, and I was really busy spending weekends with Don and Tina.

And then out of the blue, I heard from Matthew. I wrote about it in my journal:

Boundaries

I'm over it. I swear.

A week ago, Matthew e-mailed me. He's heading to see a friend in a month or two and is going to be passing through Bangor. Asked me if I wanted to meet up. I was stunned. It was very confusing after having kept my distance to have this kind of opportunity, but I e-mailed him back anyway and said I'd love to meet him (I think we'd be great friends and probably more). We e-mailed back and forth a little trying to work out the parameters of the visit (length, where he would be staying, etc.). And last night we talked.

I found out that he broke up with his primary partner, and that was the reason for his crabbiness and seclusion (understandable). When I tried to be supportive, he snapped at me saying I was being annoying. I tried to smooth things over, which worked in short order, and we started discussing his visit. I discovered his trip is taking him down to New Jersey to stay with a friend just to get a break from where he is living and all the memories there with the ex. He'd only be seeing me for a day and wanted to stay the night here (the words "free hotel" flashed into my brain, but I tried to keep an open mind and be positive about his intentions), which is essentially the halfway point between Halifax and NJ (8-ish hour drive on each side).

And then things took a huge turn for the worse. The conversation drifted to other topics about which he was very negative, cruel even, including aspects of my "annoying" personality and the appearance and behaviors of my friends. Somehow he thought it'd be okay to tell me my girlfriend was ugly. And even when he wasn't being outright insulting, I really didn't care for his tone.

I withdrew from the chat tactfully and sat watching TV ("Futurama") with Seth for a while ruminating, and the outrage startled to bubble up.

I am putting my foot down.

I don't care if he drives through my living room on the way to New Jersey.

I refuse to be treated that way.

If he can't be civil, he can sleep in his car or spring for the Holiday Inn like any normal person.

I have plenty of wonderful people in my life. I don't need someone who makes me feel this way.

Not wanting to tear the guy's head off, I took a step back, regained my composure, and wrote to him:

> If visiting me on the way to see your friend is an inconvenience or added stress, then don't worry about it. I know you have a lot going on in your life and aren't feeling well. I would much rather that you take care of yourself and feel your best than have a chance to meet you. Meeting you will either happen eventually, or it won't. I will be fine either way.

Not necessarily "open, honest communication" or the most direct route, but I was done. And it worked. With that, he stopped writing, and we drifted apart.

I was right. As excited as I had once been about Matthew, there was really nothing much there, after all, certainly no investment on his part. I felt foolish for ever having felt there was. Why should there have been? I was just some girl online.

The magic was in how *I* felt when I chatted with him. I liked the person I was when I was with him, the way I felt, the things I said. I worried I'd never be that woman again.

POLY SIGNPOST #5: HOW MANY PARTNERS IS TOO MANY?

The stigma of having multiple partners is ubiquitous. It's especially obvious in "normal" society with the standard tradition of monogamy or at least serial monogamy where people are expected to have only one sexual partner in any given time span.

Sex positivity has been in my life (as I'm sure it has been in many others) a constant struggle to connect with and accept my own sexuality, to be true to that, to take it wherever it led me, and to stop shaming myself. "Slut shaming" is a term I hear a lot in feminist circles to refer to the negativity directed at women who claim their own sexuality, who are sexually liberated and confident about their bodies.

For many years, there was a radical double standard where promiscuous men were "studs" and promiscuous women "sluts" – hardly breaking news, I know. The gap has narrowed. Unfortunately, it's by shaming everyone, male and female alike.

I've even encountered this kind of judgement in non-monogamous circles. People who are believed to have too many crushes and interests are looked down upon and judged for it. Sometimes polyfidelitous people (those in committed relationships with more than one person that are closed to new partners) sneer at those in fluctuating webs, claiming that their relationships mean more and that they are practicing "real polyamory."

Granted there weren't many poly people where I was living in Central Maine, but I did know some and witnessed the sanctimonious dismissal of a mutual friend who had 7 partners. He's clearly dirty and disease ridden, they said. And how can those connections be anything but superficial? His worst judges had 2 partners apiece.

Even after years of actively dating as a poly person, I'm still trying to figure out how I feel about these things. On one hand, judging a person harshly solely based on the fact that they have more partners than I do seems patently absurd. After all, by this logic, any given set of polyamorous relationships would be crap compared to the relationship of any monogamous person on the street. And I knew that wasn't the case.

On the other hand, as much as it pains me to admit, time is limited. Money is limited. For some people, libido is limited. Not only that, but it takes a lot of mental energy to really focus on people. Juggling a lot of partners can lead to impersonal interactions. I found this with Matthew, who seemed to be forging attractions with women for the purposes of trip planning, not unlike a hunting expedition or a shopping spree. He split himself in a multitude of directions. As a result, regardless of his true intentions, his attention came off as limited and insincere.

How much time and energy you have to divide in order to give it to those you love, or at the very least fancy, are pragmatic considerations. And of course, exposure to sexually transmitted infections enters the picture.

There is a temptation to stigmatize promiscuity because it carries a greater risk profile. Many view sexually liberated behavior as inherently threatening to sexual health. However, I've found that for the most part, polyamorous individuals practice safer sex, get tested regularly, use condoms, and most importantly, have important conversations about risk and health status and disclose, disclose, *disclose* in a way I never found in college hook-ups, the bar scene, or any other bastion of serial monogamy. Sure, strict monogamy is the next best thing to outright abstinence as far as limiting your level of risk, but practicing polyamory with an ethical communicative group of partners can come pretty damn close, not to mention the fact that many people end up in relationships that they think are monogamous but secretly aren't.

While the numbers of connections and points of contact are higher and accordingly carry a higher intrinsic risk, the key, is managing this risk. Of course there is risk involved in being sexual with other people. There is also risk involved in riding in a car or being exposed to secondhand smoke. We all determine what level of risk we're comfortable with and act accordingly to minimize it in any way we can that jibes with our goals.

In the way that you can decide not to date someone based on the fact that they smoke, you can veto someone for having too many partners.

In the way that you can date a smoker but request they don't smoke in your presence, you can request your partner take certain precautions with others or conform to certain rules.

In either case, there's no need to shame the individual. You're just not comfortable with accepting that level of risk. They are, and it's their right.

I wish I knew all the answers. Trouble is, sometimes I'm not even sure what all the *questions* are. They vary from situation to situation, from person to person.

That's why it's key to find a partner (or partners) that you can talk to. About anything. And that includes the sexy stuff. Besides, talking about it is half the fun, right?

ROB

As time wore on, it became evident that mousy Dr. Tina had a secret. She was kinky. I suppose the handcuffs should have tipped me off. And the references to nipple clamps. What can I say? I can be kind of dense sometimes.

I realized she had no clue that I was oriented that way myself when she told me, "You're awfully vanilla for a poly lady."

"You think?" I replied, grinning.

It was easy to see why she'd get that impression. Aside from group sex, Seth was pretty darn vanilla (i.e., not kinky), and though I'd been a hell of a lot kinkier in my approach early on in our marriage, over time I'd given up, conditioned against initiating or suggesting kinky acts by his consistently negative responses.

In actuality, some of my favorite sexual memories were quite kinky, like my submissive ex-girlfriend who liked to eat me out while I smoked a cigarette, flicked ashes on her back, and called her terrible names. And then there was the old boyfriend who fucked me in the ass and shoved a vibrator in me, calling me "dirty girl" while I screamed and writhed and came my brains out under the weight of his body.

One of my favorite college memories was a sort of masturbatory scavenger hunt that involved a checklist of a list of locations chosen by my friends where I was to masturbate to orgasm without getting caught. Impressively, the list included many of my friends' beds – and I completed it.

I was soon to learn something else about Tina. She had a friend with benefits back home in Cleveland. Rob was Don's best friend, and on the rare occasion that they were in the same place, whether that was Cleveland or Maine, they'd have sex, or "play" as she liked to put it.

I was shocked when I logged on to my online dating profile one day to find the following message from Rob:

> **Hey!**
>
> Heard you are friends with some other good friends of mine, Don and Tina!
>
> Take good care of them, now that they're not in the Cleveland area I miss them terribly!
>
> Also, yay for a 97% match! :D

Being that Rob was close friends with Don and Tina and wanting to make a good impression, I messaged him back right away:

> Aww, thanks for saying hi. :) I'm terribly fond of both Don and Tina. Meeting them has truly been the highlight of my year.
>
> I'm going to take an educated guess and surmise that you must be the illustrious Rob! If so, I am very pleased to make your acquaintance. If not, I am still very pleased to make your acquaintance but am wrong about my guess (yes, I know I'm a dork).
>
> Reading your profile, the 97% match thing doesn't surprise me. :) The polyamorous thing aside (which always gives me a large boost with matches), I agree with and enjoy a lot of what you say on it: The part about being separated from your tribe, hating threesome bait on OkC

- I, too, am a recovering Catholic! Actually was a youth leader back in the day. I have the skills to run horribly bland ice breakers to other pimpled teens whilst reflexively professing my love for the Lord in ever increasingly elaborate ways!

I am one of those false trustworthy and approachable sorts as well – and have a sick fascination with Scrabble.

My profile is bland city. All it's missing are the long walks on the beach... I keep attracting idiots who want to use me as a sex toy. I really need to fix it.

-Page

Rob wrote back right away:

Hah! Well, yeah, I agree we seem to be a good match and I am, in fact, the illustrious Rob, as you have noted. :)

Anyway, thanks so much for a thoughtful reply. perhaps in the future I will have the pleasure of meeting you in person! I know my wife and I are trying to plan another trip to Maine in the somewhat near future as we didn't get nearly enough time up there the last time I visited back in June.

Have a great weekend!

– Rob

It seemed like I had made a good impression, and I didn't have anything else to say, so the exchange left my mind entirely until nearly 3 weeks later when Don let it drop that Rob had congratulated them on snagging me, saying that I was terribly cute in the pictures on my profile.

I flushed. I didn't know Rob at all, but for some reason, knowing that he'd paid me a compliment totally made my day. It was a nice change after chasing partners for so long, all the while feeling like a salesperson for polyamory, to feel desirable without trying, even if it was to a perfect stranger.

I wrote back:

> Ah yes, you and your wife definitely should visit! It would be loads of fun. I'm kind of (read totally) addicted to meeting new people, and as you and Tina go way back and you and Don even further, I would have a dual interest in the matter. :)

Rob replied rather quickly asking for my chat info. I gave him my Skype username, and immediately he messaged me.

Not shy, that one.

We chatted for 4 hours that first night, discussing Don and Tina and tidbits from our dating profiles. The conversation was effortless. If anything, he was putting in most of the effort for a change. I certainly wasn't sold on the idea of Rob as a

romantic prospect, what with the sizable distance involved
and the botched online flirtation with Matthew fresh in
my mind.

The discussion started out innocuous enough. We bonded
over our love of yard sales. When talking about Puzzle Pirates,
a goofy online game that we'd both played, things took a turn
for the kinky.

> **rob**: I used to be a paid sub.
>
> **rob**: I mean.
>
> **rob**: That's not quite what I meant...
>
> **page**: I'm an unpaid switch myself
>
> **rob**: You really get me. You're amazing.

Rob confided that he'd been exploring his local kink scene,
checking out a local dungeon. He explained that while there
wasn't much of a formal poly scene in Cleveland *per se*, there
were plenty of kinksters, a large number of which were poly
or at least willing to have open relationships. I could tell he
was nervous as he shared this. When I didn't freak out, Rob
further shared he had fantasies of being a Dominant (or a
Dom). He'd had an ex who'd begged him to spank her. Sometimes, she'd curl up next to him on the couch and lay her head
in his lap and wanted him to treat her as his pet. And he'd
liked it. Intensely.

I shared my experiences with my submissive ex-girlfriend,
and told him that while I'd never been seriously submissive
myself, outside of a night or two in bed, I thought that I
could be open to exploring it with the right person. *Not that
you're necessarily that person*, I typed. *But I do think*

I have a submissive side to me somewhere, even if it's buried.

Fair enough, he replied.

I asked Rob about his wife, Michelle, and he talked about her in glowing terms, shared a few stories of nice things she'd done for him, the time she went way out of her way to rescue him when he'd totaled his car. They'd been together 14 years all told, 8 of those years polyamorous. She'd had a secondary relationship that lasted for 4 years, and though it'd ended over a year ago, her focus wasn't on dating or seeking new partners. I suppose it didn't help that she was 5 months pregnant. As hard as it can be to find someone who will date you when you're married, throw in a pregnancy, and the difficulty level skyrockets. For Rob, too. He shared that though he'd been actively seeking a new partner, his wife's pregnancy scared girls off.

It doesn't bother me in the slightest, I wrote – and meant it. After being frustrated by a string of single guys (Nathan, Mark, and Eric), I had decided that dating people who were coupled or had other steady relationships was preferable.

As I spoke to Rob, I warmed to the idea of pursuing something with him, as long distance as he might be. I'm not proud to say it, but rejection was starting to make me desperate. It wasn't just about the failed attempts to strike up a relationship with Nathan or Eric. I felt especially rejected by Seth, a more devastating blow to my self-esteem, and though I'd supported him through his fresh breakup with Megan and hit the dating scene hard looking for other possibilities to distract him (all the while feeling like bait), Seth seemed to care little about my emotional state, not checking in with me to see how I was doing and inattentive or apathetic when I'd try to approach him with my own concerns and stress. As time wore on, I felt less and less important to my husband.

I was on the brink of disaster. From the outside, I'm sure things looked great. I was, as always, a leader at work, training my peers, making good money. I had lost over 100 pounds, down to a size 14. Seth and I were practically poster children for polyamory in our small college town. Constantly on the defense about my lifestyle choices, I was his biggest advocate, reassuring everyone around me that we were more in love than ever, that he was a great catch.

In actuality, our sex life was virtually non-existent. The time we did spend talking together, he spent perseverating on Megan, the breakup, his regrets regarding their failed relationship, and his frustration that we hadn't yet been able to form a stable triad with someone.

For years, Seth had told me my love of romance, touching, and conversation was needy and boring, and that for asking for those things, I was indicating to him that I didn't want him. I told him that I *did* want him, apologized, and adjusted my expectations.

When we had opened our marriage, Seth had told me that at last I could find someone to help me meet all my needs. I'd been pleased to have the freedom to explore sparks that I felt naturally and focused on friendships, kept my expectations on meeting people, and if something developed, something developed.

Seth, however, had been unhappy with my approach and impatient, pushed me to make more contacts on online dating – complained that as a married man he was too scary and intimidating to attract potential partners online. It meant so much to him to have the opportunity to make new connections, I was infinitely more approachable, couldn't I just do this one thing for him?

I felt like bait, but I did it anyway. I went on a series of dates (besides Don and Tina) that left me feeling empty and like I was being insincere, laying a trap for perfectly nice people. I was emotionally exhausted and still starved for affection. When someone came into my life who was saying all the things I wanted to hear right off the bat, I leapt without looking. I couldn't bear my loneliness a minute longer.

It should have been a bad sign that Rob declared his love for me that night, the very first time we chatted. It should have told me that he, too, was desperate.

And two desperate people have the worst kind of chance in thinking clearly while building a relationship.

I probably should have run screaming in the other direction. If I had, my story might be very different indeed. However, that's not what I did. While I didn't reciprocate his instant expressions of devotion, I accepted them politely, reserved my judgment, wished him good night, told him I'd speak to him again soon.

As excited and engaged Rob had seemed during that first chat, I expected his interest to taper off – and sooner rather than later. After all, he lived 900 miles away, and while he seemed pretty taken with me, long-distance things rarely work out. It didn't help that he lived in a large city, and finding poly partners was exponentially easier there than where I was living. I figured he'd find an opportunity locally, forget about me, and that would be that.

But rather than tapering off, his interest seemed to intensify. He'd text or chat with me from work, letting me know he was thinking of me, share random bits of his day. It was an amazing feeling, to be pursued, doted on, showered with compliments.

As we talked, Rob shared his troubled dating history, how difficult it had been for him, even living in close proximity to a large pool of kinky folks, to find women to date, while his wife had practically fallen into her relationship.

This was becoming a familiar story.

POLY SIGNPOST #6: POLY WITH A PENIS

Polyamory. It's a woman's world.

Don't look at me like that. I'm not hating on men! I have character witnesses that will testify that I've (enthusiastically) loved me some men – despite the strange looks I've gotten from some of my friends.

That's the problem, really. The curious double standard. How much more desired females seem to be in these circles and how much people are disproportionately threatened by male sexuality. For instance, I saw a woman (who considered herself straight but mysteriously attracted to me) for a few months who was engaged to a man, who knew about me and had no problem with us seeing each other but expressly forbid her from seeing men. I've heard this policy flippantly referred to as "no penis, no problem."

It was a fairly prevalent trend where I lived, though to be fair swinging couples in Eastern Maine seem to outnumber poly-amorous couples 10 to 1, relationships that are open to women but closed to men. The cause is probably multifactorial and varying widely from individual to individual – potentially as a result of defensiveness resulting from sperm competition, the popular fetishization of female bisexuality, the desire of women in heterosexual relationships to experiment with same gender ones while still having the security of a long-term partner, vaginal fluid's lower risk profile for the transmission of STIs when compared to that of semen (though still certainly possessing risk), or any of countless other reasons.

Whatever the case, the feminist in me reared up with a vengeance – irate at the notion that somehow sexuality between

women is less threatening or counts less than sexuality between a man and a woman – that somehow heterosexual sex
is more "real" than lesbian sex. I've been there, and (for me at
least) it's bullshit.

The bias against men was even seen in the reaction from poly
friends of mine becoming extremely judgmental when I started to become involved with a — gasp — bisexual man! Not
only did my new flame have a penis, he was attracted to other
people with penises! I could make out with 10 women in a
single night (and did) without an eyelash batted – and indeed
with some lauding the behavior – but the moment I chose to
make out with a bisexual man, I was recklessly promiscuous
and needed an intervention for my risky behavior. The part
that floored me with this blatant bias was that the sexual acts
performed were identical (and very mild).

I have watched repeatedly as my behavior as a shameless flirt
earns me the title of "charismatic" or "sex kitten," and men
flirting with a similar volume are disparagingly called "collec-
tors" or "pigs."

When a close polyamorous friend fell madly in love with a
new boyfriend, she was apologetic and said, "I couldn't help it.
I really wanted a girlfriend, but this just happened."

Even so, her husband placed extremely strict restrictions on
the physical activities she could perform with this beloved
partner of over a year (much more strict that her rules for
what she can do in general with women) – although her husband has had a number of relationships with women where
many of the acts were performed with his partners.

She was openly (understandably) frustrated by this but said, "I can't blame him. Guys are sketchy," and expected that the explanation would suffice.

When I first started seeing guys other than Seth, as much as it pains me to admit it, I struggled with feelings of guilt. It was different from dating women. Because I couldn't hide behind the idea that the relationship could possibly have a future sexual or romantic benefit to my husband. When I dated men, I had to accept that those relationships were about *me*. What I wanted. And not about fulfilling any of *Seth's* fantasies. It felt so good and yet so wrong in a deep, conditioned sense (this despite the fact that my husband had a relationship on his own when he dated Megan and had no problem with my dating men).

Well I'm done with the devaluing male sexuality. No more.

As much as I love all sorts of different kinds of people (female/femme, trans, genderqueer), I want to take this opportunity to shamelessly proclaim how much I love men, how much I love penises, how much I love masculinity, how much I love and support men who love other men or are at least comfortable enough to be around other men in sexual situations – to declare I don't believe in the one-penis policy – and I like it this way!

I love you guys.

MICHELLE

I t's difficult for me to pinpoint precisely the moment that I started to consider Rob a serious possibility. I do know that the more I talked to him, the more I liked him. He'd given me his phone number the second time I'd chatted with him on Skype. At the time, I'd laughed to myself. How forward! It was one thing to trade niceties over messenger; the phone was another, a great deal more intimate. Rob had given me his number, but I had no intention of ever calling it.

And then I found myself calling Rob one night at a DRUNK party standing alone outside, Seth pounding drink after drink inside.

"Can I speak to Rob?"

"This is Rob."

"Hi, this is Page."

"Oh my God, Page! You called. How are you doing?"

"I'm good. It's good to talk to you. Oh, if I hang up or some-thing, I'm sorry. I'm not tech savvy at all. This is my first cell phone."

"Ever?" he said.

"Ever," I replied. "So there may be some problems. I've barely even used the thing, really, other than to send a few texts. It's a TracFone."

"Awww," he said. "You called me on your TracFone? You only have so many minutes on those."

"Well, they have to be used by a certain date, or they'll expire," I explained.

"Ah," he said.

"But I did want to talk to you," I added. "For curiosity, if nothing else."

He laughed. "I just can't stop thinking about you with one of those phones they make for old ladies with the giant numbers on them."

"They really make phones like that?" I asked.

"Oh yeah," he laughed. "Though I doubt you're their target audience."

His voice was nothing like I had expected. It was so light and playful, with a lilting quality, like he found virtually every-thing funny. It was infectious. He had seemed so serious in flat text, severe even. But to hear him actually speak, he seemed like an entirely different man. I preferred this Rob to the one I'd been chatting with.

We didn't talk long. After all, he was right. I only had so many minutes. Just long enough to talk a little bit about Cleveland, to tell him about the party that I was attending, kvetch about how bored I'd become with the DRUNK scene. He made me laugh even without telling proper jokes, just from his tone.

I hung up feeling the conversation was far from over, my cheeks burning. I physically returned to the party, but my mind was still with him. I knew I'd call him again and soon.

Oh shit. I was falling in love. With some dude I'd only talked to on the phone once. How ridiculous.

We started to call each other every day. Seth had a smart phone with unlimited minutes, and we quickly figured out that since he and Rob had the same cell provider that if I borrowed his phone to make the calls, I could talk to Rob as much as I wanted for free. Of course, this meant that I could only call Rob when Seth was home, which was more than a bit awkward in our small apartment, and that any time that I spent talking to Rob was time that I could be spending with Seth but wasn't.

With my growing feelings for Rob, it wasn't long before the two of us were having phone sex, something I could never get Seth to do or to not make fun of me for wanting to do, for that matter. It had been an early disappointment in our relationship as talking dirty got me hot like little else. Being judged for it? Significantly less hot.

It was gratifying, sexually and otherwise, when Rob welcomed it. Saying filthy things to Rob and masturbating while my husband played *World of Warcraft* in the next room, I felt a bit like a child sneaking around parents, staying up all night to secretly talk to boys in the dark, and quite honestly, I liked it. It wasn't that what I was doing violated our poly agreements. It's that if I got caught, Seth would make fun of me, which equated to just enough of a risk that it felt sexy to sneak around but not a true betrayal or consequences that I couldn't live with, were I to get caught. Seth would laugh at me, and that would be that.

Rob was delightfully perverted, I was realizing more and more. He confided in me that he needed a pair of women's panties to get off when he masturbated, not that he wore them, but that he used them to stroke his shaft. And not just any pair of underwear would do; they had to belong to a woman he admired and was deeply attracted to. Usually, he used one of many pairs he had belonging to his wife, but he also owned a few stolen pairs (even one from a former house-mate) that gave him a special thrill to use.

Rob relayed to me that Tina had insinuated that if he were a very good boy that he might be getting a special present from her this Christmas. I learned quickly that teasing was an essential part of the dynamic between Rob and Tina, a game of cat and mouse where they alternated roles with Rob starting out thinking he was the cat, repeatedly to be shown that he was the mouse, but Tina made sure to give him just enough hope that the hunt would continue.

I watched it with interest, though knowing I wasn't interested in that sort of back and forth. I felt sometimes like Tina had started out trying to play out an identical script with me, baiting me only to leave me hanging, but when I gave up pursuit and actually went away for a while had abandoned the game.

This is not to say that the mutual seduction between Rob and me was without tension.

From the onset, he begged me for dirty pictures, and I enjoyed stretching out complying with his request. The first photo I sent to him was a shot of my face flushed with orgasm directly following one of our bouts of phone sex. The next time, I sent him a photo clearly taken in the dark mere moments after I'd orgasmed from the things we'd said to each other. The photos progressed gradually into partial nudes, full nudes, and then finally out and out hardcore raunch, major for me, because I'd taken very few nude photos in my life and had certainly never sent one to someone I'd never met.

Another first for me was when I mailed my favorite pair of panties to him, freshly worn, smirking at the postal employee who asked me if the package contained anything harmful, my mind drifting to Rob pleasuring himself with my offering.

"Nope. Nothing like that," I said.

I eventually came clean to Seth that Rob and I were having phone sex, and as I'd predicted, Seth rolled his eyes and gave me a bit of a hard time about it, letting me know he thought it was terribly silly, and that was that.

Rob was not so lucky.

One night, when Michelle had left for the library, Rob called me on the phone, and even though we weren't having phone sex *per se* at the time, the sound of my voice as we chit chatted about our days turned him on to the point that he had undone his pants and started to play with himself. It was so subtle that I didn't even notice. All of a sudden, he sounded stressed, told me he had to go and that he would talk to me online, not even waiting for me to respond before hanging up.

Rob and I spoke a few hours later online (the tension of that wait was unbearable). He told me Michelle had come home early, having forgotten something, to find him masturbating while talking to someone on the phone. He'd leapt up, covered himself, and she'd reacted angrily, yelling at him. She was upset for two reasons: The first was Rob was clearly sneaking around and she felt deceived. While I understood where she was coming from, not all secrets are harmful, and I felt that shared secrets were crucial to feeling a true sense of intimacy with another person. But I got it. I myself could be suspicious of the motives of people hiding things.

Her second objection was that she wasn't comfortable with Rob having a sexual connection with someone else. I boggled at this. She'd been with her ex-boyfriend for 4 years, and they'd run the sexual gamut together. Rob wasn't a poly virgin either. He'd had sex with a handful of other women since they'd opened up. And as far as safe sex goes, it doesn't get much safer than phone sex.

As baffled as I was by Michelle's freak out, it was Rob's reaction to it that crushed me. Apparently, in an effort to appease her anger, he'd offered to Michelle to delete all my contact info and block me, to effectively erase me from his life.

Had I been a different sort of person, I would have done the same to him.

It always felt like an affair.

And in hindsight, that should have told me something. "She doesn't have to know how serious we are yet. She just wouldn't understand."

I thought it was romantic that he would lie to her by omission. That we'd have little secrets that only the two of us would know. I thought they were harmless and bred intimacy. He'd tell me when he'd screwed up and bummed a cigarette, knowing I wouldn't yell at him, only encourage him to do better. Adding, "Don't tell her. She'd freak." It made me proud. I was chill. I could handle the fact that he was imperfect. In reality, it should have made me nervous. Very nervous.

I became addicted to his confidence. To this feeling that he could tell me things he couldn't bear to reveal to her. Over time, I felt his loyalties shifting, subtly, then explicitly. "Tell no one this, but if I'd met you when I was dating her, I would have dumped her and gotten with you instead. You're the kind of woman I wish I'd married."

I knew they'd become poly in the first place because the two of them kept cheating on each other, that all of their extra-marital relationships had been full of dishonesty. That her ex-boyfriend of 4 years was married, and that the metamour, her ex-boyfriend's wife, never knew. That Rob had slept with another woman the week before he and Michelle were married and didn't let Michelle know for a few years after the fact. That he had broken rules with exes like "don't fuck in our bed" and "let me know beforehand."

It was arrogance to think I could be anything but part of the pattern of behavior, that somehow I could break the cycle through love, support, and my own efforts at ethical communication.

CLARITY

I had all but forgotten about Mark when he suddenly popped back into my life as the fall semester was about to begin.

excited – but nervous!

Mark just got back in town from his summer in Rhode Island yesterday. He called me 10 minutes ago and asked me to come have dinner with him tonight. Hearing his voice again was jarring and made me realize that I miss him and our talks terribly. I also think it's funny how just when I'm starting to forget about him, he resurfaces, sweeter than ever. I'm also going to get a chance to meet 2 of his closest friends tonight and see his place, which I'm super excited about. Even though he and I have been shamelessly flirting for a year now, this is only our third official "date" date (rest were gatherings with friends or him dropping by to play cards, etc.) and the first one HE asked me on (the first one I asked him on and the second Seth invited him to double date with Seth and Megan). I'm worried about how much time I'll be able to give him (time has become more of a commodity as of late), but I think with how busy and independent he is as well (and not a scrap of jealousy in that one) that the two of us will work something out.

Gahhh, I feel faint.

And... what the heck should I wear?

As excited as I was about going out to dinner with Mark, it turned out not to be the biggest news of the day:

> **page:** I'm gonna be out tonight on a dinner date, but I want to make sure you know I love you :)
>
> **rob:** ok
>
> **rob:** I was fired just a half hour ago
>
> **page:** holy crap
>
> **rob:** so yeah, kinda numb at the moment
>
> **page:** wow
>
> **rob:** yeah
>
> **page:** that's huge
>
> **rob:** quite

We talked for a while hashing over some logistics, how much of an upset it was to his life, the way the whole thing made him feel worthless.

> **page:** well I don't feel any differently about you – not that it is much of a consolation
>
> **rob:** *nods*I appreciate it
>
> **page:** I absolutely adore you
>
> **page:** you were really unhappy there. I know it was a sweet gig, but it wasn't your dream job

rob: no, but I was finally in a position of accepting it and being comfortable with it

rob: I had accepted it

page: ahh, I see. that's how it usually happens, part of the cosmic joke

*****rob** holds you

page: it makes me want to say fuck it and fly out to Cleveland

rob: *hugs* I'll be OK. I have a good family and good friends

page: I'm so glad

rob: I have some support structure at least

page: see, that's how you know you're not worthless. you have people who love you

We chatted for a while. I did my best to support him, but it's tough to know what to say in those circumstances. As strong as my feelings for him were, I was still largely an outsider to his life. We hadn't even met. I wasn't sure what I *could* do for him other than listen and reassure him. After a bit, Rob excused himself:

rob: I'm going afk going to do some work around the house

page: well if you need/want to talk about anything at all, you can call me any time you want

page: I don't care if I'm in the middle of my date, I'll answer and talk to you

rob: OK. Enjoy your date.* hugs*

page: if you wanted me to, I'd cancel

page: just so you know

rob: nah, have fun

page: <3

I went out with Mark but made a point to talk with Rob online and on the phone when I got home from my date. I wrote about the experience in my journal:

Clarity

Tonight's date went well enough. I got to meet Mark's closest friends and see where he lived. His best friend is an amazing cook and actually a renaissance man who tends a mean garden and brews a fine beer. Pretty decent artist, too. There were a lot of folks there for dinner, a delicious feast of ziti, some bizarre but very healthy homemade tomato sauce, kielbasa, and garlic bread – with cheesecake with pear sauce for dessert. I tried to do the best I could with my carborexic needs. After Mark had a few margaritas, he got me to sit on the floor with him (he was leaning against the refrigerator) and cuddled with me under the guise of acting as his chaise lounge. Unfortunately, there was a cracked tile with a sharp edge that got caught on my jeans and ripped a small hole in the seat. Of my favorite jeans. Mark inspected the damage. It was a small hole and easily patchable, he said. Plus, a nice patch would give people cause to check out my ass.

Most of the guests left after dinner save for me, Mark, his best friend, and his best friend's girlfriend. We watched *Home at the End of the World*, and Mark and I cuddled (though it was over 80 degrees in the house, and we were both drenched in sweat) and held hands.

After the movie, I announced that I should get home, and he tried to convince me to stay a little longer, but I told him I had work early in the morning. We discussed our schedules and talked about meeting up later in the week.

The whole time I was thinking about Rob. He lost his job today, and I was wondering how he was holding up. It also occurred to me as I cuddled with Mark how much less intensely I felt for him than Rob or Tina. There was just... something missing.

The possibility had crossed my mind with how whirlwind the whole thing has been with Rob that the only reason I felt so strongly for him was because he was so into me. I thought maybe I was just responding to his feelings or that I loved to be loved rather than loving Rob himself. Tonight was rather instructive in that regard. Mark's level of interest has skyrocketed as of late, and yet my feelings are the same as they always have been – more of a sense that I could relax around Mark than any deep connection.

I spoke briefly on the phone with Rob tonight after I got home from my date, and between that and the chat we had online, I gained as much personal satisfaction from that as on my date.

How peculiar.

————————-

Addendum: I did neglect to mention a few more touching things that happened that evening.

I was told by a rather sweet and precocious 4-year-old that I was a beautiful princess. When pressed by her father what sort of princess I was, she added, "Snow White but beautifuller."

And as I was leaving at the end of the night, Mark's friend told me that I was the first girl Mark has ever brought home that she's actually liked and gave me a hug. :)

It really was wonderful to talk to Rob after my date with Mark:

> **page:** I love you :) hope you're having a decent
> evening

rob: Hello love. It sucks, but I'm working on it

page: awww =/ I love you so much

page: just reading your Livejournal entry

rob: thank you dear

***rob** gooses you

page: eheeeheee

rob: I just enjoy your company in my current state. I have really few needs

page: :)the way I feel about you is about the closest thing I have to a "need"

rob: *nods*

page: talking to you really eased my mind. I could tell you would be okay

rob: thanks, I'm glad it meant a lot to you

page: I'm sorry I missed that opportunity earlier – I love you though – hope you're having a nice evening

rob: at the hackerspace working and what-not

page: cool :) I'm working out at the moment – heard the IM noise and got up heh

rob: hahaha, OK, well keep working :) I'm doing work too :D

page: I'm doing you. in my head

rob: Oooo

page: mmm you you you

rob: what about me? I'm just a guy

page: you're my guy :)

rob: :)

page: at least I like to think so

***rob** hugs you

Despite the increased stress and bleak financial reality in the wake of his recent job loss, Rob and Michelle nonetheless planned a trip to Maine in late September to visit Don and Tina and for Rob to have an opportunity to meet me in person. Besides, they reasoned, with the baby due to arrive that winter, it might be the last opportunity for them to take a vacation for a while.

It took Rob and Michelle two days to drive to my town, splitting the journey into two segments, spending the night in a hotel at the halfway point somewhere in New York. The second day, Rob slept in, and they left quite a bit later than expected, even forgetting his favorite pillow at the hotel.

Meeting Rob, I was struck immediately by how intense he was. Not loud or dramatic but completely focused, one might even say hyperfocused, on me. He spoke me to purposefully, looking at me directly in a way that conveyed a sense of confidence and personal power.

Look here, pet, his eyes said. *I own you. Make no mistake.*

And yet, there the four of us stood in the shoddy lighting of the parking lot of my apartment complex, being pestered by the drizzly weather, making small talk. The disconnect was surreal and exciting. Seth and Michelle seemed oblivious to the connection Rob and I had formed, a connection that was even more powerful in person that it had been at a distance.

Since it was after 10:00, well past the operating hours of most of the restaurants in the area, we took them to a 24-hour diner at a truck stop, a place renowned for both the quality of its food and the fact that it was the last major full-service truck stop until the Canadian border, a good 3 or 4 hours north.

We ordered up some comfort food and scarcely had time to exchange pleasantries before Rob whipped out his papers from Planned Parenthood. "HIV negative."

I blushed. "Uh, thanks," I replied, taking a quick look at them and handing them back to him.

"Just getting business out of the way."

I nodded, a bit uncomfortable and all too aware of Michelle's eyes trained on me. I quickly turned my attention to her and did my best to charm her, all the while fighting the urge to ignore everyone and everything else to focus on Rob. Opening a meal with STI results was a bit forward – and admittedly not the classiest move, but I couldn't help but be excited about how eager he seemed. The chemistry between us was undeniable.

Rob and I had originally planned to take a walk around town the first night of his visit, but it was raining when we got home, so the four of us sat around with our laptops instead, playing games and chatting. It was nice enough, but I went to bed sexually frustrated and disappointed at the missed romantic opportunity to show him my town bathed in moonlight. I worried that the entire trip would be this way, chaste, awkward, with a tension reminiscent of junior high school dances.

Seth conked out easily, but I stayed up late – past 3 – and was up early at 8, fully ready to go. I shuffled off to the shower to get ready. After all, I wanted to look nice for when I saw Rob since I was going to spend the day with him and Michelle. I'd just rinsed the shampoo out of my hair when I heard a knock on the bathroom door. I turned off the water.

"Hello?" I said.

The door opened, and it was Rob. "Good morning," he said. He came over to the shower and kissed me, deeply, passionately.

I was sopping wet, naked, and out of breath.

"I thought you needed that," he said.

How perceptive, I thought, shaken and speechless from his kiss.

He very pointedly looked me up and down, taking my naked body in. "Very nice," he said. "Very nice."

I shivered. There was a bit of commotion in the living room. It sounded like Michelle was getting out of the sofa bed where the two of them had spent the night.

"Gotta go," he said, stroking my face and darting out of the room, closing the door behind him.

I turned on the water and finished washing myself, still feeling his lips on mine, emotionally overwhelmed and burning with desire.

How did he know? I wondered. *How did he know exactly what I needed?*

I toweled off, joined my guests in the living room. Seth said goodbye to us. He was leaving to spend the day running errands for his parents, small-business owners that had recently given him a part-time job as an office manager for them. Michelle decided she wanted a shower herself, leaving Rob and I alone.

As soon as the shower started, Rob pulled me to him, kissing me again. "I bet you want to suck my cock, pet, don't you?"

I shuddered. "Oh yes," I replied.

He took off his pants in a hurry, and I went to work, excited by the sneakiness, the relative danger of getting caught. I threw myself completely into the act, savoring him, his scent, his taste, the texture of his skin on my tongue, the degree of rigidity and resistance of his cock as I moved my mouth up and down the shaft. He moaned and bucked against me, delirious. "Oh my God," he moaned. "Oh my God." When I responded by moaning against him, with his cock fully in my mouth, his eyes rolled back in his head. "Page, Page, stop," he said, gasping, pulling out.

"Oh," I said. I pulled away stunned. "Did I do something wrong?"

"No," he said, pulling up his pants. "It felt too good, so much I was going to lose control. I've never felt that before. It scared me."

Though I was a bit disappointed (I really wanted him to come in my mouth), I grinned. He'd told me before that he didn't like blow jobs, that he'd never orgasmed from one, couldn't really get into them or enjoy them.

"So you liked it?" I asked.

"It was amazing. I loved it," he said.

My ego swelled. I was still sick with desire, but things were looking up.

Once we'd all showered, we prepared to leave but quickly discovered that Rob had lost his keys. "Misplaced," he corrected Michelle. We'd figure out on the last day of the trip that they were hiding in the sofa bed, but after a fruitless search that morning, Michelle suggested he use her keys.

With that little hiccup out of the way, we set off to see Bangor, hardly a thriving metropolis but by far the largest city in my area. We were cruising down I-95, laughing and joking, the three of us getting on well, when a tire blew out. I called AAA, but they took their sweet time helping us. We were stranded for over an hour a mere quarter-mile mile from our exit.

When we finally got to Goodyear Tire, we confounded on-lookers by holding hands in various configurations. It didn't help that Michelle was 6 months pregnant and the only one wearing a wedding ring. Rob (prone to both accidents and losing things) had lost his, and I had stopped wearing mine because after losing over 100 pounds, it would fall off my hand without warning. I hadn't yet resized it because I wasn't done losing weight. It was thrilling to cuddle with Rob and kiss him in public. While we were technically surrounded by strangers, I was from a small enough town that the chance of being discovered, while remote, was just high enough to be real.

While the car was being worked on, we walked over to Best Buy and looked around. Rob lamented that he wanted to buy me a laptop but couldn't now that he'd lost his job. I wandered around the store separately from them, drinking in the strangeness, the newness. My boyfriend and... his *wife* were here with me.

Once things were all squared away with the tires, I showed them around town. They said they wanted to go antiquing, so I brought them to a few places downtown that were supposed to be good. In the wake of being laid off, Rob had been considering starting an online novelties business and managed to find some vintage electronics that he could mark up to sell on his website.

Even though I wasn't terribly attracted to her, I joked and flirted with Michelle quite a bit. In my mind, I was just being friendly, but as the day wore on, it became evident that she was warming to me, behavior at odds with the reports of her icy demeanor I'd received from everyone else I knew that knew her well (Rob, Tina, Don).

Yay, I thought. *She likes me!*

At one particularly frou-frou store, where potpourri saturated the air like an alien atmosphere, Michelle and I joked what would happen if she and I were to start making out on the carpeted stairs in front of the humble figurines.

"I can just see the headline now in the *Bangor Daily*," I said.

The three of us collectively groaned when the owner of the pawn shop asked Rob and Michelle where they were from, and when they told him Cleveland countered with, "That's in Illinois, right?"

Actually, not so much.

"We get a little creative about geography up this way," I explained to them as we walked back to their car, the three of us holding hands like a chain of paper dolls.

We headed home to meet up with Seth, and all four of us headed south together to spend the night at Don and Tina's. The four old friends caught up, with Rob and Michelle filling Don and Tina in about everything going on back in Cleveland, what old college friends were up to, their jobs, their lives.

I was lost for the most part but could follow the emotions of what they were saying and had trouble not staring at Rob as he spoke. Every time he'd meet my gaze with challenge in his eyes, I'd flush and look away.

When it came time to decide who would sleep where, Michelle asked if I'd join her and Rob in the guest room. Though I saw Tina's face light up with surprise when Michelle made the suggestion, I didn't think much of it.

"Sure," I said. Rob invited me to join him and Michelle in the shower, where I steadied her and helped wash under her baby bump. I loved showering with people, an act I viewed as quite intimate, though not inherently sexual, something Rob knew.

The three of us piled into the queen-sized bed in the guest room with Rob in the middle. Though I was extremely horny from all the buildup that morning with Rob and the looks back and forth all day and night, I was exhausted, and after going to bed disappointed the night before, I had prepared myself for another uneventful night in bed.

How wrong I was.

The door to the guest room had barely shut before Rob and Michelle started to caress one another. Rob moaned and writhed as she worked his cock in her hands. She mounted him, and they began to have sex with me right next to them.

"Please," Rob begged. "I want to fuck Page, too. You, then her, then you, then her."

Michelle stayed silent, bearing down on him, fucking her harder.

"Please," he gasped.

She fucked him even harder, not replying.

"Can't I at least kiss her?" he asked, sounding positively faint.

She nodded yes.

He turned his head, and we kissed passionately, deeply as she rode him. It was soon too much for him, and he exploded into orgasm, his whole body spasming. He collapsed into a state of delirious afterglow. I stroked his hair and held his arm close to me, preparing to drift off to sleep. I could hear Rob and Michelle murmuring to each other but lost my focus and couldn't determine what exactly they were saying. As I was dropping off the edge, I felt Rob's hands on me pulling me back to waking.

"Page," Rob said, kissing me.

What a way to wake up.

The kisses fed one another until Rob was hard again.

"Please, Michelle," he gasped. "I want to fuck Page." He looked at her imploringly.

She said nothing, stony-faced.

"Please," he begged.

She shook her head no, a smile creeping onto her face.

I was starting to get really disgusted. Why was she denying him? All the proper testing had been done, paperwork exchanged. My heart sunk. Power. It had to be power. She was getting off on controlling the situation.

Finally, when he couldn't stand it any longer, he pled with her again, this time to allow him to have sex with *her*. She complied, and he climbed on top of her, and they had sex again, while I masturbated next to them, my orgasm completely in sync with Rob's, falling, falling, falling.

I rolled over yet again to go to sleep. Rob's arms wrapped around me, and I felt myself drifting away.

But then he was kissing my ear.

"Page," he whispered. "Page, Michelle needs you."

I rolled back over. "What?"

"She needs release, too." Apparently, Rob had gone down on her to return the favor. "My jaw's tired."

Michelle nodded at me, still eerily silent (a sexual quality of hers I would never get used to, her complete lack of noise in the bedroom and inability to clearly verbally communicate about sex in the moment).

I was groggy and had a bitter taste in my mouth from Michelle's control over what Rob and I could and couldn't do. Not only that but I wasn't really *that* into her. And now, I was being asked to have sex with her. On one hand, I had every right to say no. I knew that. No one was going to force me to eat her out. On the other hand, she wasn't approving sex with Rob. If I failed to comply with this request, if I didn't pleasure her, would I ever be allowed to? Forging a sexual connection with her seemed like a possible fast track to getting the go ahead with him. Still, something felt terribly wrong.

Nevertheless, I shoved down my discomfort and kissed and sucked her clit until she was writhing on the bed, breathless, satisfied. Despite my emotional reservations about the situation, the sex itself was pleasant enough. She tasted sweet, and other than her eerie silence, nothing seemed awry.

Finally, the three of us got to bed with Rob holding me in his arms. As Seth never did this, and in fact didn't like to even touch another person while he was sleeping, the effect was quite novel and comforting, even if Rob did have an odd habit of twitching in his sleep.

We slept two or three hours until Rob and I awoke in the middle of the night, murmuring softly to each other. I don't know who woke first. One moment I was asleep; the next I was talking to him, loving him, kissing him. Sweetness quickly trended to sensuality, and we were quietly rubbing up against each other, my wetness against his cock, while he almost but not quite penetrated me as Michelle slept soundly next to us in bed. The tension built between us to a fever pitch.

Finally, Rob loudly announced, "I could really use a shower." He gently roused Michelle. "Page and I are going to go take a shower, okay?"

She murmured assent.

Rob and I rose and went into the bathroom. I was excited. Showering alone with him would be fantastic.

Rob closed the door behind us and turned on the shower. "Bend over now," he said. "I'm going to fuck you."

My entire body flushed, and I felt my pussy throb and swell. There was no question. It was a direct order. It was so wrong. We didn't have permission. Not for this. Not for him inside of me, bending me over the sink, using me like his fuck toy.

But I wanted him so badly, to feel him inside of me, his skin against mine, to be used like a slut, his slut. I wanted him to claim me. And besides, I reasoned, I just had sex with *her*, why wouldn't she allow him to have sex with me? It was practically the same thing. I hiked up my nightgown and bent over the sink as he slipped inside me. I swallowed my moans as he pounded me hard, what gasps I did make blocked out by the sound of the water.

He fucked me selfishly, not giving a single thought to my pleasure, which only made me more aroused. I fingered myself until I came, and he joined me not too long after. Though he was still sensitive, he ordered me to kneel and clean off our juices with my mouth. I was delirious with joy.

Finally, something dirty sweet, intense.

At that point, we actually did step into the shower, holding one another and kissing. "Good girl," he said over and over again. "You're such a good girl, pet."

I melted in his arms with the hot water pouring down on us, my world exploding into kaleidoscope colors.

COMPLICATIONS

After we'd toweled off, Rob headed back to bed to get more sleep, but I was flying so high on the bliss of our night together, a night of many firsts, that I stayed up instead, writing at the breakfast table. Just me and a big pot of coffee. Answering emails, finishing a piece or two, and smiling my face off.

I was alone for well over an hour before I had unexpected company.

It was Tina, and she'd been crying.

"Morning. Are you okay?"

She shook her head.

"Oh, come here," I said, giving her a hug.

She sobbed into my chest.

"What happened?" I asked.

Tina sputtered and then started crying again. After several minutes of emotional stops and starts, I finally managed to glean that Tina and Seth had broken up the night before, while I was spending the night with Rob and Michelle. Apparently, Seth, feeling that Tina had been slower to warm to him sexually than he'd like, had stepped up his overtures, forcing her to reject him, a situation she'd been dreading.

"I just don't feel that way about him," she said. "I feel terrible that I hurt him."

"You can't help the way you feel." I consoled her the best I could and then sought out Seth to see how he was doing with things.

I found him outside smoking in the driveway.

"Hey," I said.

He gave me a dirty look and turned away from me.

"I just talked to Tina. Are you okay?"

"Like you fucking care," he said.

"Huh?"

"You ditched me," he said.

"What?"

"Last night. You ditched me. To spend the night with Rob and Michelle."

I sighed. "Seth, they drove here from Ohio. I'm crazy about him. I don't know when I'll get an opportunity like this again."

"Whatever," he said. "You know how much I want to form a triad with you, to have another woman join us. You know how much I love threesomes. And for you to go off with them, and..." He stopped, took a long drag off his cigarette. "It's a slap in the fucking face."

"Ugh," I said. "I'm sorry. I never saw it that way. I was there for Rob. It's not about having a threesome. Honestly, I'd really rather if Michelle weren't there. I don't feel any special chemistry with her, and it'd be easier to get to know Rob."

"I was so lonely last night. I went to bed alone."

"I'm sorry," I said. "I wish I had known."

"I went to bed so horny."

"Now you know how I feel," I said. I had a much higher libido than Seth's, and most nights I'd gone to bed frustrated, a fate completely unknown to Seth as I was invariably happy to satisfy his urges, not knowing when another opportunity to get some action would arise.

"Oh Page, you're so melodramatic."

"I don't think that word means what you think it means," I said.

"And now you're being a bitch."

"Look," I said, my eyes filling with tears. "I just wanted to make sure you were okay."

He sighed. "She won't tell me what's wrong."

"What happened exactly?"

"I was flirting with her, and she started crying and left," he said. "That's half the problem. I have no idea."

"I'll see what I can find out," I said. "It's the least I can do to make up for last night."

The house came alive, and though there was obviously a great deal of tension between Seth and Tina, who were avoiding eye contact with one another, the whole crew headed off to shop at Marden's, a large and sprawling surplus and salvage store, to give Rob and Michelle an authentically Maine experience.

I split my time fairly equally between Tina and Seth, speaking with each party in hushed tones while looking at cheap dusty coffee mugs and assorted close-outs.

"So you think he went too far?" I paraphrased, considering a giant bottle of imitation lemon extract.

"He was clumsy. Made me feel like a piece of meat," Tina said.

"And all you want is to talk with her?" I asked, browsing coffeemakers meant to run off a car's cigarette lighter.

"It would make me feel a lot better," Seth said.

By the time everyone had checked out, I'd formed a tentative plan. Don would go off with Rob and Michelle in their car, and Seth and I would ride with Tina in hers so that the two of them could talk. I would provide moral support and moderate the discussion.

It did put me in kind of an awkward spot, but as I loved both of them, I wanted to help them in any way I could.

I was in the car with Tina, sitting behind her in the backseat, playing with her hair and feeling optimistic when Seth joined us, settling in beside her in the passenger's seat. Tina visibly stiffened.

"So," I said. "The two of you need to talk."

"I really like you, Tina," Seth said.

Tina stared straight ahead, kept her eyes trained on the road.

"I'm really sorry if I came on too strong last night," he continued. "It's just... I'd really like to see where this goes."

He paused, again, giving her an opportunity to speak. She didn't.

"I think we could be so great together. We have a lot in common," he said.

"What makes you think that?" she snapped.

He was clearly taken aback, flustered. "Well, it's just that... We have such good chemistry."

I heard sniffling from the driver's seat, and I saw Tina wipe her nose. I peered around the seat at her to see her eyes welled up with tears.

Seth glanced over at her. "Look, I didn't mean to... Oh shit. I'm sorry."

We pulled into the driveway, and Tina left the car without a word.

"Wow," Seth said.

"That was... intense," I said.

"I don't know what's so offensive about the idea that we'd be good together. I opened up, shared my feelings for her, and what did she do? Cry. Ouch."

"I don't get it either," I said. "Maybe she doesn't even know."

Don't Open Before Christmas

I t'd been a hell of a day – between the night in bed with Rob and Michelle, the dicey action in the early hours of the morning with Rob, and rather unsuccessfully facilitating Seth and Tina's post breakup talk. Seth and I headed back to our place because I had to work the next couple of days while Rob and Michelle stayed behind to spend some quality time with Don and Tina.

I was quickly alerted by Rob that despite what either of us had hoped, what had happened between us that morning was not at all okay and that I was not to tell Michelle what had happened. Completely unprompted, Michelle had made an offhand comment that she was getting closer to being comfortable with the idea of Rob and me having sex but that she thought she wasn't quite ready for it, that she needed more time to think it through.

Well, fuck, I thought. *We cheated.* While I hadn't violated any of my personal rules or relationship agreements by what I'd done with him, having cleared such a scenario with my other partners ahead of time, I still felt guilty to have aided him in violating his.

While I hadn't known for sure that it was forbidden when it happened, I hadn't made absolutely sure it was okay either.

As such, I felt immensely guilty. Happy, but guilty.

And backed into a lie.

Sure, I could come clean, let her know, but what then?

She'd probably be so pissed that we'd never get permission.

No, better to just pretend it never happened.

It reminded me of the one Christmas when I was 9 that my older sister and I opened all of our presents while our parents were out at dinner. It seemed like such a good idea at the time. We worked quickly but meticulously, gingerly coaxing the tape away from the paper so as not to mar the paper or the patterns. And we weren't disappointed with the presents! Oh, what a spread! The sweaters and designer jeans she'd wanted. A new electric blanket for me. Box after box yielded surprise upon surprise. And the crowning jewel: Dragon Warrior II for NES, what I'd wanted most of all. There it was, in its little cardboard box. I'd never been as excited to play a video game. My heart swelled, soared. I felt tears come into my eyes.

And then I rewrapped the package and put it back under the tree.

Waiting the 2 weeks for Christmas was nearly unbearable. I thought about my gifts constantly, especially playing my new game. It should have been fun, something to look forward to, but not being able to talk about it was torture. And I felt so guilty. Every time my mom asked me if I was looking forward to Christmas, I had to force a smile and avoid her eyes.

When the big day finally arrived, it was none too soon. The boxes were again in my lap. I inspected a few of the packages closely and could even see where I'd been clumsy with my earlier work, a scuff here, a scuff there. Something wrong with a Smurf's nose, Garfield's tail.

"Well, go ahead," my mother said. "Open it."

I savagely tore into my gifts, shredding the paper, distancing myself from the cool calculation of my earlier fraud. And one by one, the familiar sights. Absolutely zero surprises. Of course. But I put on a good show – partly because I was still afraid of getting caught, but mostly because of my guilt. My parents had gone to all this trouble, and what had I done? Spoiled the fun of the day for myself. Well, I wasn't going to ruin it for them, too.

By the time it was done, I felt absolutely hollow. Disgusting. I've always found that lying is its own punishment, the sense of stress and conflict, the pressure of the cognitive dissonance, the gap between my words and actions and what I know to be true. Whatever consequences another person can dole out, as scathing or punishing as they might be, are a mere shadow of what I do to myself.

With Rob and Michelle, all I could do was hope that she'd give us the okay soon.

I wasn't disappointed. When they returned to our apartment a few days later, once I had a few days off again, Michelle announced that she would allow the two of us to have sex, with one small catch: We had to use condoms.

It was a reasonable request, sure, and usually such a thing wouldn't have bothered me. In this case, however, there were a few problems with the request.

The very first was my irritation with the fact that Michelle had so easily agreed to my having unprotected sex with her the night in Don and Tina's guest room. It really seemed like Michelle's rules and regulations regarding the sexual relationship I was building with Rob were less governed by any practical concerns and more based on power and control.

I typically respond very poorly to this brand of reasoning. I find this sort of need often motivated by fear, whether it's fear of losing control of another person or a less manipulative cause like fear of losing what one has with someone, there remains the commonality of a lack of trust, whether it's in the existent partner or with the new love interest. This sort of insecurity is natural, and for me, it wasn't its existence that was troubling; it was Michelle's lack of frankness about it.

My distaste for her lack of frankness may seem paradoxical, especially when coupled with my own when I was struggling with my feelings about Seth and Megan's relationship when they were first dating without me.

However, there remains one great difference: Whatever my level of personal discomfort with what was going on between them, I didn't attempt to create rules or govern their behavior based solely on that level of discomfort, which I think is an important distinction.

The second problem was of course that Rob and I had already done so the night that he had run the shower in Don and Tina's bathroom while he had his way with me as I bent over the sink. It was too late to not breach that barrier. We were, as they say in poly circles, "fluid bonded."

Fluid bonding is the ultimate level of poly connection when one is talking sexual intimacy in non-monogamous circles, reserved for people in relationships with rules and guidelines and a high level of trust. To fluid bond is a statement. It establishes a reciprocal level of trust and sexual accountability unrivaled by most other arrangements. To enter into a fluid bond casually with a stranger or an untrustworthy individual is unthinkable. The results can be devastating with damaged health and legal repercussions (in the form of unintended children) aplenty, the waves of which can and will ripple to the outskirts of a poly web and any adjacent webs that have even a small interlocking with the affected one.

In the phenomenon called the "butterfly effect," it is believed that when a butterfly flaps its wings, it can cause a hurricane in another part of the world. Never in my life have I seen this phenomenon more readily demonstrated than in interlocked poly circles where health scares, drama bombs, and nasty breakups chew through great swaths of people (sometimes quite separated by time and distance) without mitigation.

A great mistake had been made, a far greater one than I had originally realized — and to admit it now to Michelle, to come clean to a person who so obviously already didn't trust me and held all the power to deny me the thing I wanted the most… well, I could not begin to conceive of doing such a thing.

I felt absolutely terrible. I immediately told both Seth and Tina what had happened, who agreed that it was pointless to tell Michelle and would probably do more harm than good, but still, my conscience weighed heavy.

I felt disgusting the next few times Rob and I had sex, with Michelle's permission, especially as he slipped into me un-protected, making a big show of throwing away the "used" condom (which had only been opened and set next to the bed during the act) after the fact. At the same time, our complicity only fed my sense that we had something special. We were in cahoots. We were having an affair.

Finally, the last night of their trip to Maine, a night that I spent with Rob and Michelle on the fold-out couch in our living room, Michelle gave her official okay for the fluid bond.

I was brought back to that fraudulent Christmas morning, faking joy or at least channeling my relief into joy, having been enjoying my presents secretly for several days.

But the general tone was happy, with the visit having gone extremely well, and when Rob and Michelle returned to Ohio, they talked constantly about how awesome I was. I had this on good authority from Justin, a friend of theirs who was renting a room in their house from them. They would not stop talking about me.

This even caused of a bit of stress at a party and a fight between Justin and Rob. I don't know exactly how it started, but evidently Rob had been bragging about his hot girlfriend back in Maine, all the while knowing Justin at that point was single and having a hard time finding someone suitable to date. Justin called Rob "pencil dick," and Michelle very pointedly asked Justin, "Who has a wife and a girlfriend?"

It was strange to hear about it from both sides. Justin and I had recently become pretty good friends ourselves, chatting on IRC from time to time about lots of things, though initially mostly about dieting. Justin was a big guy and shared a lot of the same struggles I had with trying to lose weight and have a healthy relationship with food. He had met with a nutritionist and was in a bariatric weight loss program prepping to get gastric bypass surgery.

Getting to know Justin was funny. The first few times I talked to him, he kept taking things in the direction of whatever I was thinking in response to what I was saying. The things he was saying were extremely familiar. As a result, I thought Justin was boring. Eventually I realized, no, wait. I'm a fucking weirdo. No one says the things I think, I feel, I say.

I made plans to visit Rob and Michelle in Cleveland for 2 weeks around Thanksgiving, and though I kept it pretty close to the chest, I was really excited about meeting Justin in person.

Where Rob made me extremely uncomfortable to talk to him (a major part of the appeal he held for me) as I felt an amazing amount of tension (sexual and otherwise) between us every time we spoke, chatting with Justin conversely was effortless. I could tell him what I needed to say, how I felt like saying it, when I felt like saying it, and Justin always responded generally well to my revelations. Not only that, but I found that he readily reciprocated, politely but frankly, speaking quite candidly about his struggles with eating and food issues and his frustrations with the quirks of the members of his chapter of Overeaters Anonymous. He was so easy to talk to. I needed that at that point, desperately so. Due to time constraints, I had become isolated from most of my non-polyamorous friends and was swamped with partners who for one reason or another required a great deal of effort to communicate effectively with.

Tina had great difficulty with direct communication, preferring to speak in riddles. I remember many times asking her if certain sexual acts were okay, to which she'd say something about a tea kettle, an allusion to a story that neither she nor Don could relate clearly to me, but on further probing, she would add, "Well, I'm not saying no." Indeed, it seemed like "yes" was the hardest thing for Tina to say. "No" as well was pretty much absent from her vocabulary. Instead she would say "eep" and wriggle away or leave the room when she became physically or emotionally uncomfortable.

For her part, Michelle needed a great amount of handling and grooming to accept me as Rob's new girlfriend. As Michelle told a friend of hers (and later related to me, not realizing how terrible it sounded), "I really wanted to dislike Page going in, but she was so nice. I just couldn't."

Every time I turned around, it seemed Michelle had a new complaint about something in her life. In hindsight, it was hardly surprising. She was pregnant. Her husband had just lost his job. Michelle was likely redirecting frustrations towards circumstances that she couldn't do anything about onto things that were easier targets to cope with psychologically:

- Directorial choices in television shows.

- Stupid things co-workers had said, especially about her pregnancy.

- Kvetching about their housemates (particularly difficult to stomach when it pertained to Justin as I was becoming quite fond of him as a friend).

- Baggage from her old secondary who had been out of the picture for a few years now.

Negativity, negativity, negativity. And the vast majority relating to topics I either had no interest in whatsoever or that I personally found offensive.

Because Michelle was highly reactive and openly admitted to wanting to not like me solely on principle, I felt like I had to walk on eggshells and tolerate a great deal more tedium and outright offensive speech than I would ordinarily. Otherwise, I was fairly certain that she would attempt to guilt Rob into breaking things off with me. I cared far too much for him to let this happen.

Even things with Seth had become remarkably strained, as he was finding that dealing with my spending most of my time and energy on other lovers was harder than he imagined it would when he'd been in a similar position. As a result, he was bitter and brooding, passive-aggressive and avoidant.

In the midst of all of this stress, it was good to have Justin as the one person I could talk to without a filter. It emboldened me, and despite the attendant stress, it seemed having multiple concurrent relationships was doing wonders for my confidence. I felt invincible, fearless.

With my newfound bravery, not too long after Rob and Michelle's trip to Maine, I came out about my sexual orientation to my mother.

It started when we were talking about one of my friends from college. "You knew she was gay, right?" I said.

Mom said, "I think so. I barely remember her."

"You know, Mom," I continued. "I have A LOT of gay friends."

"Seems it," she said.

"I'd say more than half actually, especially if you count the bisexuals."

She didn't say anything.

"You know, people who can love either men or women?"

"I've heard of that," she said.

"I think a lot of people are in the middle," I said. "A lot of people are bisexual and just get passed off as straight. Because they're married, and no one asks." I paused. "Like me, for example."

Silence.

"You okay, Mom?" I asked.

"I'm not really surprised," she said. "I always kind of knew there was something going on with you."

"I think it's more that I care about body parts less than other people," I continued. "Like, I'm more into the friendships and the personalities and stuff."

She sighed. "You talk way too much about your friends, religion, and sex. I don't care about that stuff. Let's just stick to talking about dieting, cooking, and your marriage from now on."

"Fair enough," I replied.

No drama. No wild emotion.

Like that, I was out. A huge weight off my shoulders.

TROUBLE IN PARADISE

Paradoxically, though I was quite loved, in the midst of a long distance relationship (separated by approximately 900 miles), I spent a great deal of time at home.

With my full dance card, I wasn't going out on dates very much, and as the weeks went by, I found myself growing mopey and weepy.

In the evenings I took 9 mg of melatonin and wrote until I basically passed out. I used the light from the television as Seth watched internet videos on the Playstation 3.

It didn't help that Seth's mood was growing worse by the day. He was doing passably in school, but his unwillingness to work for the majority of the last 4 years (aside from occasional part-time work for his parents) combined with his expensive tastes and our new higher-maintenance lifestyle, including a large apartment within walking distance of a major university and frequent dinners out, had been pushing us into financial ruin for quite some time, despite my well-paying job.

I'd managed to delay the inevitable by draining a sizable savings I'd built up in thriftier times, but we were running out of funds and fast. We had to move out of the fantastic party pad and into Seth's parents' basement.

Cleaning and packing for the move was no small task, one that I'd undertaken practically on my own as Seth had grown so depressed that he was avoiding me, not attending to his hygiene, and doing little else beyond attending his classes (he had a course load of 2 classes, or 6 credit hours) and playing *World of Warcraft*.

During this difficult period, Seth and I fought often. A journal entry from then describes the situation well:

draining

As is the case with nearly all periods of major change (even good change), the stress level at home is high. I'm trying to keep my chin up and stay positive. I succeed most of the time. Sorting, organizing, and packing can become rather demoralizing after a while.

I got weepy. It sucked. I was lucky to have friends to talk to.

I really do consider myself an optimist, though I'm well aware how sensitive I am to other people's negative emotions, and I'm human — as much as it pains me to admit it; I blame being raised by 2 perfectionists. Sometimes I get stressed out, and I get upset.

I've been wrestling a lot lately with this idea that I'm an emotional drain on people, that knowing me is a burden rather than a boon to the people I care about. I found last night that this wasn't entirely imagined on my part, just coming from a source I never expected. I'm committed to working things out though, doing the necessary work.

Chin up, I say.

On the plus side, I can really see the progress I've made on the apartment now. The beginning of the process is always tough on me because it's tough to feel like I've made any headway when you're just starting, but I've done enough that it's starting to feel a little sparse/empty in places around here. :)

I didn't come out and say it in the journal entry, but the "source I never expected" was Seth.

It stung. Badly. I felt quite miserable and rejected, but there was little time to sulk around and be depressed. We'd accumulated quite a collection of things we didn't need, didn't even use. The soon to be ex-apartment had an impressive number of closets, each filled to capacity with bins and boxes that were moved from our old trailer a year prior, most of them unopened and untouched since then.

Space would be limited in the new (hopefully temporary) place, so I set my sights on winnowing our possessions. Each and every day, I'd finish work in my office and then load up Hoarders on Netflix and tackle the stack of boxes. Goodwill of Bangor received half a library in those weeks. Kitchen goods went to needy friends of my sister's. We threw out or gave away more than some people own.

The pace was brutal. Seth was often hostile and offered virtually no help. Rob, who had been effusive in his praise and attentive prior to visiting me, had cooled a bit, still warm and complimentary but making less regular contact. Even though Rob and Michelle had added me to their cellular family plan and had shipped me a nice phone, he called less and less as the weeks progressed. Indeed, it seemed that Michelle texted me more often than he did.

I pushed ahead on preparing for the move, reminding myself constantly that I had the Thanksgiving trip to Cleveland to look forward to. The promise of the trip kept me going. It would be so nice to get out of Maine, if only for a little while. I was finding more and more that there was nothing for me in Maine. Most of my friends had moved away, my relationship with my family was strained at best, and there was little for culture or night life to interest me. It was hard to put my finger on exactly why I was so unhappy, but I was. I felt utterly alone, out of place.

And while I had no idea what Cleveland would be like, I was excited to have a vacation from the problems I knew.

But first there was a Halloween party to get through, hosted by DRUNK, sure to deliver much in the way of drunkenness and debauchery. I dolled myself up as Betty Boop with enough hairspray to shellac my improbable curls into place.

That night Seth hit it off with a woman named Gwen. They talked for hours, and from what I overheard and saw (though I was trying to give them space to connect when I saw them together), they were having a very lively and interesting conversation. He brought her over to me late into the night and introduced us. I really liked her. Very smart, cool, laidback.

Seth asked her out to coffee, and Gwen quickly said yes. They took out their smart phones and added each other on Facebook that very second. Later in the night, she was looking everywhere for him (I think he'd gone out to smoke). Watching her body language, it was obvious to me she was attracted to him.

It was a wonderful boost to Seth's self-esteem. He said that even if she cancelled on the coffee or the date went nowhere, it felt great to flirt and have fun, especially since she was gorgeous (she literally looked like a model) and was flirting back.

Gwen also said she traveled a lot and has been to Ohio many times and thought it was totally cool that we were both going on an adventure and considering moving there.

Eric was dressed in this adorable sock monkey costume and hamming it up and flirting with me at the party. It was like he was this giant living stuffed animal. I couldn't help but hug and cuddle him. In the process, he ended up flirting rather extensively and telling me how gorgeous he thought I looked, especially with the cute Betty Boop curls.

We kissed a bit (at least he took the monkey mask off by that point). After we had made out for a while, Eric tried to go down on me, and I had to slap his face to deter him. Even then, he still managed to lick my fishnets.

At that point, Eric burst into tears. I held him to soothe him. He talked about how lonely he was and how devastated he'd been that I wasn't "available" (not accepting poly as a viable way to do relationships) and how it was even worse that I seem even less available than before and could be moving so far away in 6 months. He had another relationship just beginning at the time he and I hooked up in the spring that he felt he should pursue (he felt like a creep that he and I had made out in between 2 of their dates). The two of them had sex, and she broke up with him right after, which made him feel like shit.

I wonder if I'm now a furry, I mused to myself the next morning, mostly joking. The scene that played out that night with

Eric was so ridiculous that it was funny. Funny but sad. I liked kissing Eric again, but I was over him and not hung up on him anymore. It was reassuring to know that he was as heartbroken as I was that it didn't work out. Not that I wanted him to be in pain, but it made me feel like less of a fool for hurting so badly when it didn't work out.

Eric was right. He had missed his chance. As time went on, I was shifting my focus more and more towards Cleveland, towards love interests who were formally polyamorous and actually turned into lovers.

Despite her obvious interest, Seth didn't call Gwen for coffee. He explained it away easily with, "She's just being nice," adding, "And besides, she lives 3 hours away even if she was serious."

I started to realize that this was a key difference between Seth and me, how we prioritized romantic relationships. For a viable fulfilling emotional and sexual connection, I was willing to conduct a relationship at quite a distance and even relocate if it made sense to, if the potential benefits justified the inconvenience.

It baffled me that Seth would continually complain that he wasn't meeting with success in dating and yet could not seem to be bothered to put even the slightest bit of effort forth in doing things like drive a few hours or compromise and settle on a partner who was nearby but maybe not his ideal. No, he wanted the perfect connection delivered to him. No muss, no fuss.

I knew for sure this wasn't going to happen in Bangor, Maine. I'd worked hard losing weight and getting down to a more ideal size, forging connections, and kept my mind open to people who didn't immediately captivate me, and even so, it had been difficult to achieve any degree of success dating as a married woman.

This was even with the distinct advantages of being female and bisexual, both of which gave me an edge when looking for partners as on the poly scene there are typically more uncoupled/available men than women, and most people consider women less threatening than men and are more willing to take a chance on a female unknown than a male one. In addition, our current society in general prizes female sexuality above male sexuality as the desirable ideal (as opposed to other cultures, such as the society of ancient Greece, in which masculine energy and the male form were the standard aspired to and idealized). And being bisexual has obvious benefits in improving the odds of finding partners.

From all reports of Cleveland, I could throw a rock there and hit someone who'd date me, given I was in the right social group – namely Rob and Michelle's.

Given Seth's fixation on achieving multiple successful polyamorous relationships and his aversion to hard work or compromise, it seemed an environment like that was his only hope.

Of course, I was working in theory, and the upcoming trip would provide valuable information as to the actual viability of the Cleveland poly scene. As I was working as a medical transcriptionist, I could easily move my job with me or find another position with a national company if I were to switch states and my employer were to be difficult about it.

It helped that we'd been considering relocating to a city for some time. Seth and I had briefly considered Boston, as I had many friends in that area, but we were put off by the high cost of living — a serious issue as medical transcription wages were frozen at roughly the same level, regardless of city or state. Therefore, a transcriptionist in Central Maine could make a pretty good living, but that same transcriptionist would be poor if she were to move to, say, New York City or Honolulu.

As I explored Cleveland as an option, I was pleased to note that cost of living within Cleveland and the surrounding areas ranged anywhere from Bangor, Maine, to Portland, Maine, depending on the neighborhood or suburb, i.e., roughly what I was used to paying for things.

In some ways, it wasn't that big of a deal. Seth and I were only leaving for a few weeks to visit Ohio. All of our belongings were back in Maine. We still had a place to live. Well, sort of. His parents' basement was pretty nice as far as basements go, but it was far from feeling like a home. And the reality that I'd spent my last $200 on bus tickets after losing our apartment was not lost on me. I was well aware I'd made a decision that probably made little sense to others. I had a long time to ruminate on this during the 23-hour bus ride southwest.

Clearly, at this point, Seth and I were not okay. Not okay at all. In the process of writing this book, I found myself looking back on this time and trying to pinpoint the exact moment when things took a turn for the worse. I have searched and searched both my memory and extensive personal journals. And every time, I've come up empty-handed. All I can do is speculate.

Part of the trouble is that despite my outward commitment to the notion of "open, honest communication," there was much going on inside of me that I barely registered consciously. Since I was barely aware of it, I was a far cry from knowing it for certain or being willing or able to communicate it to someone else.

This was especially true when it came to troubling or confusing realizations that I desperately wanted not to be true.

One of these was the nagging feeling that my relationship with Seth was far from an ideal one. Despite the amount of time and effort I'd poured into my primary relationship over the last decade, it wasn't getting any easier.

And as I continued to date others, I kept running into people I was more emotionally compatible with, communicated better with, and who seemed to appreciate my quirks in a less judgmental manner.

I was able to talk away quite a bit of this as simple NRE, convince myself that my memories of my early relationship with Seth were probably flawed and that he was probably a great deal sweeter and more agreeable at the onset of our relationship. As the old song goes, the thrill was simply gone.

It worked for quite a while because I wanted it to be true, but it only worked for so long. At the point I visited Cleveland for the first time, I had not yet reached the failure point, but I can only guess that Seth was starting to struggle with these sorts of issues.

There are a lot of problems when converting a relationship in which two people often act as a single entity into one in which they operate as largely independent agents. Going into such a change, it's easy to underestimate the impact of the practical details, shared resources, financial realities, etc.

It's not just about your attitude – about one partner being emotionally "clingier" than the other. In the strictly practical realm, when speaking of time and money, actual dependence issues may erupt and make things seem "unfair."

Dates can be expensive. If the two of you are living off a single income as monogamous people, can you afford to pick up two dinners out on the same night if it happens you both have dates?

Do you share a car? If you do, it can be very difficult for the two of you to simultaneously be on dates with different people in different places. Even if one or both of you are dating people with unlimited access to their own transportation, do you really want to be dependent on these third parties in the short or long term to get where you need to go to see them?

Who has a more open schedule? This one can be rather insidious. At the point when we opened our relationship, Seth was on summer break with no job and even during the semester only taking 6 credit hours and performing as a fairly mediocre student while I routinely worked a full-time schedule with frequent overtime. This caused problems when we tried to date Megan together – not only because of the asymmetry of the feelings within the triad, but also because of the relative inequalities in the size of the time commitment for both Seth and me, given Seth's much larger pool of free time.

Who is responsible for most of the childcare? It can be extremely difficult to find a partner who wishes to date you and also spend time with your small children. In addition, many parents of young children are quite reluctant to introduce their partners to their children.

For women who are breastfeeding infants, dating becomes even more difficult.

Another important point to consider when opening up an exclusive relationship: Are you and your partner willing to relocate to an area with a better polyamorous/kinky dating pool? Though I pose the question as more than a simple rhetorical device, to my thinking, it does beg the question: Why would you risk a stable long-term relationship for something you don't feel strongly enough to geographically relocate for?

Jealousy is only one part of the picture when considering how the two of you will function independently. It gets a lot of attention in polyamory guides, both in print and online, and while it's a worthy adversary to relationship harmony, it is far from the only obstacle.

CLEVELAND

*Me: Sometimes I feel like I'm way out on a branch,
and I feel the wind blow, and at any moment the
branch could break, and I'd fall.*

Justin: Or fly.

"What brought you to Ohio?"

I get asked that a lot these days. The honest answers always sound crazy. Desperation, loneliness, a sense of impending doom, the need to start a life that's 100% my own in a place where my family name means nothing.

So I used to lie, say something that made sense to people. "For work." Or I gave a technically true answer that revealed nothing. "I have a lot of friends out here."

The choice was a) sit in a dark hole for a couple of years, watching lit screens, eating gas station pizza, moldering in my in laws' basement, or b) come to Ohio.

I suppose there would have been other choices eventually if I had stayed put for a while longer, explored other options. But I was tired of waiting. I'd been waiting most of my life.

That first morning, the Greyhound forged through Pennsylvania farmland at sunrise, the Amish man in the adjacent seat close to dying on my watch, his cough rattling like a dish rag being wrung, and Seth snoring loudly, a few seats away, a welcome change from his protests and complaints. As I'd removed him from the tomb we shared, newly exhumed, he was out for blood or at least a little sympathy.

As a passenger, I got lost in time, plunged into flow. My eyes were flooded by the gray expanse of I-90. Twenty-three hours we rode, like a great exodus across the desert, the Midwest unfolding like a plot I knew by heart, despite it being my first time there.

At one rest stop, a worker manned a sub shop alone. I couldn't tell him when I asked for ranch that fat-free was unacceptable and chewed on my naked salad, sat alone in that terminal waiting for the bus to be cleaned.

It's just not something people typically do, at least not where I'm from, move 900 miles to somewhere random, following a hunch that you'd fit in better than where you are, acting so decisively on what amounts to a crapshoot, several degrees removed from everything you've ever known.

Seth and I crawled off the final bus in the late morning in downtown Cleveland at the Greyhound station. I texted Rob to let him know that we'd arrived, and Seth and I went out to wait on the street where no fewer than 3 taxi drivers slowed to ask us if we needed a ride somewhere.

There were a few large buildings nearby, and my head spun just looking at them. I'd been to big cities before – Boston, Madrid, San Francisco, Rochester – but as Seth feared planes and disliked driving in city traffic, it had been years since I'd spent any significant amount of time in one.

The vertigo was a bit unsettling but overall a good sort of intense. Cleveland in general hit me that way. Everything here was larger – the roads, the signs, the boisterous personalities of virtually every person I encountered, when contrasted by the guarded standoffish manner of New Englanders. And not a scrap of pretension.

Rob was by to pick us up shortly in the car to drive us to his home. He and Michelle lived on the West Side in a suburb, the kind with good schools, the kind where they fine you for not cutting your grass.

Their home was fairly large, especially when compared to the smaller homes of some of their neighbors, but much of it was unfinished or in disrepair. They were currently renting out the attic but not for much longer, and Justin was renting one of the bedrooms on the second floor, but he'd just recently bought a house across town and would be moving out in a few months, leaving both his room and the attic free.

Justin's room would become the nursery, and the idea was that Seth could primarily live in the large attic, which would have room for the king-sized bed, large TV, couch, chairs, and various other pieces of furniture that he was insistent on us moving with us if we did decide to relocate to Ohio.

The unfinished bedroom needed a little TLC, some mudding and cleaning, but would serve well as a space for me to have an office to work in and a small bed where I could nap, have amorous encounters, or even spend the entire night just sleeping alone if I so desired.

As we were turning away from my future office and being led to see Rob and Michelle's room, Justin emerged from the bathroom wearing nothing more than a towel. "Oh," he blushed. "Um. Hello, Page."

I blushed as well, covering my face. "Don't look at me. I've been on a bus for an entire day. I'm hideous."

Justin laughed nervously and basically fled into his room. Later, Justin explained that no one had warned him that we were going to arrive, and he was terribly embarrassed to be caught practically naked. Sure, the encounter was a bit awkward, but virtually everyone is awkward in a towel – especially when they're not expecting company, and I thought Justin was cute. Taller and broader shouldered than I'd imagined (there weren't many pictures of him online, and in the ones he had posted, I had a hard time judging his size). Overweight, sure, but solidly built and very strong and muscled.

Rob finished giving us a tour of the house, and then I decided to take a shower to wash off the remains of the long overnight bus ride. I had no more stripped off my clothes, arranged my shampoo and soap among the other products on the shelf, and turned on the water when Rob came into the bathroom to join me, a truly pleasant surprise. I went to kiss him, and he resisted.

"Did I do something wrong?" I asked.

"I don't think I like kissing anymore." Rob went on to explain that he'd kissed a drunk girl at a Halloween party.

"And it was bad?"

He nodded. "It tasted like beer. Beer and desperation."

"Ah," I said, disappointed.

"But I do love you, pet," he said, giving me a chaste peck on the lips.

"I love you, too."

I was a bit disappointed at this turn of events, but Rob was sweet, and the feeling soon faded. He held me for a while under the hot water before growing serious, ordering, "Bend over, pet." He took me from behind, pounding me against the shower wall. "Don't touch yourself," he instructed. "This is all for me, my pleasure."

"There," he told me when he'd finished. "Now you'll have to walk around tonight meeting my friends, all the while knowing I've marked you, that you're filled with my cum."

I shuddered, dizzy at the thought.

Rob left the shower, started to towel off. "Wash yourself off," he said. "You're filthy." He left me to reel in the wake of what we'd just done.

Once I was dry, I changed into an outfit I'd selected for just this occasion. Rob's birthday party tonight. It was a tight short black dress with red cherry blossoms all over it paired with a pair of 4-inch black leather knee high boots.

I'd picked them both up at a yard sale that summer, being sold by a hyperactive blond woman in a trailer, who told me when I tried to talk her down to $2 (from the sticker price of $3) on the boots that she was sorry, but she couldn't budge. She desperately needed the money for a bus ticket to Texas. Her boyfriend was getting out of jail, see, and she needed to get there, come Hell or high water.

And here I was, pairing them both together, the sexy result of a decision on the border of good taste. I put on a pair of black leggings underneath, just to be sure I was on the correct side of that border.

Rob's birthday party was buzzing with activity, at least 20 or 30 guests, nearly all friendly and interesting in their own right. I flirted up a storm, floating from group to group, feeling instantly welcome. Many flirted in return; one even gave me his business card.

I followed Rob around, as best I could without being creepy about it, and while he didn't overtly reject me, he didn't do much to accommodate me either, so I started to feel quite a bit pathetic in my efforts to be near him.

I finally gave up and sat in the living room instead and was soon joined by Michelle, who, in an unexpected flirtatious outburst, plopped down onto my lap. I cuddled her from behind and continued to chat with other guests.

After a bit, Justin sat down next to us on the other available cushion. He looked exhausted.

"Hey," I said. "Are you alright?"

Justin talked a bit about work stress and the hassle of running the hacker space, an organization he'd started that was basically an engineering club for area people with a technology lab, tools, electronic equipment, etc, for people that wanted to invent and make cool new things. A pretty general umbrella concept but one that he was rather passionate about. I knew a bit from Rob and Michelle as they'd visited the space and been involved.

As Justin talked to me, our faces perhaps 6 inches from each other, I found my eyes trending down towards his mouth. His lips looked soft but firm, and there was something so sexy about him. It was hard to place. A strong sexual energy. I got the feeling that he'd be fun to make out with, and if we ever did get naked, he'd probably tear me half apart.

I smiled, actively listened, but found myself having to force myself to resist leaning in and kissing him. Even in the throes of a sudden and powerful attraction to Justin, I was able to keep my wits about me and realize that making out with him with Michelle on my lap at Rob's birthday party would be a *faux pas* to say the least.

Instead, I continued to murmur to Justin, inch perilously close to his face, and let my mind wander about what his gigantic hands would feel like on me.

Oh, did I ever feel filthy. In the best possible way. I teased myself until I practically squirmed and then joined the festivities outside, where they'd built a fire in an oil barrel, hobo style.

There I discussed Dom/sub dynamics with a few other members of the local kink community, and Rob finally cuddled me, if only briefly and restlessly, like a cat being forced to. I was disappointed by this but couldn't help myself. I was drawn to him even as he was glacial and distant.

By the end of the party, I was really beginning to wonder. Was it all in my head? Did Rob even feel anything for me? I felt desperate, like I was chasing him. I'd been so excited for this night to be seen with him, to be able to celebrate his birthday and be shown off in front of the people who mattered the most to him. I knew it was his birthday, his night. I knew it wasn't all about me, but I'd built it up so far in my head, fantasizing about being paraded around like a trophy. And when it turned out instead that the person I spent the least time at the party with was Rob, the difference between fantasy and reality was incredibly disappointing.

I spent the night on a futon with Seth in the guest room, the unfinished room that would become my office if we were to move in with Rob and Michelle.

"What do you think?" I asked.

"I like it here. Seems like there's a lot to do in the area," Seth said.

"I didn't see you at all at the party," I said. Michelle had told me Seth had spent most of the night out on the street smoking cigarette after cigarette.

"I just wasn't feeling it," he said.

"I don't know why. You love parties."

"I don't know about these people," he said. "They're just... meh."

"Meh? As opposed to DRUNK?"

Seth nodded.

I sighed. "I know it's easy to forget, and don't take this the wrong way, but I do remember us talking one time about how there were plenty of people in DRUNK that we wouldn't want to hang out with unless we were drinking."

It was true. We were about as politically liberal as you get without being anarchists, and quite a few of the regulars at

DRUNK parties were pretty darn conservative and vocal about it.

"Yeah, I suppose," he said.

"You should have come and gotten me," I said. "I would have introduced you to people."

"I didn't want to get in the way."

"Oh, Seth," I said. "You're never in my way." I cuddled him close to me.

"Ouch," he said. "You're pulling my hair."

I pulled away. "I'm sorry."

Seth wasn't tired, so he pulled out the laptop. Megan was on Gmail chat, so he fired up a conversation with her. I knew I shouldn't look, that I should just keep my eyes on the book I was reading, but I couldn't help myself. I glanced over quickly at the screen. Megan wanted to know how he was doing, how he liked Ohio so far.

He'd typed back that there hadn't been much opportunity to look around, but he'd gotten a good first impression and that Rob and Michelle's friends seemed like cool people.

Satisfied that Seth was doing okay, I rolled over, put down my book, and went to sleep.

Michelle was an interesting tour guide, to say the least. Since she was really into true crime, she gave us a special introduction as we drove around Cleveland, pointing out the various places people had died under unusual circumstances. Here was the site of a murder-suicide over a girlfriend (must have been *some* girlfriend). Here was a particularly grisly motorcycle accident. Here a mysterious corpse was hauled up out of the river.

I took it all in as we drove to our final destination, a munch at a diner bordering Cleveland, one of those places that are open all night to serve the bar crowd. Of course, it was Sunday afternoon, and the main dining room was crammed full of perverts.

A munch, in the BDSM world, refers to an informal gathering at a restaurant or bar where kinky folk can get together to simply meet and greet and/or discuss some topic of the lifestyle. In my experience, when you get enough perverts together, discussion of kinky antics inevitably ensues, even when there is no expressly agreed-upon meeting topic. And even when there is one, the actual conversation often deviates from what was set out. Imagine that. Deviants deviating. Go figure.

I took a seat between Michelle and Seth at the end of a long buffet table. When faced with the prospect of attending, that morning Rob had been stricken mysteriously ill, further feeding my worries that our levels of interest in one another were woefully mismatched. His absence was particularly troubling in that quite early on in our relationship, not long after I'd formally decided I was interested in being his submissive, he'd expressed to me that he was eager to bring me with him to one of these. And now here I was at the round table without him. A pet without an owner, a sub without a Dom – and accompanied by two vanilla (non-kinky) people to boot. Lovely. Well, at least they were poly. We cuddled in various configurations.

I spent most of the meal chatting with a couple near to me. The submissive was bright eyed and feminine, skilled with makeup, a bit glamorous and quite friendly. Her Dominant, conversely, was brooding, heavily inked, a man of few words. "It's so nice to meet another submissive who's chattier than her Dom," she said.

"Oh?" I said. I realized she was referring to Seth. "Oh! My Dom's at home. This is my husband. He's vanilla." I fought the bitterness in my chest rising up. What was so wrong with me that I had traveled 900 miles to see him, and Rob couldn't be bothered to come eat dinner with us and introduce me to the community? Why wasn't I worth it to him? And how could I do better?

First the cold shoulder at his party and now this. I resolved that I would confront him with these concerns when we arrived home. I'd be brutal if I had to. No sooner had I thought this than was I gripped with anxiety. What if I lost him? Maybe I was already on shaky ground. What if it was all just a matter of time? Would I drive him away by being pushy? Then again, I had to know. I was going crazy not knowing. I would bring it up.

I climbed the stairs, steeling myself for the conflict, running through all the ways I could approach the talk. But as soon as I saw his face, I knew that the discussion would have to wait. Something was clearly wrong.

"Rob, are you okay?"

"My mom called while I was asleep. She's been talking to my sister. She told Mom about us being poly, and there's this crazy message on my voice mail where Mom's talking about calling off Thanksgiving. I can't deal with this."

I climbed into bed, cuddled him a while. "I wish there were something I could do," I said.

"It's fine, pet," he replied.

As much as I hated to see him stressed, it was nice to have Rob physically close to me, to feel like he welcomed my touch. I snuggled in his arms. "Are you going to call her back?'

"Yeah," he said. "Just gotta figure out what I'm going to say to my mom. I'm not ashamed. At the same time, the whole thing pisses me off."

Apparently, Rob had dated his sister's best friend ages ago. In fact, she was the very first person he'd dated when he and Michelle became poly. While they had a good date and ended up in the bedroom, things fizzled out relatively quickly because (according to Rob) while the girl was attracted to Rob, she didn't want to share him with Michelle. Even though the fling was short lived, when Rob's sister found out, she was livid and said she felt violated that he'd dated her best friend, someone she considered off limits. Many years had passed, and Rob had assumed it was all in the past, that his sister didn't care anymore. Apparently he was wrong.

Complicating matters even further, the two of them had a strained relationship even as children with some inappropriate behavior towards one another, something his sister had been exploring in therapy for years. As the older sibling by 4 years, Rob owned up to the fact that his actions as a child were wrong but would qualify this admission by adding, "to be fair, she started it." The story goes that his parents discovered what was going on between the two of their children and beat the hell out of Rob to deter future misbehavior and sent his sister to a counselor with no therapy for Rob, and that was that, leaving quite a bit of confusion in the dynamic between Rob and his sister and pain and stress in their relationship.

Though I had known this about Rob for quite some time as he had confided it to me relatively early on in our relationship, and it was something that I'd accepted about him wanting to keep an open mind and delighted he felt comfortable enough with me to be honest about something like that, what he did to his sister was major. Even as I comforted him and as much as I felt his disappointment about the upcoming holidays and frustration with the fractured family dynamics, I believed and still believe his sister had every right to be angry with him.

But I did what I could. I held him, listened to him, scratched his back as he planned his next move.

My trip to Cleveland was a nice change of pace, sure, but it wasn't a vacation in the strictest sense. I still had to work. Luckily, my position as a medical transcriptionist allowed me to easily telecommute. While staying at Rob and Michelle's house, I spent most days typing at a basement workstation set up where Rob's gaming computer usually was, so I could take advantage of his kick ass monitor. It was a nice spot, tucked away in a corner in a quiet, well-lit place, and even in unfamiliar surroundings, I found myself able to be quite productive.

In stray moments, however, I did puzzle about Rob and his hot and cold attitudes toward intimacy and also, to my surprise, Justin. The more I tried not to think about Justin, the more I found my mind traveling back to him and the sudden sexual intensity between us I'd felt at Rob's birthday party. Was it all in my head? It was entirely possible. I had expressed my interest online in no uncertain terms prior to meeting in person:

> **page:** in the interest of full disclosure, i think you're really cute

> **justin:** Aww, thank you

> **justin:** As are you

> **page:** though I probably won't do anything about it because I'm seeing too many people as it is

> **justin:** lol, I won't take offense

> **page:** I was thinking after I got to town and settled down sometime in the future, I'd probably work up the courage to ask you on a date or something

That said, Justin had given absolutely no indication since I'd arrived that he viewed me as anything other than a friend. Still, even as a one-sided urge, it was far too intense for me to ignore. I wanted to explore it further. But how? How to bridge the gap? Sure, I could restate my interest in him as I had before, but I hated to go the same exact route, and the fact that he wasn't giving off any obvious positive signals was playing games with my head. Not to mention I can be pretty direct when the situation calls for it, but I hate to beat something into the ground. So I got creative.

I texted him, *Are you a kisser?*

Justin texted back quickly, *Lol. I can be. Depends on the situation.*

I smiled. Non-committal but friendly. Okay. *Excellent. I need someone who's a kisser in this town, and you seem perfect.* As soon as I pressed send, I realized that could come off as kind of creepy. Oh well. Too late now.

He responded with a smiley icon.

Well, he wasn't overtly horrified. That was good. And Justin seemed pretty tolerant of my particular brand of forward. Another plus.

Not only that, but the next time we physically crossed paths in the house, he didn't pounce me or anything, but he was warm and friendly and didn't seem at all offended.

Okay, I decided. *This has promise.*

Not long after, I visited a BDSM dungeon for the first time. I felt immediately energized by the environment at the club, energized but not anxious. Instead I was comfortable, a bit dazed perhaps, overwhelmed by stimuli – so many people to meet and talk with, scenes to take in, things to learn.

After I'd signed in at the door, I was walking by a row of couches and was immediately knocked off my feet, pulled to the side. Before I had time to even register what had happened, I found myself on Justin's lap in a sort of half-cuddle, half-hug position.

"Hey pretty," Justin said.

I giggled and blushed and fought to regain my composure.

Justin was so strong. Pulling me in like that had been effortless. I felt that familiar desire creeping up within me, so intense that it scared me. Much stronger than Rob. Much.

This was a dangerous line of thought, one that seemed extremely disloyal. Especially here at the dungeon, with my wanting to train as Rob's submissive. True, things were moving slowly with Rob on that front – and on most fronts, really – but the distance was a huge factor, and I was sure Rob had his reasons and that my patience would be rewarded.

I flirted a bit before politely disentangling from Justin and following Rob to the main play space to observe.

brief trip update

OR "A Veiled Tale of Punishment Gluttony"
(Because the martyr was the messiah after all.)

I had my first dungeon experience last Saturday. It was fantastic to be exposed to so much truth, so much vulnerability around every turn. I also greatly appreciated the separate lounge area for when the rooms became too overwhelming. Though Rob and I kept things low key, I loved being there with him sharing our impressions, being physically near him in the face of all that intensity (which I found myself absorbing through sheer voyeurism),

seeing him, being seen with him. I especially enjoyed watching the dynamics of scenes
where masochists were like exquisite vio-
lins the tops were playing beautifully, the
pain virtuosos.

The whole experience of the last few months
has a distinctly dream-like quality to it. For
one, I'm still in shock by how much positive
attention my physical appearance has attracted recently. It's really the subtle things, people
smiling more often, checking me out, flirting
with wild abandon. I was virtually invisible to others at my heaviest weight (well at
least until I spoke). And on the relationship
front.... yeah... I could not have imagined a
better situation.

Though I really try not to be a slave to labels, I'm feeling more and more that the title
of "pet" is a rather apt one for me and really
captures a large chunk of my fundamental
essence, sexual and otherwise – or somesuch.

When we were talking before bed last night,
Seth said he's really grown to like this place
and will miss Ohio when we return back
to Maine.

Not that I'd write about it in my journal (after all, my lovers
could and did read it – well, everyone but Seth, who always
maintained it was pointless to read my writing because I

told all of it to him anyway, talking his ear off), but trying to figure out what was going on in Justin's head was becoming a real source of anxiety. He could be so shy and standoffish in person, making me feel like he wasn't he slightest bit interested in me and then without warning make a spontaneous and overtly flirtatious gesture like he did at the dungeon. What was the deal? Was he just messing with me?

Not only that, but I wasn't sure I had enough to offer Justin. I was stretched pretty thin between Rob and Seth, even if things with Tina and Michelle were a great deal more casual and low-key, more akin to friendships with benefits than full-on love affairs. Justin was single, spent a great deal of time alone, and though he'd expressed interest in polyamory as a relationship style, he still expressed a good deal of trepidation regarding actually taking the leap and starting connections.

And I'm sure it didn't help that while I was seriously considering moving to Ohio, I still for all official purposes lived in Maine and could at any time completely vanish, never to return.

"Good news," Rob said. "I just got off the phone with my mom."

"Oh?" Michelle perked up.

"Yeah, she and dad are coming to dinner again."

"Well, that's a relief," Michelle said.

"Basically, she was worried that I was into men," Rob said.

I exploded with laughter. "What?"

"Yeah, she Googled polyamory and apparently found some stuff about bisexuality and flipped out thinking I was having sex with guys."

"I don't even know what to say to that," I said.

Seth rolled his eyes, stepped out for a cigarette.

"Well," I said. "Oh noes! Not the gay! Can't have you catching the gay!"

Rob petted me on the head. "It's not exactly the most enlightened outlook in the world, but it does solve the immediate problem."

"True," I replied.

"It really would be easier if I were bi," he said. "I'd have an easier time finding partners."

"Maybe. Though you gotta remember it could be more confusing, and there's the potential for more headaches, too."

"I suppose," he said. "It also took quite a bit of reassurance to convince her that Michelle was really okay with it."

"Did you tell her that about Michelle's ex-boyfriend?" I asked.

"No," he said. "Didn't want to tell her without asking her if it was okay to first. Though I did tell her about you."

"What?!" I asked. "You told her I was your girlfriend?" I felt a mixture of terror and pride. This could make things a heck of a lot more stressful at the dinner, but at the same time, he thought enough of me to tell his mother about us?

"Well, no not exactly," he said.

"Oh," I said, feeling a bit disappointed and confused. "What *did* you tell her?"

"That I was considering dating you."

I laughed. "I suppose that's *technically* true. Well kinda. Or not at all."

"Don't be mad," he said.

"Oh, I'm not," I replied. "To be honest, it'd be a bit much for me to deal with all at once, especially with how badly she reacted to the mention of 'poly' in the first place. I'd probably end up super defensive and make a bad impression."

As it was, things went rather well with Rob's parents, Michelle's too, who also joined us for dinner, having made the long trek from Michigan.

Rob's mother was a bit critical and overbearing but nothing I wasn't used to – having been raised by perfectionist parents and spending quite a bit of my early years as a member of a small-town Catholic church. Rob's mother seemed quite pleased by my Catholic upbringing when Rob brought it up relatively early on. She complimented, too, my taste in clothing and my expertise in my profession as we chatted about medical issues. We commiserated on our shared philosophy that teenagers these days are horribly deprived of love and that this deficit causes great problems for society, pervasive and ubiquitous. We delighted at our mutual love of clams.

In fact, the back and forth between Rob's mother and me dominated the flow of the dinner table conversation. I observed Michelle blatantly squirming in her chair and remembered her bitter words prior to the dinner, "With my luck, she'll like you more than she likes me."

It was a point of contention, a sore spot for Michelle, that Rob's mother had never really liked or accepted her. Michelle couldn't pinpoint it exactly, just that his mother had been quite critical about her in virtually every aspect and had never really warmed to her in the way that she thought a mother-in-law should.

Later, feeling that I may have hurt her feelings, I tried to touch base with Michelle, but she bristled and stated everything was fine but not before adding, "I told you she'd like you better than me."

Still, Michelle and I managed to put on a good show for the parents, in an attempt to assuage his mother's concerns that Michelle resented the arrangement.

Rob told me later, after his mother had called him on the phone, "She likes you a lot. She said, 'Page is great. She's a really nice person.'"

"Well, of course I am," I teased, smirking.

Rob laughed. "I don't know how you did it, but you seem to have charmed my mother. Nobody does that. I'm kind of impressed."

I shrugged. "I'm good with mothers."

I got to exercise my mother-charming skills again as we spent the next few days with Michelle's parents. Rob's folks lived about a half an hour away, on the other side of Cleveland in a different suburb, so they just came over for the evening for Thanksgiving dinner. Michelle's parents, however, were from

Michigan and had quite a drive, so they were staying at a hotel and tying the holiday into a short visit to justify the trip.

Michelle's parents were quite a bit older than Rob's. Michelle was an "oopsie baby," born much later than her older siblings. It was immediately clear to me that her parents still treated her like a baby.

Michelle's mother in particular was a real piece of work. She had absolutely no filter whatsoever, making jokes about Michelle's weight, calling her "the fat lady" without even a slight smile on her face. Keep in mind that Michelle was almost 8 months pregnant! In the right tone of voice, this could have been playful, but both her deadpan delivery and Michelle's wincing in response ruined the effect.

I'm a talkative person myself and have a high tolerance for people who are really chatty, but Michelle's mother was another story altogether. She talked things to *death*, going on and on about the most inconsequential minutiae from the commonplace to the relatively obscure. She was opinionated and often wrong but not easily corrected – or even interrupted for that matter.

Despite my immediate discomfort being around her and distaste for her communication style and way of dealing with other people, I did my best to be kind, humor her, make a good impression. I actively listened and paid attention. Before I knew it, Michelle's mom had warmed up a great deal to me, clutching my arm and leaning in close when she talked, giggling like we were old friends, even as I found her more and more obnoxious.

Michelle took us to a thrift store in a rich suburb so I could marvel at the deals on designer clothes and scoop up some real bargains. The selection was amazing! I found a number of cute retro dresses with spaghetti straps, lace, and polka dot patterns. I stood before one wall loaded with finds, mesmerized by its bounty, a swirling sea of vintage delight.

I was so taken with the sight that I didn't realize that Michelle's mom had sidled up beside me until I felt her hand on her arm. "Now Page," she said, her voice dripping with motherly wisdom and concern, "Those are SUMMER clothes."

I felt a chill go up my spine. Really? Really? Annoying was annoying, but she'd gone to the overbearing mother level. Aggravating enough coming from one's own mother, but this... This was utterly ridiculous.

I was tempted to turn to her and say, "Not when you're a slut, ma'am," but caught myself just in time.

Instead, I said, "Maybe, but buying out of season is the only way to get the deals."

"Smart," she replied, positively glowing with motherly pride.

I was impressed when I first visited the hacker space, Justin's venture. It was located in a pretty rough neighborhood (when the price is right, the price is right), but the building was huge, plenty of square footage, and I was amazed the first time I visited that everywhere I looked was another machine or industrial component – an engineer's paradise. Rob had a workstation where he set up his laptop and started to work on something. I was curious but didn›t want to pry. Seth drifted off to mingle with some of the others (mostly guys) and check out the equipment.

One of the hackers who had been at Rob's birthday party (where we'd discussed computer game design) greeted me and came to my rescue.

When Rob had first mentioned he was part of "hacker culture," I'd bristled. I knew better than to blithely ask, "Hackers? Don't you guys steal bank info?" but my internal reaction was similar. When Rob had invited me to speak at a hacker convention, I'd hesitated before replying, "Well I don't 'hack' per se."

"Of course you do," Rob had replied.

"I *barely* program."

"Oh, being a hacker's about a heck of a lot more than that," he'd explained. "Hacking's about messing around with stuff. Some people hack computers. Some hack art. Some even hack people."

Indeed, the more I learned about hacker culture, the more I found it was a place for people fascinated by the intersection between art and technology, between creativity and design; in another word, a hacker was a modern-day tinker with few boundaries for their endeavors.

Not to mention that even the computer hackers were for the most part far from criminal (though I of course do not know everyone and therefore cannot vouch for everyone), and many of them were actually employed in the realm of information security (or info sec, as they say among themselves), breaking down systems in the employ of companies in order to more effectively know how to safeguard them.

"Hackers get a bad rap," Rob said. "But we're reclaiming the label. We're taking it back."

I saw this ingenuity at work at Justin's hacker space, where people worked on their separate projects with intense concentration. The exact nature of their respective projects might have been lost on me, but their energy was not.

One particularly interesting project involved a 3D printer they were building, a long and involved and quite labor-intensive project but one that would allow them to create a nearly unlimited number of objects made of plastic with nothing more than a computer design. I was fascinated to hear Justin speak of it, the logistics involved, the possibilities. Not only that, but Justin was so passionate and excited when he spoke of the project that I couldn't help but be attracted to him.

The hours passed effortlessly, and despite lacking a lot of the technical knowledge, I felt a kinship with those geeking out all around me. Even Seth had a good time, inspired to construct a PVC bass guitar.

I got a taste of one of the more unique realities of dating as a polyamorous person one evening when Rob, Justin, Seth, and I were playing a tabletop role-playing game called *Fiasco*. There I was, surrounded by my husband, my new lover, and my chief potential love interest all in one space, interacting with one another, playing a game. The turbulence within me was profound. I felt my love and energy shifting from one target to the next, each attraction distinct but undeniable. It was not at all true what they said. You *could* love more than one person at a time – differently but with intensity for each.

This turned what I'd been told my entire life (by my parents, the media, peers, etc) on its head.

After the game, I hung out with Justin as he showed me pictures online of his new house.

"It's beautiful!" I said. "You can tell even from just the photos."

Justin beamed. "Thank you. I'm really happy with it."

"And I'm happy for you!" Even though I was practically naked, wearing nothing but a short satin slip, I stood up and gave him a hug. I loved the way his body felt against mine. I started to melt.

I felt Justin pull away from me slightly, and my heart sank.

Well, that was it. Justin clearly wasn't into me.

Later when Rob, Michelle, Seth, and I went out to get some supplies, I announced suddenly in the car, "I'm over Justin."

Seth laughed. "I'll believe it when I see it."

"No, really," I said.

"What's up?" Rob asked.

"I dunno. It's just... different in person."

Rob smiled, and I thought I saw a wave of relief wash over his face.

"Totally understandable," Michelle said. "I was worried about you overbooking yourself."

I stared out the window, feeling heartbroken. It was nothing. Less than nothing. Justin and I had nothing together, the beginnings of a friendship, what I thought was a mutual crush. Why did I feel such a sense of loss?

Sometimes losing what never was, the potential for greatness, hurts far more than losing something that's had a chance to fully develop.

My heart ached thinking about what could have been with Justin. How could I have read the situation so wrong?

Even after I resolved that I was over Justin, I found myself second guessing my announcement when we all went out to dinner the last day of the trip. I was sitting at the table, holding hands with Rob when he started to make a big show of pressing some small bruises on my arm. It was an overt display of dominance, of his hold over me, working me like a control panel, summoning up pain to his whims. Sure, it smarted, and I was slightly embarrassed, but mostly it aroused me. I caught Justin's expression out of the corner of my eye. It was unmistakable. Envy.

I realized then that I was far from over Justin, even when I'd spoken up and told my other lovers I was. I had *wanted* to be over Justin, quite a different thing. Or at least *thought I wanted* to be over Justin. And now I wasn't so sure anymore.

If it sounds convoluted, it's because it is. Feelings often are. Romantic attraction is not some simple equation, especially in polyamory. Rather, it often involves the interplay between one's own feelings, the perceived feelings of the love object, and the attitudes of the network of each person's lovers and friends. Nothing happens in isolation, and all of these elements come into play.

Physically, I was on board. I knew it. There was just something about Justin that was so warm and manly and solid, and I wanted to touch him as much as possible. But as far as my feelings were concerned, that was another story. I liked him a great deal, but I just couldn't read him. He was an introvert, and the mixed messages (and general lack of messages, for that matter) I was getting were confusing me to no end. I had no idea what sort of cards he was holding, and I was scared to push too hard, ask too much, and scare him away, as had happened to me before in the past with other people.

Not only that, but I was having a hard time figuring out Rob's level of comfort with my interest in Justin. When I'd ask Rob, he'd simply reply, "I'm not threatened," but that was far from a complete picture of his emotions, and when I'd press for more information, Rob would lead me around a path of circular logic and tautologies.

For her part, Michelle would reply, "The idea of you dating Justin makes me uncomfortable," but wouldn't go so far as to forbid me, and to be quite honest, everything made Michelle uncomfortable, the weather, her co-workers, parties, attitudes of fictional characters on television, municipal corruption, city zoning laws, when other girls got more attention, finances, and pretty much everything Rob did. Life in general made Michelle uncomfortable. Uncomfortable was her natural state.

As conflicted as I was about Justin, there was one thing I was sure about.

Cleveland.

I wrote an e-mail to my supervisor to start the relocation paperwork and get my tax situation all squared away. I would move to Ohio the following April.

Since Don and Tina were in Ohio visiting their parents for the Thanksgiving holiday, they very generously offered to give Seth and me a ride back to Maine with them. It was cramped, but we made good time, a mere 14 hours broken up by a few quick breaks for meals. On the ride home, Seth became more and more visibly upset. At first I attributed this to sleep deprivation (after all, we'd had to awaken quite early to set out for the long drive), but as time wore on, and he became more vocal, it became quite evident that there was something more going on.

With a bit of prompting from Tina, who had somewhat randomly inserted herself as a mediator (though I was glad on some level as it signaled she had become a great deal more comfortable with their breakup over the last few months), Seth admitted the problem.

"It's nice that you're happy and all, Page, but every time you get into a relationship, it... it just sucks."

"Oh, honey," I said. "Practically everyone gets insecure. It's natural. I know I did when you started seeing Megan alone."

"No!" he snapped. "It's not that. I'm not jealous."

"Okay," I said. "It'd be okay if you were. I love you, y'know."

"If it's not jealousy, then what is it?" Tina asked.

"Well," Seth said. "Every time you get another partner, Page, it means I'm one step further away from my dream."

"Huh?" I asked. "Your dream?"

"Of being in a triad with you and another girl."

Something felt terribly wrong with what he said. I knew it instinctively, but I focused on the practical element to what he was saying as it hit me first and was easily articulated. "I could still do that, even as it is. I have enough time."

"Not really, not for what I want. You could do something with me and a new girl what? A night a week?"

I nodded. "Sure. Thereabouts. And regularly, too. If she were local."

Seth frowned. "That's not at all the amount of time I had in mind."

I sighed. "Why does it matter so much to you?"

"I told you. It's my dream. It's what I want more than anything."

Again something was bothering me. It was just at the edge of my mind. I found myself suddenly thinking of all the times Seth had called me needy or dependent for wanting a hug, a conversation, a walk together, a kiss when it hadn't suited his needs. How he looked down on me for being "clingy," considering himself superior in that way, self-contained.

It came to me. "Seth, you never asked me what *my* dreams were," I said.

"Your dreams?" he asked.

"You never stopped to consider I might have fantasies of my own. You always just assumed they were yours."

I could tell what I'd said affected him. We sat in the car in silence for a while, not sure what to say, Don's audiobook blaring on about courtly love.

Poly Signpost #7: Ex Ex Ex Ex Ex Ex - Oh?

I have a bounty of exes, ex-girlfriends, ex-boyfriends, an ex-fiancé, an ex-husband.

In short, I'm a lot of people's crazy ex.

I love so hard it hurts.

I spent my childhood terribly lonely. I was out in the country, far from my school friends. The other members of my household found me obnoxious and weird, and I was often encouraged to hold my tongue, tone my behavior down, or go away.

I'd lie in bed and talk to the wall, pretending I had a best friend. We'd kick up our legs and make a blanket tent. Sometimes he was a girl. Sometimes she was a boy – but I was always loved, breathing the stale air under the comforter and feeling this phantom presence.

I dreamed of a Great Love, that person I could say anything to and would know where I was coming from, patient, kind, passionate, intense. I wanted harmony, intimacy. A mutual admiration society. I wanted someone I could pleasure until the brink of disintegration, someone who would tell me their secrets and who I could entrust with mine. Someone I could dive into again and again, each time finding more beauty than the last. I wanted to be wanted – not just tolerated but wanted, desired, welcomed, savored. I wanted something to do with all the love I had inside of me, to be able to dote when I felt the affection welling up within me. I wanted to be lost in each other, to be brought over the threshold of identity when our bodies wrapped around each other. I wanted to fuck with my entire body, my heart, my soul. Even the filth, the degradation, the shame had to be personal and intense. I wanted mutual vulnerability. I wanted to be inseparable, intertwined mentally, physically, emotionally. There was no such thing as too close. I didn't see the point of anything other than close. I didn't want casual.

And most of all, I wanted to give. Really, that's what hurt the most, not being able to find someone willing to accept everything I had to give.

"Why are you looking at me? That's kind of creepy." "What? Make out here? We're going to get caught." "You're a little intense." "Don't you ever think of anything but sex?" "Shut up, I need to get some sleep." "You say the most messed up shit." "You're so needy. It's exhausting." "It's obsession; it can't be healthy."

All I want is for you to look at me when you come. I want to see the sun rising in your face as I touch you. Let me look at you. Love and sex are inseparable to me. I'm broken, I know. I'm a pervert. I'm not asking you to be the same way as I am; just let me be me and let me love you. I care, and I'm trying. I know you don't want to try, but please don't punish me for trying. Is it wrong to be obsessed with my own happiness, with your happiness, with our happiness?

Every time I'd try to make it work, convinced that this could be the Great Love, not wanting it to pass me by, doing everything in my power to keep relationships held together – well past the point where I was miserable. *What if this is it?* I'd think. *Do you want to let a little unhappiness keep you from the greatest connection of your life?*

So I'd use my pliancy to fill in gaps, stretch myself over the defects in each relationship, overloaded, stressed, my partners intuitively pushing their luck further and further until inevitably a line would be crossed, and it would become unbearable – and in many cases, the situation would actually become dangerous. I would then leave without warning, knowing I'd tried as hard as I could, leaving stunned partners in my wake.

My exit seemed to come out of nowhere. As far as they were concerned, I was fine with the way things were. It wasn't that I hadn't complained. I did. It's that I remained calm, spoke logically about my concerns. I never yelled or got angry. Even on the rare occasion that I gave an ultimatum, I spoke gently, often with my head down, embarrassed by the hard stance I didn't want to have to take.

My words were ignored.

I know what I would say now, if I could go back:

"Look, you don't have to yell or get firm with me for me to listen to you. Why should I have to do the same? I'm not even talking about agreeing with what I say. I'm not even being heard."

"Communication is a 2-way street. You can demand the truth all day long, but if you make yourself impermeable to unpleasant information, that's not my fault."

Maybe it's madness, but I'm growing to realize it's benign madness, and it need not be eradicated but directed appropriately.

All relationships end, and most end before one or both partners die. Odds are you'll break up eventually. And that's okay.

Far too often I see a pattern where people are desperate to assign blame, where they are compelled to vilify their ex. Maybe it's a form of defensiveness lest they be stigmatized for "failing." Maybe it's to assuage and externalize their disappointment that the relationship didn't turn out to be what they had hoped it could be.

Whatever the case, I bet you're somebody's crazy ex, too.

Learning to manage poly well is a process that takes many things. Parting ways gracefully is a skill few have mastered.

THE BASEMENT

O ver the ensuing months, there was so much I could tell no one. I wrote copiously, chronicling my frustrations on a number of fronts. With the decision having been made and officially announced to work to move to Ohio, my focus shifted away from Maine. I knew I would miss little to nothing there. Most of my friends had moved away after college to get jobs in other places, do other things, have other lives.

I was looking forward to moving on, moving up.

But for the time being, I was stuck in Maine despite feeling I had no business being there. The icing on the cake was being stuck in my in-laws' basement in a studio apartment with no windows during a brutally cold winter. I tried my best to be optimistic:

new place

The new place is rather cozy, so cozy I'm finding myself content to stay in all night (something very new). The only real problem with the apartment is it's a little cold (which only really bothers my fingers as I type as the rest can be covered), and we have to share a bathroom with Seth's parents (who live upstairs). But we even have a fridge and microwave now, which has totally helped meal planning.

One nice thing is that there are no windows in our space, so it's pitch black in the mornings, leading to optimal sleep regardless of the hour. Seriously, I'm sleeping like a log, which is highly unusual for me (I attribute this both to how dark it is down here and quitting caffeine). This morning I finally got to the point where I could walk in absolute darkness to a light fixture to turn it on (switches are located far from the bed), which was a big breakthrough.

The only major problems with our living situation are the bathroom sharing thing I already mentioned (because I hate feeling like I'm in his parents' way), there being no dishwasher (which has changed the character of our meal preparation but is still doable), and hot water having to be switched on 1/2 hour before use (as they keep it off). His parents have a rather sizable tile shower (with 2 shower heads, almost a locker room style) that could easily shower 4 or 5. However, there is no tub on the premises, and the nature of the shower heads (limited directions for pointing and not able to be detached) makes it more difficult to wash, though not impossible.

—

On the money front, Seth has lost the job with his parents, but this wasn't entirely unexpected as I was surprised that they could afford to pay him in the first place when the initial job offer was made. In better news, I'm getting a pretty decent holiday bonus at work, which should help offset things a little bit.

Also... I may have left my heart in Ohio...

I bought myself an LED color-changing nightlight and made friends with the toaster oven as our microwave sadly tripped the circuit breaker downstairs every time we attempted to use it, resulting in a mini-disaster as our computers, along with everything else in our apartment, shutting off until we could reset it.

No Hot Pocket is worth that.

When faced with our dire financial straits, Seth had already taken the fall semester off school ostensibly to work and after a short job search had given up and gone to work for his parents. Once we moved in with them, they'd let him go. Business wasn't that great, and free rent was a big help anyway, so I wasn't terribly surprised or upset with them.

But then Seth didn't get another job. In fact, he wasn't even bothering to look.

When I did mention my worries about our financial situation, things took a turn for the worse.

"You got a sec, honey?" I said to Seth.

"Sure, what's up?" he replied.

I levelled with him. "I need some help from you. I've been feeling a lot of stress lately. I don't know how we're going to continue to pay the bills with just my income. It's been a few years since you've worked steadily, and it's just getting harder and harder for me to make it work, especially with all the changes they've made at my job. And I get that it can be difficult finding a job, but I really need you to try, and at the very least, I need you to stop asking if you can buy things that are extras, like in-game gold or character transfers on *WoW*. I hate saying no to you, and it wears me out."

"You're so fucking selfish!" he replied.

The suddenness of his ire disturbed me. I hadn't anticipated this reaction. I really thought going into the conversation that I could share my feelings, plant a seed, and maybe we could problem-solve later. After all, I had started this discussion on my afternoon break from work, thinking it would only take 5 minutes or so, tops.

"I am?" I said.

"You KNEW when you got together with me that I'm depressed, and you married me for better or worse!"

"I understand that you're depressed, and I know that's not easy for you."

"Like hell you do," Seth replied.

"I love you and I care, but sometimes it's hard to give you the space you need to sort out your depression because it directly affects me, especially this financial stuff."

"Oh, of course it's all about you," he said. "I never thought you'd be the one to betray me, Page."

"How am I betraying you?"

"If you feel like I'm such a burden, Page, you should just go off to Ohio and leave me the hell alone. I don't want to live with you anymore. We'll get separate bank accounts."

"That's not what I –"

Seth stood up suddenly. "I need to fucking get out of here." He stormed out of the basement apartment. I collapsed on the bed, sobbing.

A few minutes later, he returned. "It's a blizzard out there."

"Do you need help cleaning off the car?" I offered.

He shot me a dirty look. "Don't fucking talk to me," he said and sat down to play a game.

I dragged myself back to my workstation to finish the remaining 2 hours of my shift.

After I got out of work, we hashed things out and apologized to each other. He said he didn't mean the things he'd said in anger. We agreed on therapy to help him both with his severe depression and our issues as a couple.

Unfortunately, I was still stressed out (as my stress predated the fight) and didn't really get to address it. I stayed up until about 3:00 that morning, having to take melatonin to get to sleep, even though I had been sleeping horribly the last few days.

I woke up at 8:15 in the upstairs bathroom, my clothes a mess, completely unaware of how I had gotten there.

Apparently when the alarm went off at 8, I stumbled around in the dark slipping and falling several times in a chaotic fashion crying out, "Help me, help me," over and over again. I had lost bladder control in the dark, and my night clothes were streaked with urine.

I had to mop up the floor before work.

When the initial fight had broken out, I complained about it in an IRC chat room that I used to communicate with Rob and Michelle and a handful of their other friends. Justin responded quickly by private messaging:

> **justin:** Oh boy... Sounds like maybe you hit a big trigger for him and he's lashed out because of it
>
> **page:** yeah, I feel like an awful person right now. I really tried to use neutral and diplomatic language
>
> **justin:** I can see why he feels that way then... But you aren't an awful person, you were trying to communicate your feelings
>
> **justin:** He's obviously been feeling bad about it, but probably feels very stuck
>
> **page:** yeah, I don't even mind if he doesn't contribute as long as he's not asking to buy a bunch of stuff and then yelling at me when I say no. he got really mad I said no to his spending $30 to transfer his alliance warrior to horde the other day, but we're living with his parents because we can't afford our old place! that seems like a bad idea
>
> **justin:** Ah. Sounds like he's gotten a bit entitled too

page: oh yes, I honestly didn't even address it with
full force. I was very gentle, and he flew off the
handle

justin: I don't know what his depression is like, but it
doesn't sound under control :(

As Seth became more hostile and standoffish, Rob and Michelle were increasingly harder to reach, so in addition to talking to Justin, I reached out for support from another source: My mother. Now that Seth and I were going to be moving in with Rob and Michelle, I knew that it would become more and more evident to my family that this was more than your average friendship, so I wanted to at least lay a groundwork for my mother to understand in the event that she found out that I was polyamorous.

I also desperately needed to spend time with someone who didn't resent my presence, even though I wasn't quite ready to reveal to Mom how strained my relationship with Seth was becoming. My parents had never really been wild about Seth, and I couldn't bear the "I told you so."

When I called Mom up and asked her if she wanted to go to dinner, she quickly agreed.

She was driving me back to my place after dinner and talking about some of the TV shows she was into and asking me what I thought of them. I didn't know most of them since I only watched shows that were available online and even then was usually pretty behind.

I then took a shot and asked her if she'd seen *Sister Wives*.

She said yes, she had.

"I hate that show," I said.

"Me too," she agreed.

"I mean, it's such a double standard. If he gets to have 3 wives, then they should all get to have three husbands. It's only fair."

"Yeah," she said. "It's not right at all. That guy is such a pig. They even asked him how he would feel about them having other husbands, and he said he'd hate it. What a jerk."

"Not that I'd know what to do with three husbands," I said. "I can barely handle one sometimes."

She laughed. "Well, I don't know," she said. "If they fulfilled different needs."

I was taken aback. This was sort of a polyamorous way of thinking, at the very least poly-friendly. I'd mentioned Rob and Michelle to her at some length, basics of who they were, what they did for work, that they were expecting a baby, and some of the more interesting characteristics of their life. I took a shot.

"Well, Mom," I said. "All the sex stuff aside, that's kind of what Rob and Michelle are for me. They complete my family. Like, I think they have a lot of good qualities that will help Seth and me live a better life. They like to chat and shop and stuff, which are things Seth doesn't like to do. At the same token, I can help them with their new baby and be a good emotional support for them and help with the chores. They're really important to me."

"Hmmm..." my mom said.

"Not that we're swingers or anything," I added. This was disingenuous, but technically true, if horribly misleading.

"I'm happy for you," she said. "They sound like good people."

I did my best to stay sane, but living with Seth had become quite a nightmare. He'd reversed his sleeping schedule so it was completely opposite mine, with Seth getting up around 6 p.m., a half an hour or so after I got done work and staying up until 6 or 7 in the morning playing online RPGs: *World of Warcraft, Everquest, Aion*.

Seth began to not wash his clothes or body and often smelled. He ate whatever he wanted, whenever he wanted.

Despite not having a job or doing any sort of chores (cleaning up our space or cooking dinner), he continued to smoke about a pack a day and routinely buy large bottles of Captain Morgan's Private Stock to take with him to DRUNK parties. More and more, he didn't want me to go with him to those parties, saying he preferred to get drunk without me there.

Despite having a rent-free situation, confusion over a broken lease meant we were still on the hook for the rent at our old place until April of the next year, so we were saving perhaps a few hundred dollars a month by not having to pay for utilities. Desperate to scratch up enough funds to be able to pay for a professional move to Ohio (no small cost) and the repairs I knew our older car would need to make the long trip west, I staggered payments on the old apartment, cut back where I could, and allowed myself few to no day-to-day luxuries to try to offset Seth's expenditures.

Even after the initial large fight, we went on to have a series of smaller ones, all running in this same theme. One fight began because he kept on insisting that he have money to do character transfers between servers and buy gold in *World of Warcraft* and because I pointed out just how bad of an idea and how unnecessary I thought this was. After the dust settled, Seth went and did it anyway.

I was cooped up in a tiny apartment with someone who resented me, waiting for my life to begin somewhere else. In many ways, it felt like I was serving a jail sentence.

With so much time on my hands, my sympathies for Seth began to wane, and I started to reflect on my experiences with polyamory in a distinctly different light, responding to his apparent loathing for me not with self-loathing (as I might have in the past) but with self-love:

Me Time

I went to my second exercise class tonight, and it was awesome. Okay, Zumba's a little dorky, and I'm far from knowing what the heck I'm doing, but I can really feel I'm getting a good workout, and the time flies – and the adrenaline high has been superb afterwards... Tonight I came straight home from class and cooked a delicious pork and broccoli stir fry with a smile on my face.

I love the exercise, sure, and I have a feeling that I'll see the visible results on my body in the upcoming weeks, but more than anything tonight, I was struck with the notion that I was doing something for myself, by myself. And that was so freeing.

Most of my early experiences with polyamory involved sitting at home alone trying to not go stircrazy as my husband saw his girlfriend at that time (Megan), who lived a good jaunt away (about 40 minutes), so he'd leave while I was still working about 4:00 at night or so and then come home at about 1 or 2 in the morning from seeing her. Sometimes this happened 3 or 4 nights a week. I'm not gonna lie. It was challenging at first. So much of my identity had been wrapped up in "Seth and me." I didn't quite know what to do with myself when presented with that much time alone. But I pushed through.

About 6 months ago, my luck with dating started to change – rapidly. I went from having just Seth to having a total of 4 partners in the span of just a few months, not counting 3 others I was seeing on a more casual basis and another first date I went on. And of course, I had to maintain my friendships as well during this time period. To be frank, I was busy and a bit strained.

I realize now that my relationship with myself was the first thing to suffer.

Polyamory, for me, has been about focusing on the only true "primary" I'll ever have: Me.

Figuring out who I am, speaking for myself, being assertive, figuring out what I feel and why I feel it and being honest about that to myself and others. This has been especially important as I've started dabbling in submission. As Seth says, "No, nobody loves a martyr."

Not even the martyr, really.

Something about being on a regular exercise routine again gave me that much-needed reminder.

Over the Christmas holiday, Michelle went into labor, and before long, baby Callie was born. Both Michelle and Rob texted me extensively during the labor process, telling me they wished I could have been there in a flurry of contact that contrasted sharply with the weeks before. I was ecstatic and excited for them. Then, paradoxically, once Callie was born, I found myself feeling like I should go away, like I was extra, unwanted.

As I told Michelle on IRC one night, I got an impulse to go and hide and let them be a "family." To run away.

I suppose I was feeling like an outsider maybe?

It's like when you see an animal giving birth: You're careful to keep your distance. You don't want to intrude on something sacred. Something that isn't yours.

Don't get me wrong. I was happy for them – elated, overjoyed! I found myself beaming from ear to ear.

But yeah, at the same time, I was struck with this urge to flee, this feeling that it didn't involve me, and I had no right to be in the picture.

Just as I started to come to terms with the birth of the new baby, things with Seth precipitously took a turn for the worse.

One evening when Seth was swearing at the Netflix because it kept disconnecting, and I said, intending to be reassuring, "Don't worry. At least we have Netflix and aren't in a hurry to watch this."

"You're so fucking condescending!" he exploded at me.

I went numb as he unloaded on me with a litany of my faults.

"My depression is all your fault," he said. "You drain me. You're singlehandedly ruining this relationship."

"The problem is that you don't try. You bring nothing to the relationship."

"You only financially support me so that you can hold it over my head. You don't really love me."

"You're manipulating me out of selfishness. You manipulate every fucking conversation I have with you. You're domineering. It's all your fault our relationship sucks."

"I used to love you before you became such a bitch."

I didn't fight it. I sat there and took it all, with tears streaming down my face. Interrupting him seemed like it might turn dangerous, and the pain of all his accusations paralyzed me.

Because even though they felt false, they could be true, and I hated the idea that I could be this person that he thought I was. Because I thought she sounded pretty terrible.

After an hour of silence, he came and apologized. "Page, I'm so sorry. I'm broken."

"Oh honey," I said. "I get that you're in pain. It's just so hard."

"What's hard about it?"

"Well," I said, "It's just… the things you said. And how you said them. It's not something I can deal with. That felt like abuse."

Seth started to cry. "I know. It was unacceptable. I'm so sorry."

"I can't let that sort of thing happen. I love you, but that needs to stop. This calls for therapy. I'll go with you if you want. But if you don't get therapy, we're gonna have to get separated."

"Of course," he said. "That I can do. That makes sense."

"I've been thinking about what you said, and it's hard to hear, but if you really feel that way, that I'm selfish and manipulative, then I need help, too."

"Well," he said. "It'll be hard to change your ways, that's for sure."

I felt a slight sting at this but focused on keeping my cool. "You're the only one who has ever said these things to me, Seth."

"That's because I care about you, Page. I'm the only one who cares enough to tell you the truth about you."

Later I stopped to wonder about all this. I'd been supporting him financially for years. I'd faced personal demons and
taken on intense social stress to help him achieve his sexual
fantasies. I did all the chores. Our sex life had never been as
frequent as I'd wanted, and as of late, it was on life support.
It dawned on me: If I really were some kind of master ma-
nipulator, how would I ever have ended up in the situation I
was in?

I started to get a sense that a lot of his insults might actually
be projection, and it might be that he was manipulating me. I
feared that he was using his diagnosis of depression to control
me. I felt like a terrible person whenever I'd think this though.
I'd been through the depressive gauntlet myself with brain
weasels aplenty, and even though certain familiar aspects
were missing in his case, who was to say that everyone's illness
played out the same?

Even after we made up, I felt distant. I wasn't sure what I was
doing in the relationship and couldn't feel much of anything
for him. "I still consider you a friend," Seth said, but even
those feelings were hard for me to find. The trouble was that
even without the large fights, all he seemed to do on a daily
basis was blame me. He had become a largely joyless proposition for me.

I wasn't sure even therapy could fix it. We were broken even
for broken.

POLY SIGNPOST #8: DON'T FORGET TO OIL YOUR HINGES

One thing that is plainly obvious is that there are certain people who date more than others. Their dance card is fully booked. They meet a new cluster of friends and are suddenly dating two-thirds of them.

There's a good chance this person has a hinge personality.

A "hinge" in the strictest sense among polyamorous folk is a term used to denote someone who is involved with two people who are not involved with each other. Say Sally is dating both Matt and Steve, but Matt and Steve are not involved with one another romantically (some words to describe Matt and Steve's relationship with one another would be "metamour" or "other's significant other," though other terms exist). Sally is the "hinge" between them.

I started to notice patterns as I dated and became friends with more polyamorous people. Certain people were much more likely to be hinges than others. And I was one of those people. For whatever reason, I was a born hinge.

It sounds like a pretty good deal, in theory! All those lovers, all that fun! After all, the "harem" fantasy is built on just such an arrangement, taken to extreme numbers. And I'll admit it had its moments with fabulous group sex in which I was the common link or went on back-to-back excellent dates. A metamour and sometimes lover would complain bitterly of envy for my situation, the amount of attention and love that I seemed to garner effortlessly.

But it wasn't all wine and roses. Being a hinge has its challenges. For example, I supported and processed with both parties during their breakup while still being romantically involved with both of them (as in the case of Seth and Tina). If you think that was complicated, you are right.

Being involved with four or five people at a time meant someone was always having some kind of crisis, drama, or at the very least a bad day and needed support.

It took a great deal of my time and mental energy to communicate with my partners, offer emotional support, commit to memory all that they had told me, and not confuse conversations I'd had with one person with another as the idea of being inauthentic or treating them generically or interchangeably bothered me on a deep level. As one would expect, I wasn't perfect. Many people have trouble with these behaviors when conducting a romantic relationship with one individual, let alone several.

If you're involved with a hinge personality, it's tempting to be envious of them. It's tempting to be harsh when complaining that they're busy, that they make mistakes. While I'm sure your frustrations are real, if you want to continue to have a long lived, healthy relationship with this individual, it would behoove you to rethink this course of action. There are ways to express concerns in a way that is supporting and loving and relatively devoid of personal blame. It's also important to make sure you're supporting them as well, that not every conversation is devoted to what they're doing wrong but also a celebration of what you have together with them.

Unless of course you find that the situation is simply not working for you, you don't feel like they are capable of giving you what you want or need from them, and then the best bet in my opinion is a civil breakup.

If you are a hinge personality, make sure you take time to yourself and guard it. It's easy when in the throes of multiple relationships to forget that your primary responsibility is to yourself. Not only that, but cutting corners in your self-care will inevitably translate to your not being able to give your best to your partners.

Hinges get a lot of action, but they're also under a tremendous amount of stress.

And they might not always squeak before they break.

THE EMOTIONAL AFFAIR

With Callie in their lives, I knew Rob and Michelle would be quite busy. Rob had postponed his job search until further notice to stay home and take care of Callie and was often online working on his side business, the website for his novelties store, and making preparations for a yearly convention he and Michelle organized. The convention was a labor of love that did little more than cost money but afforded them an annual opportunity to meet up with friends who were spread out all over the country – and a few even in other parts of the world.

But despite being online quite a bit, Rob rarely chatted with me, and when he did, he often seemed aloof and preoccupied. I wouldn't have thought much of it, chalked it up to new parenthood, lack of sleep, distractions posed by the work he was doing on the computer if not for the fact that he managed to find plenty of time to browse Fetlife and comment on pictures of pretty girls there.

I voiced my concern, and though he reacted with kindness, he switched immediately to kid gloves, a maneuver that insulted me. He took my observation as being a jealous one. It wasn't.

I was upset that he wasn't interacting with me. I was sexually frustrated, emotionally burdened by Seth's brooding and seeming contempt for me, and just plain lonely. The cross country move filled me with anxiety, and though I would be seeing Rob and Michelle for my planned February trip to Cleveland, I had been away a month and still had another month to go. Snowed in with someone who despised me. In a cold basement apartment with no windows, where the days dragged by, and I struggled not to lose my mind.

Further raising my suspicions that Rob was just plain old ignoring me for some reason (who knows exactly why) was the fact that Michelle continued to chat with me incessantly online or via text message, whether she was at work or at night while she was watching TV and breastfeeding the baby. While I appreciated the support, Michelle and I didn't have nearly as much in common as I would like, and I found a great deal of the things she talked about (city politics, the plot lines of TV programs, etc) tedious, and her constant attention served to underscore just how much Rob *could* be talking to me, if he truly wanted to.

I hyped up my attention, sending nude photos to Rob, trying to take my flirting to a new level of filthy.

And yet he remained distant.

To make matters worse, when I voiced my concerns to Michelle, she'd reply that she wished he'd pay more attention to her, too, and then tell me I was being weak and that she worried about my ability to really handle a relationship with her husband, or anyone, really, if I cracked under so little pressure.

Well then. I was on my own.

Except, not quite. Ever since Justin had volunteered to be a supportive ear that first big fight I'd had with Seth, he'd been a constant presence in my life online, always checking in with me, saying hi, chewing the fat. Though I liked Justin a great deal and still entertained the notion of furiously making out with him when I let my mind wander there, he'd recently struck relationship gold and had fooled around with four different beautiful women in the past month: a law student, a bubbly redhead, a goth girl from the dungeon, and a girl from the hackerspace. Some of it even involved multiple girls at once. It wasn't simply raining for Justin; it was pouring.

It was nice in a way. The pressure was off, and I could be myself. I could talk to Justin with no worry that it was going to affect my chances with him. I figured life would do a good enough job of that. With so many dating prospects, I felt it certain that one of them would eventually coax him into monogamy, and sensual and open minded as Justin was, he often spoke of wanting a primary more than anything, wanting someone to come home to, when it was all said and done. I already had two serious relationships as it was. The idea of my filling that position in Justin's life was unthinkable, and short of being able to do that for him, I knew that there was nothing I could do to ensure that he and I would stay together in any long-term sense of things. I could be replaced at any moment by a woman with more availability. He said this was not the case, that he'd make room for me, that he was actually very excited for me to move to Cleveland, and that he was already developing feelings for me, but I would not be dissuaded.

Instead, I listened to him talk about his other relationships, his worries and frustrations. He asked me for advice on how to let a girl know he loved her. And Justin was there for me, as I worried that Rob was more in love with the idea of me than actually in love with me, a feeling that grew more and more by the day. Justin also served as a reality check when Seth would say I was a bad person for some reason or another, that I was manipulative, cruel, thoughtless. Whatever the charge of the day was, I'd run it by Justin, who would promptly debunk it with evidence to the contrary, remind me that Seth was depressed (Justin had struggled with depression himself in the past and knew of what he spoke).

It kept me sane to see a "hey beautiful" from Justin on days that were otherwise full of waiting, guilt, and despair. Justin was something to look forward to, even if it never went anywhere.

Little did I know, Justin was telling the other girls he was seeing that he was having an "emotional affair" with me and that something deeper would surely develop when I moved to Ohio.

That was a nice surprise.

POLY SIGNPOST #9: WHAT'S THE RUSH?

I f there's anything I've learned from polyamory, it's that the quickest way to destroy a relationship is to try to make it into something it's not, to force it into a box that it doesn't really fit in, and to slap labels on something and assume that those labels give the relationship value.

No, no, and no.

What you end up with is damaged goods in a mislabeled package that end up absolutely where you didn't want to send the damn thing in the first place.

That said, it's an extremely easy trap to fall into. Long before we personally experience romantic love, we are inundated with descriptions of what love is, how to know if your love is "true" (whatever the blazes *that* means), and that love has inherent rules and implicit ways by which we can measure the strength of these feelings.

Here's the secret: It's not true. A broken clock keeps better time.

Which is not to say that the pattern doesn't sometimes hold true, that we don't find these ideal relationships in their proto-typical, described form, "in the wild," so to speak. It happens.

But common wisdom is just that. Common. Prevalent, found everywhere, familiar. It is not particularly worthless or worth-while, in and of itself.

Absence makes the heart grow fonder. Opposites attract. Birds of a feather flock together. It was love at first sight.

Lust is instant; love takes time. You can't hurry love. Marry your best friend. Don't shit where you eat. You have only one soulmate. You can fall in love only once. Any two people can fall in love, if they just make up their minds to. You need to be happy alone. No man is an island. It's better to have loved and lost than never to have loved at all. Only fools rush in. If you love something, set it free.

Okay, everybody just shut up for two seconds.

It's a cacophony of voices, often conflicting and profoundly unhelpful.

I've discovered that the less you think about love, the less you worry about it and what is and is not, the more likely it is to find you.

My Own Primary

So many times, I've gone through my life trying to be the person I thought the other person wanted me to be, to appear attractive to him or her, to play the game, and to feel how I thought I should feel once I'd managed to ensnare someone somehow. It was all I knew.

It worked okay in monogamy. Even though I was fundamentally miserable with my partners, I managed to satisfy a lover with little to no conflict for decent stretches of time.

But then, polyamory was a different story. Juggling so many relationships, I was suddenly unable to keep up appearances. About the time things with Seth took a turn for the worse, I stopped trying to look good all the time and started to be me, whatever that meant, however good or bad that looked to other people.

It was then that I discovered the love I had been waiting for my whole life.

Me.

Every day I was fighting to save my marriage, a relationship that I had up until then had complete faith in. The unthinkable was happening. I realized then that for good or bad, I was my own primary. Even though I'd lived most of my life worrying I'd end up alone, I was finding that I quite enjoyed my own company and preferred it to dealing with people that I found annoying or draining. There were worse fates than being alone. It was far more troubling to have anyone I couldn't stand monopolizing my time and criticizing my character, even if they were admirers I felt I couldn't abandon out of sheer courtesy and honoring promises I'd made earlier, with a different set of values.

I stopped caring so damn much about what others thought and started caring what *I* thought. And that's when love really found me.

The days dragged on in the windowless basement apartment with excruciating slowness. Adding to the agony, Rob soon informed me that he would be going on a lunch date with the same bubbly redhead who Justin had been seeing quite a bit of, a curvaceous woman with an infectious giggle. She was an artist and from all accounts quite adorable. Seth had developed a crush on her just from her Facebook photos. I felt hopelessly out of my league.

Rob was incredibly sweet about the whole thing, even gave me a chance to veto the encounter, something I never would have felt appropriate to do, but I got that he was trying to be thoughtful. I had about a week to stew and worry that things would soon be over with Rob, that he'd replace me with this local girl, decide I couldn't move in with him in April like we planned, and I'd be up shit creek, planning a move to Cleveland but suddenly without a place to stay. Lovely.

I knew on some level I was catastrophizing, but I also knew what a fast mover Rob could be. Hell, 8 days after first chatting with me on Skype, he told me that he was so in love with me that had we both been single he would have run off and married me, sight unseen. And compared to me, Rob had so little relationship experience that it was entirely likely that as much as he thought I was some kind of special soulmate to him that his abundance of initial affection had just been inexperience talking. The fact that Rob seemed more and more distant to me every day wasn't helping to reassure me.

I could see all too vividly losing both Rob and Justin to the redhead, and that terrified me.

There was nothing I could do to stop it if it were going to happen, and I could tell no one of my worries, ashamed of my insecurities.

I eagerly counted the days until my February visit to Cleveland. It could come none too soon.

BREAKING FREE

No one lauds the joys of Cleveland in February, but that trip will forever stand out in my memory. For starters, I flew for the first time alone, quite a feat for a person as directionally challenged and spatially unintelligent as I am. I was armed with a book of crossword puzzles and a steady stream of texts from Justin, who kept me company during my layover. I made sure to check with airport employees (who seemed relatively bored) about the locations of my gates and stay focused on boarding instructions. Somehow, miraculously, I made it to Cleveland in one piece.

I was met at the airport by Rob and Michelle – and Callie, who was rather cute but about as oblivious to my presence as one would expect from an infant of younger than 2 months. After a quick dinner at Denny's (I'd gone straight to my first flight after getting off work and was starving), we headed back to their house. Rob promptly gave me a stuffed kitty cat with huge anime eyes that made adorable mewing sounds. I named her Pussy Galore after the Bond character. Plus, who couldn't use an excuse to say "pussy" more often?

I was floored by this random gift. What an odd turn of events, after such prolonged radio silence, to be wooed in such a way, with this small kindness from Rob. I didn't quite know what to think.

Michelle was still home on maternity leave, Rob was still jobless, and I'd managed to actually get the week off work this time, so we spent quite a bit of time together.

Michelle had been co-sleeping with Callie as it managed to keep the baby from screaming her fool head off if her mommy was next to her in the night, so Michelle slept in the nursery with Callie, and Rob and I were left to sleep alone in the master bedroom. It was wonderful. We stayed up until 4 in the morning working on crossword puzzles and making our stuffed cats talk to each other.

The sex was frequent, though Rob still seemed alarmed if I moved or spoke at all (something I was having a hard time adjusting to, but I imagined came from how quiet and passive Michelle could be in bed). While he made a few kinky over-tures, he seemed quite reluctant to ramp things up. After the second or third encounter of the trip, he broke into tears as he held me, complaining bitterly about Michelle's complete lack of sexual interest in him since Callie had been born. I did my best to be sympathetic and caring, but it made me feel like he didn't value his sex with me as much as his sex with her, and that I was, as they say, chopped liver. In that moment, I found myself questioning my attachment to Rob with a new gravity.

This would become a pattern.

The next real push away from him came from his pointing out my "saggy tits" in the shower.

"Excuse me?" I asked.

"Well they are," he added, throwing in a quick aside about how he used to be proud of the fact that his beer belly didn't sag – and now it does.

Hm, I thought. *Parading your perceived misfortunes does little to engender trust with me.*

I pulled into myself. *This is not a flaw, my body – you perceive it as such as you perceive your own to be flawed. However, it is only with my express consent that I have to surrender to this truth that you perceive – and this I refuse.*

Basically: *Fuck that.*

On another occasion, after what I thought had been tender and passionate love-making, Rob leaned in and whispered, "Page, you really need to clean out your ears."

I realized more and more I wanted out, that I felt like I was deserving of more than I was being given – that Justin, who had no formal relationship with me beyond friendship, who I had never even kissed, treated me far better than those I shared a fluid bond with.

But despite my newfound perspective, the fact remained that I was paralyzed by honor, owned by the promises I'd made. Intent gave way to new perspective – to their broken promises. And that childhood premise that "two wrongs don't make a right."

I wondered: Why then does breach of contract require only one party defaulting?

Are there clear offenses for which we can take a step back, say "mulligan" or even "it's done?"

Do boundaries exist in the realm of romantic absolutes? Is honor something we earn and carry and lose by virtue of our misdeeds?

I wrote about it in my journal:

Empty/Full

So far vacation is going really well. I'm feeling very relaxed and happy. Somewhere in the mix is confusion.

I've been doing a lot of thinking the last few days I'm here. Overall, I think I have fewer bad feelings, less anxiety, less fear – but these things for me indicate attachment, and with the loss of attachment is a form of loss. You lose all of it, the good and the bad. You lose, and your mind is quiet. Meditation, centering, balance – peace is often cited as achieving emptiness. Which makes me wonder if that's the best we can ever hope to accomplish – nothingness, lightness, freedom... is that the goal after all?

An empty room with a single cot... a clean slate.

Pain is a sensation. Pain reaffirms who we are.

I get it now... Pain is acquired so much more easily than pleasure – and if pleasure is incapable of being obtained, bring on the pain.

I understand it now.

I finally get myself.

At the very least, I continued to feel like Rob was more in love with the idea of me than the reality of me – and conversely, that I had been more in love with who I believed he was than who he actually was.

I wasn't so sure things were going to work out in the long run, and I wanted to be okay with it. Although I still hoped they would.

Justin was sick most of the February trip, but we texted and chatted online throughout my visit. I did, however, get to see him relatively early on during a trip to the dungeon, where I met the bubbly redhead for the first time. She was just as adorable as I imagined. Justin managed to snuggle us both for a brief period of time, and she was warm and flirtatious. I even got the feeling she was as attracted to me as I was to her.

Well, this could get interesting, I thought.

Though she and Justin seemed rather cozy, I noticed an awkwardness, a lack of connection between her and Rob, though it was a small relief now framed by my growing doubts about my relationship with him.

The last day of the trip, Rob took me to the airport at 4 in the morning to catch my early flight home. He stopped the car right next to the curb even though the airport traffic cops were right there. He jumped out and kissed me in the freezing rain.

It left me so confused. I felt suddenly that for once he was the clingy one, at my mercy, and I didn't know quite what to do with it.

I didn't want it nearly as much as I had before.

Something had definitely changed within me.

Seth was excited and even quite sweet upon my return. He'd missed me quite a bit in my absence, had a chance to ponder life without me. It seemed the separation had done us some good.

It didn't escape my attention, however, that I had been happiest alone, navigating airports, cradling Pussy Galore in my arms.

Though I had only seen Justin briefly in person during my visit, the week after my return to Maine, he was throwing a private kink party at his new house. When I rued that I wouldn't be able to attend, Justin offered to set me up using Skype, so I could telecommute to the festivities via web cam.

At first I laughed the offer off as hopelessly dorky, perhaps even too dorky for me (and that's saying something!), but over the course of a few days, I changed my mind. I put on a black dress that gave me amazing cleavage and tuned in at the appointed time.

Numerous strangers, acquaintances, and friends flashed and flirted with me. Among the guests were Rob and Michelle, who had questionably decided to bring Callie to the party. After all, a main feature of the event was the viewing of a myriad of strange and terrible pornographic films, and an orgy later broke out in the basement. In their defense, at 8 weeks old, there would be virtually no chance of Callie remembering the party, but it was still disconcerting to see a baby there on camera, clinging to Michelle's shirt, wide-eyed in the bacchanal.

Rob frequently texted me to tell me how beautiful I looked on web cam and even brought over a friend to the laptop a bit later in the evening to introduce us. "This is Page, my hot girlfriend from Maine."

It was wonderful to see Rob and flattering that he seemed so proud of me and so eager to show me off, and I gushed in return.

But I also knew it had been a while since Rob had last bothered to set up Skype to talk with me. We'd last Skyped 3 months ago in December and hadn't done so *regularly* since November. We'd barely even spoken on the phone, for that matter. Even our online chats had dropped off precipitously.

And it certainly did not escape my notice that it had been Justin, not Rob, who had been responsible for making sure I could attend the party in some fashion rather than stewing alone in my apartment.

The connection between my computer and Justin's dropped out a few times, and for a good while, the guests would jump in and renew it, but after the fifth or sixth time, I was out of luck. Surely, the gathering had gotten sexy and drunken enough that the novelty of "the pretty girl on the computer" (as I was called) was no longer a priority, and there were more pressing and physically gratifying matters to attend to.

No worries. I'd had quite a good time.

THE RISE OF JUSTIN

Though he was quite fond of the bubbly redhead and very busy between both managing the hacker space and working full time, Justin nonetheless continued to reach out to me on a regular basis. I would often process with Justin about my shifting feelings for Rob and my failing marriage.

"I wonder how it all works," I said.

"How what works?" Justin asked.

"How 2 people can move in different directions at once. Where one becomes more attached and the other less."

"That has to be tough," Justin said.

"I don't want it to end, "I said. "But I don't fear that it will. It seems like everyone moves on a different schedule."

"Awww."

"Rob's… my imaginary friend. I miss sleeping in the same bed as him, staying up doing crossword puzzles and giggling."

"That's sweet," Justin said.

I quickly began to feel like I could tell Justin anything, including these anecdotes of questionable taste from my February trip to Cleveland:

> **page:** oh my god, Rob and Michelle are so weird
> sometimes

page: we were at Tommy's eating dinner, and Rob blurts out "I went down on Page in the shower"

page: Michelle says "In the shower? why the shower"

page: and Rob says "it was very pleasant"

page: and Michelle says "we have a perfectly good bed. you didn't need to do that in the shower"

page: I just sat there mortified :P

page: those two

justin: lmao. That's hilarious

page: oh my word. ok... so I love showering with people. no big secret, but I'm pretty much always willing and love it

justin: I haven't done that since... my ex-girlfriend like 3 years ago.

page: so Rob says, "Hey, Page, wanna take a shower with me?" and of course I agree.

page: (awww, I'm sorry)

page: and then Rob says, "erp, gotta use the bathroom, one sec" so I wait a few minutes, and then he's done and it reeks so I have this dilemma.

page: I love showers, but I also don't want to essentially linger in his colon

page: so I grab my bottle of Fructis and start smelling it vigorously. Bit of a dilemma, yes... "must... find... air freshener..."

page: and Rob says, "Oh, Page, you're huffing shampoo. That's love."

Virtually every time I'd log in, Justin would be there with a greeting, wanting to know how my day had been, what I was up to.

In fact, when I was reading old chat logs while writing this book, I saw that from December 2010 to April 2011, the total data from the private messages between Justin and me was over *5 times* that of those between me and Rob.

Rob, the guy I was sleeping with, fluid bonded to.

Rob, the guy I was moving to Cleveland to live with.

Rob, who wanted me to be his human pet, his sex slave.

Just as things seemed to be returning somewhat to normal with Seth, they reached a new all-time low after Seth behaved very badly at a DRUNK party.

The low point of the evening was when Seth asked me if I'd be cool with this girl, Laura, giving him head at the same time I was doing it. I was disgusted. So much was wrong with Seth's suggestion. Laura had a boyfriend she cheated on repeatedly and had been with pretty much all the guys in DRUNK. They also talked about Laura in disrespectful ways when she wasn't around in a way that made me feel bad.

I told Seth "no," and he blew up and started to rant, demanding why. I reminded him of our rule that physical activity that serious shouldn't happen for the first time drunk since it's legally shady at best, and poor decisions are made when drinking.

He went off. "OH, THERE ARE NEW RULES, ARE THERE?!"

Seth stormed outside.

Several people told me as they reentered the house after a quick smoke that he was out there bitching about me.

When Seth came back in, I also pointed out that Laura was in a monogamous thing and that he didn't want to help her cheat, did he? Plus, he had no idea what her sexual health status was. I told him it wasn't just about me, that the rules existed for more than just me. I also reminded him of Rob's refusal of a girl when she offered to give him head at the Halloween party and that I had to be responsible out of respect for my other partners.

Meanwhile, Seth refused to speak in private, so the DRUNK peanut gallery kept interjecting with all sorts of unhelpful nonsense as I tried to square things away with my husband.

One bullshit point they kept making: I was getting so much action that certainly I was being selfish to deny my husband this chance! It was so much harder for men, surely I could accommodate him this opportunity.

My rebuttal: "Desperation doesn't justify reckless behavior."

But it was when Dan turned me to me and said, "Page, you've just had so much more success than Seth. It's only fair this way," that I finally snapped.

I yelled at him and everyone else who could hear me. "You don't know what you're talking about! Everything I've been doing has been about what makes *Seth* happy. How I could get *Seth* a girlfriend. Even Tina was someone I wanted for *him*. And I met Rob and Michelle through her."

"And so fucking *what* if I've had more success dating. I've been working on my body nonstop for 2 years. I've busted my ass. Literally."

"I can't believe you have the *nerve* to call me selfish. I've been 100% supportive of Seth. You don't even know the half of it."

"I'm sick of being berated for having a boyfriend or wanting to move to Ohio."

I'd had it. This was the one thing just for ME that had come into my life. I knew I'd acted honorably enough and that they should all just shut the fuck up.

But the misery went on for a couple of hours until Seth pulled me aside in a back hallway and started to grovel.

"Page, I'm so sorry. I'm such a pig. Can you ever forgive me?"

Seth blamed the alcohol and told me he would quit drinking when we moved to Ohio.

We drove home about 2:00, early for him to leave, because I had to work the next morning.

When we did get home, Seth got online and drunkenly shouted things at his *WoW* guild on TeamSpeak, so I couldn't really go to sleep.

I stayed up a few hours and had low-carb pizza and talked to him a little.

And then while we were talking, he saw Megan come online and got on to IM her. He was drunk enough that he was reading everything aloud without seeming aware he was even doing it. He started by saying how much he missed her. But quickly tried to proposition her for his birthday to give him a joint blow job with me. And then Seth told Megan that I clearly didn't want him to have fun so that I probably wouldn't even do it for his birthday.

It gave me whiplash. This was all after apologizing to me for "acting like a pig."

As he wound down, he kept repeating that getting head from 2 women at a time was his "one dream."

I told him that if he wanted to have lots of casual sex in whatever manner he saw fit that he was welcome to as long as we severed our fluid bond but that I wasn't comfortable with his desired level of risk.

Reasoning with a drunk person rarely goes well. I was all for having fun, but I hated it when he drank this much.

"I'm sorry things were so shitty last night," Justin said.

"Thanks," I said, "I think Seth just needs to not drink so much. I can't trust him when he's that drunk. He already thanked me for saying no to doing stuff with that girl last night. He's horrified that he suggested it. To be fair, he was seeing double at points last night, that's how drunk he was, but it was still very stressful."

"Wow..." Justin said, "That's pretty drunk. He shouldn't drink that much."

I sighed. "I hate feeling like a cock block or a bad guy. His friends were acting like I was being unreasonable, but they're swingers that fuck anything that moves basically."

"Page, you weren't a cock block. And they did that because they were drunk. But like you said, they only do it drunk. Which is silly."

"Right," I agreed, "And I was actually being asked to PARTIC-IPATE as well, so I certainly had a right to say no."

"Absolutely."

"This morning, I talked with Seth, and he agreed that if Rob had behaved like that, he would be upset with him. And to Seth's credit, he did ask and even though he berated me, he didn't do anything. Though..."

"Hmm?"

"I think Seth's upset because he doesn't get special treatment sometimes," I said, "Upset that my sex rules apply to every-one, including him, but that's the only way it makes sense. How could anyone trust me if I made exceptions for certain people? Ugh, these sorts of things make me want to be celi-bate. I hate governing other people's behavior."

"I'm sorry," Justin said. "I'm glad you held your ground. Last night wasn't your fault. It was just a bunch of drunken shittiness."

"Thank you. I don't mean to dump this on you, but it's really nice to have my feelings validated."

"Of course," Justin said. "To me, Seth's behavior was childish, and more like a tantrum than anything else."

I sighed. "Seth likes DRUNK, but he only hangs out with them to drink. He doesn't make friends easily, and they're some of the only ones he's had. I think they're a bad influence on him, as maternal as that might sound."

"I would agree," Justin said.

"I said to Seth this morning that I don't want the kind of future that the people in DRUNK have. I don't want my future full of old drunks. I asked Seth if he wanted to be an old drunk. He said yes, and I told him I didn't want to be married to an old drunk. You know what he said? 'Divorce me then.'"

"Wow," Justin said.

"I thought we were through this shit." I sighed. "I'm wondering if my husband has a problem with alcohol. I don't know if it's depression, or alcohol, or just his personality."

"I wish I knew what to tell you," Justin replied. "If he says he wants to be a drunk, then definitely an alcohol problem, but given his depression, I imagine that's a major contributing factor. I know my whole family has anxiety and depression issues, thus lots of drunks."

"I just don't know what I'm supposed to do," I said. "I can't take this sort of thing. It's just too stressful."

"I can imagine," Justin said. "It puts you in a really hard place."

"Especially on top of everything else recently."

"Everything else?" he asked. "I imagine you're stressed living with your in-laws and prepping for moving again."

"Right," I said, "And the verbal abusiveness that Seth only just stopped. There was a solid month where he was cruel every day for no good reason."

"Oh Page."

"Yeah. It's been bad. He's been lying about money, too. It's hard to trust. I need to get stuff fixed with Seth."

"Yeah."

"I think what I need is an expert to help me determine how much of it is his depression and how much is his taking advantage of me. Someone who can help work through things."

"It would probably involve going in as a couple," Justin said. "Would he be willing to do that?"

"Yeah, actually."

"Yay!"

"He was unwilling to go alone," I said, "but was more open to us as a couple because he thinks it's mostly my problem, I think. I mean, it could be."

"Could be, but I'm doubting it," he said. "From all you've told me, you support him emotionally and financially, and he's taken advantage of that."

"Well, I don't need him to be perfect," I said. "I just want him to try."

"Yeah."

"Hopefully a third party can help."

"It can give some external validation, yeah," Justin said.

"If he gets short or irritated with me for no apparent reason, they can point that sort of thing out or whatever they'll do, and they can help me learn how to talk to him in a way that'll work better," I said.

"Page, you care and love so much."

I blushed. "I hope that's ok."

"Um, yes?" Justin replied.

I didn't need to see his face to know that he was smiling.

Throughout all the chaos, Justin was the one constant. Attraction or not, it was wonderful to have a sympathetic ear. My stress and anxiety about the upcoming move reached fever pitch when Seth and Rob got into a disagreement about the recarpeting of the attic space, where Seth was slated to live. It was damaged from the previous renter, who had allowed her cats to urinate all over the space, and tensions ran high as Rob tried to figure out how to get it replaced quickly and cost effectively and Seth expressed an unwillingness to move in with things in such a state.

At this point, Justin had become my best friend, and like always, talking to him gave me just what I needed:

> **page:** welp, if they all decide to kill one another, let's you and I run away together, Justin, ok?

> **page:** we can go to... I dunno... Columbus or something

> **justin:** lmao. Okay :)

> **page:** we'll just go sin. it'll be ok. lmao

> **justin:** lol

> **page:** I'd have to text Rob. lmao

> **page:** "Gone to Columbus for sex vacation with Justin, brb"

> **justin:** lmao, I can only imagine the reaction!

> **page:** hilarious and hot. oh my word. wouldn't be my most mature moment :)

> **page:** you'd probably refuse me cuz of the drama because you're a grownup

> **justin:** lol. You don't know, I might be caught up in the whirlwind of page :)

> **page:** ahaha

page: if I managed to survive the fallout, 'twould be an epic story

page: my friend Mark has done things for the story alone

page: you deserve better than to be a revenge fuck in some twisted story though :)

justin: I've told myself that to get through some hard times: "will make for a good story"

justin: lol. But it would make for a good story :)

page: I'm just amused at the thought. don't even really need to do it. it makes me laugh because it's the opposite of how I normally behave

justin: You and me both :)

page: exactly, it would be our Thelma and Louise moment!

And with that, "Columbus Sex Vacation" became our first major private joke, a symbol for rage-quitting the tougher parts of poly and just going off and doing whatever.

It was an absurd notion, but it kept me sane during my darkest days.

As Rob and Michelle continued to deal with the challenge of preparing their house for Seth and me to join them in the upcoming weeks, they often bitched about Justin and their other friends, many of whom I had befriended on my trips to Ohio and would write messages to from time to time, trying to foster connections in the area where I would soon be moving.

One day in the channel where the three of us would often chat, Rob made a point of frankly advising me not to share their criticisms of others with anyone, not even Justin. I assured them that I wouldn't and shared with them the most questionable of my disclosures to Justin, to give them a full picture.

Rather than being happy for me that I was getting to know people in the area, the fact that I was developing a friendship with Justin did not sit well with Michelle. At all.

> ***page** is pragmatic in social affairs

> **page:** honestly, it doesn't paint me well, but I'll be brutally honest with you

> **page:** when I get all weepy and emo about missing Rob, I talk to Justin and whine. poor guy

> **page:** I hate admitting it because it makes me look pitiful, but yeah, there ya go

> **michelle:** can I be honest and say that the level of weepy and emo disturbs me?

> **michelle:** it makes me fear how strong you really are as an individual... and that even being around him a lot won't stop that... :/ and I fear how easily you get along with people

> **page:** you fear how easily I get along with people?

michelle: to the tune of friends barely speaking to us but spilling their guts to you

page: I'm a sensitive person, Michelle, but that doesn't make me weak

page: it's hard to understand my baggage without having lived it

page: I resent the implication that I'm weak, to be quite frank, because being able to feel and accept your unpleasant emotions is part of being emotionally strong

michelle: but the level of emo you have expressed is scary, the level of weepy you've shown me. if that's continued toward Justin, that's excessive

page: how so? why is it scary?

michelle: because you don't trust me or Rob if you keep questioning so much

page: I'm not you

michelle: no, people like you. so you aren't me.

page: oh goodness. people like you

michelle: yeah, that's why they constantly stab me in the back?

page: they do it to me, too. I've lost a lot of friends over the years. I can't tell you how many friends I've burned through. I have a lot of exes. It happens. It's part of knowing people

michelle: to lose friends people have to be your friends in the first place

page: please don't be jealous of my ability to make friends

page: it's all I had for years, when I hated my family and was on drugs, when I wanted to die

page: it's the only thing that kept me going

michelle: now I feel like I've lost Justin too, because he's talking to you about all the stuff that we used to talk about, and now you're talking to him about things that we used to talk about

page: so he's your friend? he belongs to you? I did something wrong?

michelle: he doesn't speak to me, and he just went back on a promise

page: you mean cancelling coming over to work on the drywall?

michelle: yes

page: well he IS sick with a migraine

michelle: how is that a friend?

page: my friends do that to me a lot. Even my husband does really. I have to count on myself a lot

michelle: but I'm fighting a headache and dealing with Rob's moods and whatever today and it's just building up

page: yeah, I hear ya. lots of stress. I'm not your enemy. I'm gonna be there

michelle: then finally confirming how bad things are upstairs, but it's just another case of make one friend and lose 3, or whatever ratio it always seems to be for me

page: I'm not weak though

michelle: re: Rob you are.

michelle: it feels like even though I told you about the losing friends to other friends, you did the same thing to me.

page: you don't trust me, do you? if you're insecure about me as a friend

page: what did I do to you? other than try to make a new friend?

michelle: you meet someone one time that I've seen multiple times, and they're sending you messages, inviting you places, etc

page: I know almost no one in Ohio! I'm just trying to make friends

michelle: I have only the people I work with

michelle: yeah, we get a lot of people at parties, but we don't have any good friends.

page: this is not a thing I'm doing TO you, Michelle. trying to make friends is not some sort of attack on you. you can't possibly say this is something I'm doing to wrong you in some way by being social. that's patently unfair. I'm just being myself, and I'm certainly not being friendly to other people in some attempt to be malicious to you

michelle: you now know nearly as many people here as we do, so don't say you don't...

michelle: we're minor celebrities, and look how we're treated

Things took a turn for the weird when Rob jumped into the conversation:

rob: I'm not going to scroll back because Michelle asked me not to

(How bad of a sign is this that Michelle didn't want Rob to read what she'd been writing to me?)

rob: point is this: people don't give a shit about us except in regards to what we can do for them or who we can introduce them to

rob: people don't ask "Hey Rob, what are you up to?" it's always about something else

page: look, I never meant to hurt anyone by making friends

page: this is upsetting. I can't stop making friends. I'm a person who makes friends

page: it's not meant as an attack on anyone. I'm just a friendly person

michelle: but they go out of their way to message you

page: how is that something I've done to you?

michelle: and it just makes me feel like a failure

rob: that's not the point, I don't think. it's not that it's done anything to us. it's that you don't see that people are being super super friendly for you for reasons that are other than just wanting to be friends sometimes, and it's not to say you can't be friends or won't make lots of friends :P 'cause you will and I'm glad.

As you can see, Michelle's asking Rob not to scroll up has sent Rob on a tangent about people's ulterior motives that has nothing to do with what Michelle and I are actually discussing. He wandered off, and Michelle and I continued the fight:

michelle: you have it so good and yet it's always "woe is me"

page: I'm not weak for getting emo

page: I really resent that you said that

page: that I'm weak about Rob

michelle: well, I think you are, and I said it

page: you have no idea what it was like to live my life

michelle: what does that have to do with us?

page: "you have it so good"

michelle: you don't know what it's been to be
me either.

page: I recognize this

page: I'm upset because you insulted me, with words,
directly to me, not by some reading of what
your actions mean, like the fact that you've
made friends

page: Seth keeps asking me what's wrong with me,
and I don't know how to explain

page: Michelle, right now, I'm crying because I care
about you, and I've pissed you off by just being
me, which is a hard thing, and I don't know
what it all means

***page** goes outside a minute for some fresh air but
will leave the laptop open

page: Michelle, what do you want from me?

page: how can I concretely change my behaviors in
order to serve you better?

michelle: I don't want you to serve me.

page: ok, how can I concretely change my behavior in
order to be a better friend to you?

michelle: I just feel like a failure right now and took
out some of it on you.

michelle: I feel like the success you have just keeps enunciating that I suck

We talked for a while longer. Michelle continued to bristle and vent, even as her anger cooled. I did my best to let her know that she was still my friend and figured that this was an isolated outburst and would eventually die down.

It was a bizarre notion to me. I'd never had anybody get upset with me for making other friends – regardless of any underlying causes of insecurity, or as Michelle often called them "abandonment issues." I'd say that it seemed like grade school stuff, but I'd never even gone through this scenario in grade school.

Regardless of how Michelle felt about it, I continued to pursue friendships in Ohio, including my strong one with Justin. After all, as much as Michelle complained about it, when I asked her what she wanted me to do, she'd stop short of asking me for any changes.

Still, it concerned me, and it was yet another stress heaped on top of the pile of things I was dealing with.

I discussed it with Justin the following day:

> **page:** honestly, I don't know if anybody else would stay in this situation sometimes :P

> **justin:** *hugs*

> **page:** it would drive most anybody away, ya know?

> **page:** I mean, new baby, wife having issues and being snippy, crazy depressed boyfriend who lost his job

justin: *hugs* Yep, I know. It would all depend :)

justin: Hopefully having lots of people who like and love you here already is helping a bit :)

page: yes, and I thank you for being one of those people :) you are truly special to me

justin: Awww

***justin** blushes

page: I got really upset that my friendship with you upset her because it was making me so happy and has nothing to do with her

justin: Indeed. Thing is, she never really shares any emotion or thoughts with me :/

page: I guess she only really does with me and Rob, and when she does, she seems to have no idea how to phrase them so they aren't scathing

justin: Well, she doesn't practice :) And she lets them fester

page: yep, so I'm gonna hang in there, I think

page: I think I'll be helpful for her as a friend

justin: :)

page: though I doubt she'll realize how much I'm helping – but that's ok

page: you have to do things because they're right, not for the credit

> **justin:** *hugs* You're wonderful
>
> **page:** awwww, why am I wonderful? for sticking in there?
>
> **justin:** For being you, yes.
>
> **page:** awwww. I don't need to be wonderful. I just want everyone to get along and be happy :P

Complain as she might, there was very little Michelle could do to keep me from talking to Justin. The idea of anyone in a peer relationship (friend, lover, spouse, etc) dictating who I could or could not be friends with rubbed me entirely the wrong way, so even though the growing connection with Justin made Michelle uncomfortable, I pushed forward regardless. Even if Rob himself had objected, the idea of being prohibited from flirting as a polyamorous person, let alone being denied or guilted out of a friendship (!!!) was much too tight a rein on my behavior. It wasn't going to fly. So Justin and I grew closer and closer over the weeks leading up to my move. And I kept up with the emo, Michelle be damned.

Besides, Justin had become not just a friend, but my best friend, and as the days wound on, he was becoming even more:

> **page:** in my head... you're like my "pretend boyfriend" or something
>
> **justin:** Dawww
>
> **page:** my brain is a strange place
>
> **justin:** I'm a figment of your imagination!

page: you're pretty cute

***page** should stop hitting on you...

justin: :)

page: I'm embarrassing myself

justin: You're allowed ;) If I can hit on you

page: but of course

justin: Then we win!

page: well you have many other interests, and everything's socially complicated... and I should probably stop pretending you're my boyfriend in my head. I'm putting carts and horses in the wrong order

justin: You can do whatever you want, it's in your head. And I would love to be your boyfriend. I know things are complicated though. Thus why I don't push at all. If it's meant to be, things will fall into place.

page: hmm, Justin, I may be wrong, but if you and I ever got the opportunity, I think we would melt into a huge puddle of love

***page** is embarrassed now

justin: Daww. Don't be embarrassed. I feel a good attraction for you, we have a lot of similar viewpoints and ideals.

justin: :) I know you're worried about Rob, and it's not the same as him, but you still have my love :)

page: oh goodness :)

***page** blushes

justin: *hugs* :)

justin: Well you know that I love you.

***page** faints

justin: lol

page: I love you too

page: a lot of the process is figuring out how my new life will be and how you'll fit into that

justin: *nod*

page: but I really think you're swell and unique :)

justin: I have no worries. Awww

page: and omg, if I like how you kiss, you won't be able to get rid of me

justin: lmao, That's a good problem to have :)

As the move drew closer, I came to feel more in control of my life. As had started on my trip to Ohio in February, I continued to see that no matter what I did, I wouldn't be able to please everyone. This was not only true in general but particularly so when considering Rob, Seth, and Michelle. As stressful as it was to be pulled out of my former way of thinking, where I would sacrifice everything for a lover's happiness, the stress had given birth to a much stronger sense of identity for me, one that continued to develop and grow every day.

page: I just gotta solidify the pet thing with Rob and figure out you're so triggery for Michelle

justin: *nod*

page: I'm looking at you as a long-term prospect though. I mean that sincerely, as crazy as that might sound

justin: Awww *hugs*

page: your basic essence is just so wonderful :)

page: I think you will be fun to play and explore with in your own right, and we will go different places

justin: :)

page: you are special to me

page: if you weren't, I wouldn't bother – because 1) time component 2) extra work because of Michelle, etc, but I want you, and I'm going to work for it. I want you to be part of my life.

justin: *hugs* You're special to me too page. :)

***page** hopes she didn't creep you out

justin: lol, not at all. Makes me all warm and fuzzy :)

page: oh good :) you just make a lot of sense to me :) I dunno. It's hard to explain. it will be fun :)

justin: *nod* I know what you mean

page: I like it that you're autonomous, too :) like I wanna connect meaningfully, but I don't want to own you

justin: *nod*

page: well you've heard me talk about autonomy a lot. you know how I feel about such things

justin: Yep. Page just wants to be free :)

page: yes yes :) not alone but free :) and everything's up for negotiation

page: just remember, like if you want something or
   don't want something, etc

justin: *nod* We shall communicate

page: haha, we shall, and we will be adults and little
   kids all at once :)

As Justin and I became closer, Rob continued to maintain distance. I found myself growing hypervigilant. I was on the look-out, analyzing each and every one of Rob's online behaviors in attempt to avoid being blindsided. All of my efforts led me around in logical circles.

I wanted to completely trust and let go so badly, but at the same time, that was what caused me to get hurt in the first place. I set out on these little empirical missions in my own mind that could never be proven.

I could look at things with Rob in so many different lights. I could prove anything when it came to him and me.

I could focus on his largely unsuccessful history to establish romantic relationships with other people.

I could find a way to make all of his words seem like delusion, manipulation, and coercion.

I could find a way to make my feelings seem like desperation, insecurity, and pure lust.

Or I could focus on the fact that he made me laugh and that I never quite knew what he was going to say.

Or the fact that I had moments where I wanted to simultaneously hit him in the face and kiss him because I'm was disgusted, irritated, and in love with him all at once.

So I did all of the above.

And I got damn confused.

I was ambivalent about Rob, sure, but I wasn't ready to give up. I still remained hopeful that once I actually got to Cleveland and we started living together that things would turn around. Rob was hard to reach online, but he was a new father, and it was the busy time of year for their side business.

Besides, it could be that the long distance played games with his emotions, too, and that talking to me only caused him pain because it made him miss me more.

A few weeks before the big move, Justin asked me if I was going to an annual kink festival that was being held in Ohio soon after I was due to arrive. He thought I'd have fun, he said, and he was willing to take me.

> **page:** ok, yeah, then I want to go – just have to double check the cost with Seth and see if he wants to go, too

> **page:** it's spendy enough that I think he'll just say "go with Justin"

> **justin:** Ok :)

> **page:** but I want to check

justin: *nod*

page: I really, really want to go though :)

page: that would be awesome if I could go with you :)

And then upon further reflection, I added:

> **page:** I'm gonna email Rob and ask him if he wants to go :P

justin: :)

> **page:** he probably won't be able to go (childcare, cost, etc), but I thought I'd ask him

> **page:** though I'm sure I'd have a great time with you :)

I was right that Seth wasn't interested. Rob, however, was another story. He really wanted to go but couldn't justify the expense since he hadn't yet found a full-time day job, and his disposable income was understandably low as a result.

Seth suggested that I could pay for both Rob and me (about $200 for the weekend, a multiple-day event) and consider it my birthday present from him.

> **page:** I talked to Michelle re: the kink fest and asked if she planned on going. She said probably not but that she might encourage Rob to go.

> **page:** I explained to her I wanted to go to some of the classes really badly – and didn't want anyone to feel left out if I went alone and mentioned I was sure I could find a ride (without mentioning you specifically) if I went alone

> **page:** she mentioned that she thought you were going with me :)

> **page:** trying to be considerate so she doesn't feel left out, re: my conversation with her the other day

> **page:** but also so she'd be ok if I went with you

> **justin:** :) You're so considerate

> **page:** I try!

> **page:** it's hard to be considerate when you don't have all the facts, and no one has all the facts, but I do try

Justin had called me considerate. But was I so considerate? Within a handful of hours, I'd worked it out so that I had tickets to the event and had crossed my T's and dotted my I's as far as the pragmatic realm, cost, timing, transportation and cleared things with Michelle, the most emotionally volatile member of my web.

But in the process, I'd managed to write Justin into basically a friend role when it dawned on me: He had been asking me on a date.

I had been considerate to everybody but Justin.

By the time I realized this, it was too late. Non-transferrable, non-refundable tickets had been purchased. Plans had been made.

Not only that but for all things kink, Rob had "dibs" in a sense. I was his pet (and he my Owner) on Fetlife, and he'd spoken on occasion of his plans to collar and train me.

Still, I couldn't help but feel that Justin was getting the raw end of the deal.

Still, I couldn't help but feel that Justin was getting the raw end of the deal.

THE MOVE

The professional movers came 3 days before we left Maine, taking roughly 95% of our possessions with them: our bed, the bulk of our clothes, anything that was easily boxed and packed onto the truck. We were left with a week's worth of clothes and fragile electronics that needed babying (TVs, computers, etc) and would journey with us in the car. We slept upstairs in the guest room for a few days.

Going away parties were the worst, first with our local friends and then with Seth's family. We said goodbye over and over again. But our course was set, and there was no going back.

We'd scheduled our arrival in Ohio to coincide with Rob and Michelle's technology convention and planned to caravan with Don and Tina, who were also attending. It promised to be a hectic few weeks as I was getting done at my current job literally the evening before the move, and with the 2 days of travel (to break the 14-hour drive into 2 segments), we would be getting to Cleveland the day before the convention.

From there, I would attend the convention, which normally would be a relatively leisurely and social affair but instead I was presenting as a speaker, my first time doing such a thing, so I was pretty stressed out about it. Not only that, but the day after the convention, I was scheduled to start my new job.

Though I'd hoped to have a few weeks off between jobs, my new employer desperately needed the help and had been insistent that I start as soon as possible.

But it seemed a small price to pay for a new adventure, the beginning of a new life, a welcome break from the routine I'd established.

We drugged the cat with the giant pills the vet had given us, crammed our car full, and set off for Don and Tina's an hour south.

In a move of dorky brilliance, Don whipped out walkie talkies to facilitate our caravan. Tina and I quickly abused these, chatting to pass the time. It was great fun. Aside from the inevitable traffic nightmare in Worcester, it was a fairly straight shot to our hotel in Albany. Every few hours, we'd have a quick stop to get out and stretch our legs and let Tina walk their beagle. Our poor cat spent most of the trip yowling and appeared to be hallucinating, as he was pawing at things that weren't there, even once we got him out of the car and set him up with a litter box in the hotel room. Incense and peppermints.

We made it to Ohio the following afternoon, parting ways with Don and Tina that morning while they were headed off to his parents' place to visit with them and drop off their dog. When we arrived at Rob and Michelle's house, the energy was frenzied and chaotic. A few volunteers were present, making preparations for their event, including Justin. Seth and I quickly unloaded our car and got everything up into the attic, setting up food, water, and litter for our cat, who promptly decided he needed to roll around in the litter box like it was a giant pile of money, yowling and carrying on. The rest of our stuff wasn't due to arrive until after the convention, so until then, Seth and I would sleep in my room.

Rob looked harried and distracted. He barely seemed to register our presence. His first words, after we'd made the 15-hour journey were, "Don't bother talking to us until the convention is over."

I would soon find he was only half joking. I wasn't thrilled about it but tried to be understanding, knowing that the convention was a major undertaking for them and a huge financial investment.

After we got the car unpacked, Seth and I were starving, and since Justin was there helping out to get ready for the event, we asked him if he'd like to grab dinner with Seth and me. Justin was game.

We also checked with Rob to see if he wanted to come to dinner with us. Rob said he was too busy and had to stay at the house, so we told him where we were going and said goodbye to him.

Rob even said, "Have a nice time," and smiled as we left the house for a pub within walking distance.

When I returned from dinner, I glanced at my phone to find a string of angry texts from Michelle. Apparently by going out to eat, we had ruined Rob and Michelle's dinner plans because they didn't feel right ordering out for so few people – so they weren't going to eat anything. They were going to starve, she wrote.

I came up the stairs to find Michelle sitting in the nursery in the dark in a rocking chair, sobbing, letting me know how inconsiderate I was to have ruined their evening. And to make matters worse, I had stolen a helper from them in their hour of need, depriving them of Justin during a 45-minute meal break from volunteering for them.

This was only the first act in a long line of passive-aggression – where I would check with one or both of them and be told something was fine, only to find out – no wait, it wasn't fine at all, and I was an inconsiderate asshole for taking them at their word, not seeing the hidden signals and inquiring further.

We were off to a terrible start.

I did what I could. After talking with Michelle, I walked to Dunkin' Donuts and picked them up donuts and coffee as a peace offering. I told them both I'd meant no harm, that I'd been starving after the trip, and that if Rob had offered the slightest bit or resistance or let me know that they wanted to order something as a group that I would have just gotten a snack or something.

Michelle said nothing but did smile as I handed her a cup of hazelnut coffee, just the way she liked it.

This seemed to do the trick.

The convention started the next day. Rob and Michelle were human blurs, bustling about. I dolled myself up, schmoozed, socialized, had a great time. My talk went off without a hitch.

I spent two out of the three nights of the convention sleeping with Rob and Michelle in their suite. It should have been nice to cuddle and unwind with Rob after the long days. However, they were out and about until about 1 or 2 in the morning every morning and up early for administrative duties. Not only that, but Callie's crib was in the room where we all slept, which significantly limited sexual opportunities. Still, Rob, Michelle, and I snuggled, and I relished the closeness.

"Page," Rob said. "I know this is crazy right now, but before long, everything will settle down, and I promise you I'll take you out to coffee. We'll have a real date."

I was so happy my heart almost burst. That was exactly the kind of reassurance I'd been looking for.

The second night of the convention, I was sitting on the bed in the suite watching Callie while Rob and Michelle tended to a minor emergency when I got a text on my phone. It was Justin.

You are sexy and beautiful.

Awww, thank you, I wrote back.

Whacha doing? he wrote.

Sitting around in a satin nightie, I flirted.

Sounds hot. You should come see me.

I felt a thrill go through me. So forward! So unlike Justin!

Oh, I wish I could. I'm stuck babysitting.

The next day I made sure to stop by the temporary hacker space Justin had set up so that attendees could hardware hack and solder their convention badges, adding lights and other fun doohickeys to them. I'd seen Justin a bit during the convention, but he'd been preoccupied with his duties, and after Michelle's outburst after the initial dinner when I'd first got to town, I was trying to take it slow with Justin.

However, his out of character messages had piqued my interest, and I was compelled to find out what had prompted his sudden boldness.

The mystery was short lived. I overheard Justin talking about how much he'd had to drink the night before. Well, that explained the texts.

I lingered at the hacker space for several hours, a few feet away from Justin, under the pretense of another friend teaching me the basics of Python programming and the fundamentals of object-oriented languages. I did this to be close to Justin without coming across as desperate or clingy. Justin seemed to barely pay any attention to me, his eyes glued on his monitor.

The irony, as Justin later told me, is that Justin was perturbed with me because of this since I had earlier mentioned his teaching me the same things and had no inkling that I was sitting there getting that lesson in order to be near to him.

In short, I was being totally idiotic, and my plan had the opposite of its intended effect. Justin seemed oblivious to my presence, and I left the space feeling like his flirtation the night before had been a booze-filled fluke.

I wandered around for hours talking to people, trying to find Rob and Michelle. I found them schmoozing with a bunch of attendees in the con suite, the hospitality room that the convention provided for people to lounge and mingle with one another. I quickly realized I was surrounded mostly by people I didn't know, and Rob and Michelle maintained their distance from me, even as I tried to stay relatively close to them. I felt out of place.

I knew technically to some people I would be considered Rob's mistress, though we'd worked out the details between the three of us, and everything was consensual. While the majority of con-goers were liberal, and polyamory seemed to be much more common in that circle (and most geeky circles) than in the general population, I felt it essential to be relatively discreet and follow Rob's lead as to how affectionate to be around other people.

And in that moment, he completely shut me out. It was more or less a repeat of his birthday party.

Fair enough. I was disappointed and totally wired on free hotel coffee.

I walked in circles around the hotel until about 3 in the morning when I texted Justin, on the off chance that he was still up. He was.

Can I come visit? I texted.

He sent me his room number.

Justin greeted me warmly, though he seemed completely exhausted, staring like a zombie at the muted hotel TV after he let me in and crawled into his bed. I took a chance and crawled in with him. I put my arms around him, and the two of us snuggled a bit, not saying anything. Then he began to open up about some of the stress of the weekend. After a few minutes, I kissed him softly on the neck and moved his hand onto my breast.

He removed it. "Not now."

"Oh. Oh, fuck. I'm sorry," I said.

"No worries," he said.

I held him for a while longer, the two of us barely speaking, holding one another, until he started to nod off and needed to turn in.

I left Justin's room but knew I wouldn't be able to sleep. I was still too wired and distracted by the intensity of what had just happened. It felt amazing to cuddle with Justin, but why had he rejected me? Maybe he was like Nathan and only wanted to fool around when he was drunk?

I found a few other attendees in the lobby, online friends of Michelle and Rob's, and I spent the rest of the evening into early morning chatting with them, not wanting to wake Rob and Michelle or Don, Tina, and Seth, let alone explain where I'd been. Let them all assume I'd spent the night in the other room.

After closing ceremonies, we all helped Rob and Michelle tear down the convention equipment and unload it back at their garage. Afterward, the core group headed to a diner for some lunch. Again I experienced the surreal experience of layered polyamorous relationships when Rob spent a good deal of the meal with one arm around me and the other around Michelle, and as Justin drove me home, I took the opportunity to hold hands with Justin as he reached over to shift gears.

The very next day, my new job started, and though the new position was exciting, the adjustment was extremely stressful, especially coupled with all the energy it was taking to adjust to the move. As I wrote in my journal:

Fuck

There's something wrong with me.

I know myself, and I am ill.

I'm keeping it together enough to do what
needs to be done, and I'm doing the things
that need to be done, but my inner life is all
fucked up. It's hard to explain, and I'm not sure
anyone would want to listen to the full extent

of it even if I could piece it together enough to convey it to someone else.

I'm not unsafe or anything. Just screwed up.

I know I can make it through, just be a stoic, man it up, keep putting one foot in front of another. I just hope I get better eventually. Getting by, that I can do. Getting better is the part I don't know I can count on.

I wrote that about a week after I'd gotten into town, soon after starting the new job, a bit depressed and shell-shocked by adjustment required by the move. Justin called me that night to check on me. We talked for about a half an hour or so, a good reassuring conversation between friends. He obviously cared about me, but between the stress I was dealing with and the way he'd shot me down in his hotel room the last night of the convention, I'd dialed back the flirtation with Justin to lower levels. Still, it was wonderful to hear from him and know he cared.

When I got off the phone, I saw I had a text from Rob that read *you busy?*

When I went downstairs to find him, Rob told me he'd been horny, but when I hadn't responded right away, he'd masturbated instead. Rob then waved me away so he could work on his website. That was the first time Rob had sought me out in 3 days.

We lived in the same house.

I was dismayed to find when I'd moved in with Rob that he and Michelle spent nearly every evening in front of their large TV, Rob sitting at his desk using his computer, Michelle on a couch across the room using her laptop. I'd come down to visit them the first couple of nights but found myself quickly growing bored with the activity, or lack of it. After all, they were doing this, in all places, a windowless basement – the exact situation I'd been trapped in all winter.

Instead I started to spend evenings in my upstairs office with the door open, making myself equally available to Rob, Seth, or Michelle, whoever wanted to drop by and spend time with me. The sunlight poured in through the windows, and I looked out on the wide suburban streets with a mixture of overload and fascination. It was so much louder than back home, and there were so many more people.

Several days passed with no visitors until one evening Rob and Michelle literally danced into my office. Rob had his stuffed cat in hand, making it assume all kinds of ludicrous poses, a one-cat conga line. Rob was not a small guy, but he was prancing, and Michelle (whose normal facial expressions ranged from dour to blank) was grinning and joining in the weird victory dance.

"Page! Page! Page! Guess what?" Rob said.

"What?"

He beamed. "We had... relations. First time since the baby!" Rob's favorite euphemism for sex.

"Oh, that's great," I said.

And they danced out of my office.

Though I'd been happy for them in the moment, disappointment instantly set in. They'd left so quickly. Why come up and tell me if they were just going to turn around and leave?

I made a point to talk to Rob about my concerns and my feeling that things had changed somehow, that he seemed to have cooled towards me since I'd moved in with him.

"Rob, I'm worried. I feel like our whole dynamic has changed."

"You know, Page, I'm not so sure we even have one yet. We've been long distance all this time."

My heart sunk. I felt like we had been so intimate, emotionally and physically. The kink connection meant the world to me. I moved across the country to be with him. Here I had been thinking this whole time that we had this big thing worth upsetting my life for, and now I worried it had all been in my head.

"I see," I said.

"I do love you, Page," Rob said.

"What does love mean to you, Rob?"

He considered this. "It means a lot of things. I enjoy your company."

I sighed.

"You're the first girlfriend I've ever had, really. Michelle was too young and dependent to really be called a girlfriend when she came into my life."

"But what about the girl you dated before me?" I asked.

"Oh, her? She never stayed more than 24 hours at a time. She was more of a friend with benefits," Rob said.

"Ahh."

"It's all a lot for me, too, that you're here. I'm still adjusting to the fact that you're here, you're so sweet and dote on me, and you're able to take care of yourself. I'm not quite sure how I fit into all of that," Rob said.

I was devastated, but I smiled. "We'll figure it out," I said.

Seth was adjusting well to the move, more or less, though he wished he knew more people in the area. I saw a post on Fetlife where some people from the dungeon I'd visited on my previous trips to Ohio were starting a group to hang out, play board games, and shoot the shit.

They were meeting up at a coffee house to play *Munchkin*. Seth thought that sounded like fun, and at my urging, he posted to the group's message board and joined them for the geeky card game.

When Seth came back from hanging out with the group, he seemed markedly happier. "I feel kind of out of place some-times because don't really know what to say when they talk about the kink stuff, but they're cool people."

The second time he went out to hang out with them, the group stretched the festivities further into the evening, so Seth returned to the house to pick me up when I got off work to bring me to where they were hanging out. And wouldn't you know it, it turned out to be Justin's house. Justin at that point was volunteering extensively at the local dungeon, and it just so happened that a few of his friends had been the ones to form this new social group.

Justin gave me a brief tour of his house, including his spacious attic. It was unfinished and had a look that was sufficiently distressed that, as he pointed out, it would make a rather sinister kinky play space if one were so inclined. I laughed a bit, turned towards him, and found myself desperately wanting to kiss him – with the same intensity I'd felt the night of Rob's birthday party. I tilted my head, tried to lean subtly forward. Justin began to move, and I thought he might kiss me, but instead he was turning around to head back down the attic stairs.

I would find out later that the sexual tension wasn't all in my head. Justin later told me that as he'd followed me up the attic stairs, he'd had an intense urge to grab my hips, one that he'd quickly dismissed as highly inappropriate.

After the tour, Justin and I joined the other guests in the living room. A few of them I knew, but most I hadn't met. I was introduced, made small talk, told a few jokes, and quickly found that I liked them (in fact, a few of the people I met that night remain among my closest friends). We played *Apples to Apples* and had a few snacks but mostly chatted about sex, kink, relationships, and our various love lives. I insinuated that I was rather busy dating practically everyone – or at least that's how I felt most days, that my relationships and dating in general were fatiguing me.

As I sat next to Justin on the couch, we inched closer and closer together (on my part it was conscious, if subtle) until I was stroking his arm and eventually cuddling with him with my arms around him, the two of us so close I was practically in his lap. It didn't progress beyond cuddling that evening, but still it was so prolonged and intense that I floated for days.

That evening, when I got home, Seth, who had been seated in a recliner across the room from where Justin and I sat together and had been treated with a prime view of the cuddling, remarked that it was one of the most adorable things he'd ever seen, that Justin and I were completely, utterly blissed out.

I hopped online to chat with him late that evening after I'd gone home:

> **justin:** *hugs* :)

> **page:** why hello there :) thank you for a lovely evening. of course, now I'm all hot and bothered

> **justin:** Awww. Would have helped with that...

> **page:** it would have been a little strange to just start making out

> **justin:** lol. Indeed

> **page:** well my pants were kinda falling off, and I was going commando – so that coulda gotten dicey at any minute :P

> **justin:** Although funny lol :)

> **justin:** I tried really hard not to just start kissing you this evening :)

page: oh yeah? that's hot. i thought about texting you to meet me downstairs :P

justin: Oooo. Nom nom

page: just for a few minutes. long enough ;)

justin: I wanted to kiss your neck really bad, unless that sounds weird :)

page: doesn't sound weird. I would have gone crazy

justin: :)

page: probably just gone limp and had my eyes roll back in my head

justin: \o/ Awesome

page: the way you touched my neck was making me crazy, but that was probably obvious

justin: Awww. A bit :)

page: I was so focused on you tonight. I know I was supposed to be social, but I was really, really into you

justin: You were social :)

page: yeah, but I just wanted to go somewhere alone with you and start kissing and undressing if I'm being totally honest. That's where my mind was

justin: Same here :)

> **page:** so when are we gonna have a proper date?
> hmm hmm?

Since I was going out of town to a convention with Michelle and Rob to work at the table for his novelty business, I made plans with Justin to go out to dinner with him the day after I returned from my trip, a Monday night.

The coffee date Rob had promised still hadn't happened despite my alluding to it at regular intervals. I knew my time was a potentially limited resource, and since Rob had been there first, in one sense, he had "dibs" on my time over Justin. But now that 2 weeks had passed, and Rob still hadn't delivered, I was through holding my entire calendar open for him, sitting around bored, waiting on the off chance he'd decide it was time to go out. Besides, Rob and I would spend all weekend together. I'd even taken time away from my day job to volunteer to help him with his business on the trip as Sunday was normally a work day for me.

When Rob and I were preparing merchandise for the show the night before we left for the trip, I let Rob know about my plans. "I'm gonna grab dinner with Justin when we get back."

I scanned Rob's face for concern, but he seemed relatively unphased by the news.

"I'm not threatened," he replied.

In retrospect, I suppose this seems an odd response.

At the time, however, I took him at his word, that Rob was fine with the date. Besides, the heads up was a courtesy. I didn't need his approval/permission. Our relationship wasn't like that. We had no such arrangement (nor did I at this point have such a rule with Seth).

At the convention, the days were long, and we were mobbed with customers. I did my best to flirt and be friendly to drum up some business (after all, it was a convention targeted to sci fans and open source aficionados, and I was, as Tina always said, "geek nip," i.e., cat nip for geeks), but although we generated a lot of interest and had our fair share of traffic, Rob was rather disappointed in the overall sales figures. I suppose it could hardly be helped, as Rob was launching a novelty business in the midst of a recession, a risky venture in the best of times. Still, he was rather down.

"You know, Rob," I said one evening as we walked back from a polyamory panel discussion, "That talk brought up a lot of frustration I felt this winter. I'll fess up. It made me totally crazy when you'd flirt with others or talk about being with other people. The thing that got me through that was looking forward finally being with you full time. I thought it was going to get better."

"And it hasn't," he finished.

"Yeah," I said. "I don't know what it is. I feel like you're already stretched too thin as it is between work, your daughter, and your marriage. We haven't even gone for coffee."

"Page," he said. "From here on out, I think I'm only going to have 3 women in my life – you, Michelle, and my daughter."

"That's not what I meant," I said.

"You're important to me," Rob said.

"That sounds great," Michelle said. "I think Page was right."

But something felt off about it. The next day I told Rob it wasn't my position to judge whether he was too busy or not, that it was his life and his choice to make, to draw conclusions about the wisdom of adding new people in his life. Furthermore, I stressed that it wasn't that I was prohibiting him or that I would do such a thing (not my style), only that his comments that he was interested in more made me uncomfortable, an important distinction.

After all, I had a date scheduled with Justin, something I was greatly looking forward to, and what kind of hypocrite would I be to prohibit Rob from seeking other relationships when I was doing so myself, regardless of whether Rob and I were spending enough time together or whose fault that was?

I made sure to mention the date with Justin again on the ride back from the convention as Rob, Michelle, and I made the 3-hour drive home to remind Rob as well as to make sure I brought it up in front of Michelle. Rob again said that he was fine with it, and if I was going to date someone else, he'd prefer it to be Justin because he was one of their best friends, and Rob knew Justin was a truly good guy and wouldn't hurt me.

With that bit of business out of the way, I was good to go. It was a wonderful first date.

From an email I sent to Tina (who drank up every detail like a champion voyeur) about how it went:

```
From Page

To Tina

My date with Justin
```

It was wonderful. He's a great kisser. Phenomenal. We went to a nice little restaurant that sells soup and salad. Then we went to Walgreens and picked up some drinks (I had Diet A&W root beer) and went back to his place. We ate our soup and chatted until we ended up kissing on the stairs. When he went into the bathroom for a moment, I stripped down to my bra and panties and climbed into his bed. I told him to turn off the light. He got in with me, and we kissed and fooled around for about 4 hours by moonlight. He gave me 4 cookies (all very soft play with his hands and kissing my shoulders, breasts, etc). He also spanked the heck out of me, etc, while I stroked him. I finally made him cookie after a few hours (I was teasing him a lot) with some lube and my hands. It actually arced up and hit the window blinds. Apparently it felt wonderful. :) He held me, and we spooned and talked about how happy we were to have each other, various things, etc. He says he's never had this deep of an emotional connection with another person, that he loves me dearly, and that he's ecstatic. I really love Justin. :) He's a fantastic human being.

I don't know when we're going to have another date again because we're both so busy, but I had an amazing time.

("Cookies" is a euphemism Tina uses for orgasms. She never told me why, but the best I can figure is that if you're really, really good, you get a cookie.)

I came home from that first date with Justin beaming. Seth had been on a rather odd sleep schedule for a while, where he'd stay up all night and then sleep most of the day, so the two of us went out to an all-night diner to have some pie.

"Aren't you going to ask how my date went?" I asked.

"You're grinning from ear to ear," Seth said. He leaned in close to me, "Sometimes I like to pretend that this place is run by vampires," referring to the diner.

I giggled. It seemed my good mood was contagious. Justin was among the friends Seth was making in town, and Seth had told me several times he liked Justin. It didn't hurt that Seth now had several prospects of his own, cute poly girls he could talk to he'd met through the folks he had begun hanging out with. Seth's spirits were much higher than they'd been in a while.

"So, Page," Seth said. "How was your date?"

"Great," I said. "He's a wonderful kisser."

Seth put his hand on mine. "That's all I need to know."

Michelle wasn't quite so happy for me:

> **page:** I need to be honest with you. I've developed feelings for Justin, and I don't think they're going away. I'm going to do my best not to mess up anything with this, but I thought you should know. Even if I have to wait a while to explore things with him because we're both so busy, there's a connection there

michelle: I noticed. it's obvious

page: I've been trying to fight it, but I can't

michelle: it's what's been bugging me

page: I'm losing

michelle: I've given up

page: I think acknowledging it will help me keep it in check and better manage it. fighting it just makes me and everyone around me nuts

I let Rob know the same, that the date went well, that I would see Justin again, and that I had feelings for him.

Rob thanked me for telling him and rushed off to do something else, but it was clear he was upset. He was cold and terse, without his usual playfulness.

rob: Also, page, I am not as upset anymore as I was when you came downstairs. I figured out my issue and I can deal with it. My issue was this, don't tell me I'm overcommitted and stretching myself and then go add another relationship on to your own life when I'm the one that doesn't have a 9 to 5 job :P

page: exactly. that was what I was talking to you about the other night. I was telling you I was wrong to say that

***rob** nods

To be fair, 9 to 5 job or not, Rob had a lot that he was dealing with. Frustrated with the sexual side effects, he had stopped taking his Cymbalta in February. When he'd stopped the medicine suddenly, he'd developed a strange buzzing noise in his head, a noise that weeks later was still present. And though the plan had originally been for Rob to be a stay-at-home dad to Callie, he'd had to put her in daycare after finding he couldn't deal with the stress and frustration that ensued.

To put it lightly, Rob wasn't operating at 100% – thus my concern.

Even Michelle seemed a bit better after a bit of time to process what I'd said:

> **michelle:** so, I must commend you for msging me re Justin even if I'm not thrilled with the idea since I kinda already knew and am glad you were honest about it. just shitty timing, heh

With that bit of housekeeping taken care of, I was pumped to go to the kink festival!

Up Early

Apparently my body is under the impression that 4 hours is enough sleep. Or silly allergies + the cat jumping up and down on me with his peg legs = this. Whatever. No biggie. Coffee's brewing, and the cat is putting the moves on me again. The big annual kink festival 'round these parts starts tonight, and I'm rather excited to be attending with Rob. It should be a fantastic time.

In other news, I've started seeing Justin and am excited about him, though we're taking things slowly because of all the parties involved and the limited time on both Justin's and my ends of things (forgive my awkward phrasing).

———

Ahahaha, as I was writing this entry, the coffeemaker failed and started spewing coffee everywhere even though I made sure to close the lid down tight. Okay, it's more frustrating than humorous. I'm just glad Rob was around to help me contain its brown geyser. Blech. Perhaps some tea is in order to soothe my throat.

—-

It's the little things

Quick update potentially of little to no consequence to people who are not me: After the coffee fiasco this morning, Rob went and found a brand new coffeemaker he had in the house and got it all set up so I could use it – we're talking within the same hour it happened. Yep, that's love.

The kink con started out wonderfully, with a first night of delicious debauchery. Rob and I had a great time flirting and playing at the play space. Justin was there with the bubbly redhead (who he was still seeing). The redhead confessed an attraction to me, and Rob and Justin egged the two of us on until the redhead and I had a rather gratifying and exciting make out.

Rob and I returned to the house disturbingly aroused and had sex on the downstairs couch.

Sadly, while the first day had gone quite promisingly, the good times with Rob were soon over.

When the second day of the kink convention came, Rob slept in so late that we missed most of our classes, and at the play party that evening, he got rid of me several times, telling me to go make out with Justin, disappearing into the bathroom to text Michelle.

At the end of the festivities, I asked Rob if he'd had a good time. He replied me that he wished Michelle had been there. After shelling out more than 100 bucks for his event ticket, I was devastated.

But all was not lost. Despite Rob's behavior and the disappointment it brought on, I had a good time with Justin, whose own date, the bubbly redhead, had flaked on their scheduled plans and wandered off to play with someone new.

It was not until Justin realized my pupils were dilated, that I was slurring my speech and not at full verbal capacity, that it became apparent that anything was amiss.

I had entered subspace for the first time.

Sure, there were plenty of attractive folks around, but I had been in a mellow headspace. This head rush had blindsided me.

Cue a fisting class complete with an exquisite demonstration. Cue making out with more than one person I'm attracted to – then being laid on top of by multiple people while my hair was pulled, my shoulder bitten, my neck kissed, my shoes stolen, and my feet tickled – followed rapid fire by verbal cuing by two men I'm extremely attracted to, in a dizzying disorienting succession. Endorphins flooded into my system, each wave potentiating the next.

Justin held and kissed me, escorted me back into the quieter lounge area under the red lights. Gradually I returned from being lost at sea, became more coherent. Part of me wanted to stay adrift. Even so, all night I felt on the edge of delirium, and even the following day, I felt a little different.

I have never felt that fucked up without drugs before. I would not have believed it possible. All those little things added up over time into a net cumulative effect that fucked the hell out of my mind. Apparently when being tickled, I was yelling French curse words (something I do not recall).

Subspace is a marvelous discovery and a place to which I've already returned. Calibrating such things would prove to be an utterly exhilarating process.

Unfortunately, Michelle was getting more controlling by the day.

I'd left Tina behind when I moved to Ohio. We missed each other, but Tina was really supportive of my choice, was genuinely happy for me, and handled my moving away extremely well (I suppose it helps that we'd had more of a friends with benefits sort of relationship that was pretty fluid as a matter of course).

Tina was really curious about my sex life out here in Ohio and asked me questions so regularly about what I was doing, so I geeked out and created a special Google Calendar called "Bed Notch" (like notches in your bedpost) for her where I'd record who I had sex with, what position, etc., for her licentious pleasure. It only included Seth and Rob, for the time being, but who knew what the future held? It was all in good fun, and I cleared it with Rob and Seth.

When Michelle got wind of Bed Notch, she demanded that I add her. The first thing she did was read over my recent activity and figure out Rob had lied to her about re: omitting a sexual encounter we'd had. Then she used the information she found on my calendar to harass him and start an argument.

I shut down Bed Notch not long after, even though it disappointed Tina greatly, because Michelle used that info against Rob and additionally criticized the manner in which I documented my sex life, complaining that I failed to record the time of day the encounters occurred.

Justin and I went on another date. My reservations about going too fast were starting to fade. My feelings for him were getting stronger the more time spent together, and the more Michelle sniped at me or tried to push me, the less I cared what she thought.

> **justin:** I had no clue we'd be so compatible. I knew I liked you a lot, but you're dating a friend, etc.

page: I've been looking for someone like you

*****justin** blushes

justin: And I you... You have your shit together. You understand yourself and me.

page: um, the sex. it is great. and there is no sex yet

justin: Exactly. Dear god the sex is great

page: you're gonna want a fluid bond, aren't you?

justin: Maybe eventually... but I know the pragmatics don't line up right now, so it doesn't bother me.

page: I'm gonna want one

*****page** admits it

page: stupid pragmatics

justin: I admit it'd be hot. I haven't had a true fluid bond in years

page: pragmatically speaking, you're the person I'm probably going to want to have sex with constantly because your libido's like mine

justin: That... probably excites me more than it should :)

page: I get really hot thinking about fluid bonding with you...

justin: *nod* So do I. It was hot dirty talking about it last night :)

page: well ok, no shit talk. no PR. here we go. you have the libido, you drive me insane. I want to fuck your brains out. I have very little sex life with Seth. I've explained this

justin: mmhmm. *nod*

page: sex is pretty good with Rob but intermittent due to his average libido and issues with time, sleep, health, and Michelle. also, the fluid bond disproportionately benefits him because he's not terribly concerned with my pleasure – both due to his lack of energy for concern about other people in general – and our dynamic which is built on frustration

page: also of all my lovers, Rob's the one I trust the least. I mean, I trust him a lot but I also could see him sneaking off with one of his exes, etc. as much as he professes he would never do such a thing

justin: *nod* Because he has that impulsiveness... the thing that excites and scares you

page: right

justin: (I have to admit, I love being in each other's heads)

page: :) so my risk vs rewards ratio with you in a pragmatic sense is worlds better than his. that's the no PR, no shit version

justin: *nod* I'm so not used to someone wanting me... so my first instinct is to say "you don't have to sleep with me". But I want it so bad, and I can tell you do too. So all of this is very novel for me

page: now, the problem with that is that dissolving a fluid bond is an act of war and there's a factorial degree of difficulty involved in getting *you* to trust Rob's judgement in being fluid bonded to him through me – and the idea that Michelle and Rob would accept you as a risk (given especially that they think you're some kind of pimp) is almost unthinkable, therein lies the rub

justin: Indeed

page: you've worked this out in your head?

justin: As you've talked about it, it just makes sense. And the dynamic just isn't there for all of us in a web. There isn't quite enough trust/healthy communication there. It's something that *could* happen, but it requires a lot of work.

page: right. I could *easily* see it working with you, me, and Seth, etc. I mean, just the dynamics

justin: *nod* Even if it was just Rob... he could probably deal or at least accept. But add Michelle with him, and it goes a bit nuts.

page: so in order for us to be fluid bonded, something would have to change

justin: Yes

page: now, that said, I could probably end up with some sort of compromised quasi-fluid bonded status with you, but it would take a great degree of negotiation, which I would pursue vigorously of course

justin: Yea, I suppose it doesn't have to be true/false huh...

*****justin** hugs you

justin: You are amazing, you know

page: oh? what brought that on?

justin: *nobody* has ever fought for me... gone through trouble for me. *worked* for me... It's enough to make me almost cry.

The New Relationship Energy was glorious. As I wrote in my journal:

Let me tell you about my new boyfriend

My new boyfriend has giant hands and smooth, smooth skin. He is an engineer, an inventor, a renaissance man. He is a genius who was raised by hippies in a town without stoplights. A former child prodigy. Brilliant and visionary but humble about it. Generous, adaptive, creative, sincere, kind. He has a young face and an old soul.

He is superlatively sex positive and passionate with a taste for the bizarre and all things bright and beautiful, new and shiny. An autodidact, a fellow polymath.

He's so tactile he can see with his hands, mend things, fix things, create. He is capable, skilled, mindful, tactful, ethical, and giving – and open. Imminently reasonable.

He has the mind of an architect and the soul of a poet.

I love him and am in complete awe that he loves me, too.

Michelle waited for me at the door as Justin pulled the car back out into the street to go to work. She rolled her eyes at me.

"If you're not fucking him, then what the hell are you doing over there all night?"

I averted my eyes. "Sleeping, for one."

"You sleep like shit," she snapped. "You're back up in a couple of hours."

"Not when I sleep next to him," I said. "I can relax around him. I'm not sure why, but I can." It was true and no small thing. I never managed more than a couple hours of sleep in one go. Something would invariably startle me awake and keep me there; sometimes it was my own mind conjuring echoes.

But with Justin? I felt completely safe. Cared for, even. It wasn't an emotion I could remember having, aside from some fuzzy memories of being rocked to sleep by my mother or carried upstairs by my father when I fell asleep on the couch. And I'm not sure even now that those memories aren't just dreams.

"That doesn't even make sense," Michelle said, and her dismissal was so profane and offensive to me that for a moment, I felt adrenaline surge through me and wanted to hit her.

"Besides," I said instead. "There are a million things that aren't fucking that you can do if you have enough imagination."

It was petty, but I didn't care. I knew the rules of our agreement and that I was squarely within them, having done nothing risky STI-wise. Making out, hand jobs, some light kink, all things I could to do at will when the mood struck me.

I brushed by her to get to the kitchen. I needed to make coffee, shower, start my own day working at home. She grabbed her keys from the table.

"We'll talk later," she said before heading off into rush hour.

> **page:** I want you. I'm so in love with you. it's ridiculous and awesome. I didn't even know this kind of love existed

justin: I know... It's still surreal sometimes :) But it's so strong and real it can't be ignored

page: you make me feel so beautiful

justin: You are :) In many ways

page: :) I want to pleasure you for days

justin: *shudder* Only if we can take turns ;)

***page** squirms

page: you love me so much, with an intensity and passion I'm not used to

justin: Ditto.

page: but you know, i could get used to it :) though it tends to color everything and I'm already worried about the implications. radical changes of perspective have been known to change one's inner landscape. you make the rest of the class look bad sometimes :P

page: you're the center of my sexual universe at the moment

justin: Ditto. I just want to make love with no time and not come up till we're done :)

page: I love how everything flows with you, how we stop and talk or cuddle, etc, just naturally, and then go back to things

justin: Yes. I love that too. No hurry, no time limits

page: there's no performance. it's genuine

page: I shouldn't have said anything about the turmoil bit of things. that's really my business to take care of, not yours

justin: *hugs* You can talk about *anything*

page: awww, thank you for that

justin: I love hearing about your inner process

page: umm.. hmm...

justin: I honestly get more respect for you each time we talk about what you think

page: you are dwarfing my feelings for Rob. it makes me feel like shit in a way

page: I shouldn't compare. it's just that while that's a great relationship, there are so many issues, and he doesn't know himself, etc. again, i shouldn't compare

justin: It's hard not to... and I know you won't let that... hurt him? We're human, we compare...

page: I still enjoy my time with him, etc

justin: Yes. I know it doesn't mean you don't love him

page: I get a distinctly different sort of enjoyment out of him

justin: and I'm very... flattered... embarrassed? Strange feeling that

page: yes, it's just... holy shit. like.. basically the stakes are higher here. you are much more invested than he is in me. you work on a different level than he does. does that make sense?

justin: Yes

page: I'm realizing it more and more. he just doesn't invest as much in people as I do. I've known in some sense for a while

justin: You've mentioned it before, I think.

page: you know he told me something interesting at the kink con that stayed with me. I asked him what the most triggery thing I could do for him would be, how I could hurt him essentially, and he said it would be if I pursued a girl I knew he liked, seduced her, and didn't invite him along, which was interesting. It made me see that he thinks of me on some level as a rival

justin: That is interesting

page: it's peculiar. usually that kind of jealousy is far more prevalent in same-sex friendship

justin: You know, I was a bit envious of your attraction to other people... but I don't feel that anymore.

page: no? why's that?

justin: Dunno. Changed when our connection really took off.

page: yes, see? for me, that almost signals to me that my connection with Rob isn't as strong on his end as I would have hoped

"You look like you're dying to talk to someone about Justin," Seth said.

"Oh? What makes you think that?"

"You just get this look on your face whenever you say his name... or anyone else does."

"Sorry," I said, embarrassed.

"No, it's okay," Seth said. "Go ahead. You look giddy. What were you guys talking about?"

"Oh, the last few hours?"

"Yeah."

I smiled. "We've been making all these plans for unconventional dates. Like going to the free clinic to get tested. That could be oddly romantic."

Seth laughed.

"Or prom night in Columbus. With hideous corsages and all! A Columbus Sex Vacation. That one's kind of a long-running joke. I'd just rage quit this whole mess and text Rob and Michelle 'be right back, gone with Justin on Columbus Sex Vacation.'"

"Oh, that is all so you, "Seth said. "Fucking weird but so you."

I laughed.

Seth added, "He really does get you and love you. I'm so happy for you."

As Justin and I continued to date, I started to want a more serious physical connection. The tension was killing me. I wanted to have sex with him. I knew I had to talk to Rob, as per Rob's one rule: "if you're fucking anybody else, I want to know about it before it happens."

I dreaded bringing it up, the awkwardness of it. But as it turns out, I soon got a good chance.

One morning after an overnight date at Justin's, I basically collided with Rob as he was coming back from the bathroom.

"So you and Seth went to Justin's last night, huh?" he asked.

"Yeah, a bunch of us watched *Dr. Who*, and Justin talked to me a bit about some of the stresses running the hackerspace."

"How's Justin doing with that?" Rob asked.

"As well as could be expected. It's a lot of logistics to deal with, but he's hanging in there."

"You spent the night, right?" Rob said.

"Yeah."

"Have you guys had sex yet?" Rob asked suddenly.

"Not yet," I said, "but I think we're going to pretty soon. It's trending that way. We're really compatible. He's clean, got tested for a full STI panel as part of his bariatric screening labs, not sure when it'll happen, but I'd say anywhere from within the next week to next month."

"I see," he said.

"I just wanted to give you a heads up. Justin and I have made out a lot. I guess I'm just a ho, right?"

Rob cracked a smiled, changed the subject. We chatted a little about his baby, and I kissed and snuggled him. He seemed okay.

I awoke the next morning to cryptic passive-aggressive messages on my phone from Michelle.

Rob's reaction was nothing compared to Michelle's. She fought with me via text for days.

> **michelle:** am I wrong to feel like I should have been treated somewhat as an equal all this time? That I feel like I deserved even snippets of your time? I feel like I should have been a higher priority than Justin.

> **michelle:** if the only thing you're doing for yourself involves leaving to spend time with Justin, how is that for you?"

> **page:** he makes me so happy

> **michelle:** you need to be happy for YOU not BE-CAUSE of others

page: well you can appreciate and enjoy what people give you

michelle: I feel like you don't give a shit about how I feel

page: well I do care, but I also care about myself

page: and I know what I need right now

michelle: I don't think you do...

michelle: which is why you constantly beg for encouragement and reinforcement

page: from you?

michelle: from everyone

michelle: you get everything from everyone.

page: wait? am I avoiding you or following you around asking for reinforcement?

michelle: grrr

michelle: yes, I'm pissed off that you went after Justin, yes I'm pissed off that you're getting codependent with him and claiming it's for your independence.

I was LIVING with Rob and Michelle. Not only that, but they had been actively REJECTING my offers to hang out and ignoring me when I did reach out.

And they had mouths – they could have certainly asked me to do something. It wasn't like they had been asking "Hey, you want to go out tomorrow night?" and I was answering "Nope, too busy banging Justin."

Plus, I was going out with Justin 1 to 2 nights a week. That's not being codependent – that's called dating.

I also seriously disliked that she said I "went after" him. Justin was a grown man with his own feelings. It unfolded very naturally and very mutually.

> **michelle:** I'm pissed off that all the time I was talking about how I've had trouble with him in the past you were getting close to him and not telling me.

As far as all the "trouble in the past," she had in passing once or twice had said "oh, I really should hang out with Justin more, we used to hang out more, and I miss that."

Plus, it shouldn't have been a surprise that I was talking to Justin. I did a lot of it in front of her, in a group chat that had another eight or so members other than Rob, Michelle, Justin, and me.

It was only after I started to speak to Justin in private chats with any frequency that I let her know that I had started talking to him a lot, and her response to being told this was to completely flip out on me.

I tried everything I could, reassuring Michelle, reasoning with her, defending myself, checking out emotionally, problem-solving – and all of it backfired.

> **michelle:** you're happy stepping on my feelings
>
> **page:** oh goodness

page: no, I just trust you to take care of them, own them, and manage them – reach to people for support, make your own connections, advocate for your own happiness – and sometimes that means chilling out if a friend needs a little space

michelle: I say things and you turn them so that they can be your way. I talk about my feelings and you make it about you. you beat things into the ground and interrupt people. you're ruining this relationship.

page: I don't find blaming people for things productive

michelle: I wasn't placing any blame

There were a thousand points I could have turned back when the poly web began to burn. But incrementally, inch by inch, I didn't want to. At every turn Michelle objected, insisted I was in violation of rules that I never agreed to, never would have agreed to.

I know it wasn't exactly the most mature decision to leave to spend the night at Justin's again, but with things so tense at home, I worried about my sanity.

I was rewarded with a wonderful night, which I later recounted in an another one of my emails to Tina:

```
I had sex with Justin last night. Twice. It was
wonderful. Prior to the vaginal sex, he tied
my wrists behind my back and went down on me.
After I came, we talked and held each other. I
ended up getting on top of him, at first only
```

squeezing my Kegel muscles while I held his
hands and then fully moving to have sex with
him for a while and then climbing off suddenly.
He got frustrated, pinned me on my back, and
shoved my legs next to his head. We are a good
fit. He can hit my cervix. Second time, I started on top of him facing backwards so I could
masturbate, and then I finished him off with
my mouth.

Very, very wonderful.

I am a very happy Page. He's a keeper,
that Justin.

However, rather predictably, my problems were still there
when I returned. Michelle hadn't cooled off in the interim:

> **michelle:** when I tried to look at your calendar as-
> suming you would be around last night, you
> weren't

> **michelle:** you want what you want and to hell with
> everyone else.

In hindsight, I realize I could have said the same thing to her.
Although I didn't and wouldn't have if I had thought such a
thing. It was bad enough as it was without openly baiting her.

Instead, I did my best to be clear, gently, while still advocating
for my needs:

> **page:** michelle, we might not just be a good fit. our
> poly might not be compatible with each other.
> there are many different kinds.

page: I absolutely need a certain level of freedom, of autonomy, or I'm terribly unhappy

page: and Justin isn't "new" per se, as much as we didn't realize how we were growing together and just thought we were friends for the longest time

page: I really didn't mean for it to happen – he and I just have this natural chemistry, and it's a deep connection

page: I think what I've realized that Rob is seeking, struggling to get all his needs met – same with you, and things are such with commitments, scheduling, etc, that they aren't – even with me in the picture, they aren't

page: I could really sense that, feel that. I think both of you would like more emotional support, far greater than I can provide – even if I made it my full-time job

page: honestly, learning the area and meeting new people is super important right now to me, as I'm not from here, and I guess you did not trust me as my intentions as much as I thought you did, which is ok

page: and whatever will be psychologically healthy with you guys is okay with me

page: if you just want to be friends for a while (or however long) or whatever, I totally get it

page: your marriage and your baby should come first

I suggested to Michelle that the four of us have a "family meeting" to hash things over. Michelle refused and said she wanted to talk to me and only me, one on one. With how poorly our chats had gone though, I really wanted there to be other people there. There was a definite practical aspect to it since we were discussing time sharing, an issue that affected everyone else. And I didn't say it to Michelle, but I was concerned she'd use the isolation to bully and berate me and try to manipulate me. Other people would help prevent her from getting carried away.

I held my ground, insisting that I really wanted the household to talk, that it was important to me.

Michelle responded by dropping me from Fetlife, changing her orientation to straight, and setting her kink status to Vanilla.

"If you noticed the changes in my profile, at this point I no longer consider myself poly," she wrote in a status update.

Talk about passive-aggressive.

It made sense in a way. She kept reading into my actions meanings I didn't mean, after all, and instead of approaching me with an open mind to get clarification, she came at me angry, assuming I meant the worst.

I did wonder what this meant for Rob and me – if I was now considered a mistress.

As I wrote to a friend, who inquired as to Michelle's sudden status changes:

> I haven't gotten to discuss with her whether
> this means that I'm technically cheating now

```
with Rob and need to break things off with him,
but my guess would be that it does. I'm doing
fine, just a little irritated... Lots of unspo-
ken rules and expectations, and I've broken
promises to her that I never made, etc. It's
sad. A lot of pragmatics need to be worked out
here as this is where I live, but I do have
friends who have offered to take us in (and our
4-year-old cat).
```

Eventually, Michelle did agree to meet as a group but stipulated that Seth not attend since she felt like it didn't involve him. I agreed to the compromise.

I met with Rob and Michelle that night to discuss the state of things.

"So we'd like to set some expectations," Rob said.

I started out the meeting firmly. "I will not stop seeing Justin. Know that before you make your list of expectations. I will not accept that."

"Oh?" Rob said.

"I could see your concern if I were just hooking up with some guy," I said. "But this is not just SOME GUY. This is Justin, for fuck's sake. He's a wonderful human being, and I love him. How could I not love him?"

Rob nodded. "He's a really nice guy," he said.

Michelle rolled her eyes. "Maybe a little TOO nice."

"Agreed," Rob said.

"Oh please," I said.

I could tell it threw them off guard. They weren't used to my copping an attitude like that, but I'd reached the limit of my patience. I was done with their transparent blame-shifting. They were clearly insecure, and I knew it couldn't be easy. But insinuating that Justin was up to no good in an underhanded attempt to discourage me from seeing him? It was stupid, and I wasn't going to put up with it.

I talked about how negative the atmosphere in the house had been, reminded Rob of all the times I'd been available, even sought him out, and he had barely registered my presence.

"One thing you gotta know about me," Rob said, "Even when I'm happy, I still bitch. And I have a really hard time asking for help when I need it."

I frowned. "Sounds like an assertiveness problem to me."

"Perhaps," he replied.

What had been trying as a series of texts and chats from Michelle seemed absurd when exposed to the light of day. With Rob present, she was far less vindictive, and when she was harsh, I was able to easily correct her. I felt emboldened.

"You have to remember, Rob, that you told me that of all the people I could date, Justin would be the one you'd want me to date because you knew he wouldn't hurt me," I said. "That meant a lot to me. That's really what pushed me over the edge and told me I was right to trust my feelings about this and that I could trust you to take it well."

"Well I didn't mean to date him right now," Rob.

Michelle piped in. "Yeah, he said later."

"Actually, Michelle," Rob said. "I didn't give any time frame, and as you recall, you didn't even hear that conversation. You had headphones on."

Michelle sighed. "I can't believe that single conversation held so much power."

"You guys should both probably stop saying things you don't mean," I said. "It's really a terrible way to communicate. I can't read your mind. I can only go on what you say, so you have to make your words count."

Rob frowned. Michelle began to cry.

I felt I was getting somewhere. "I repeat: Don't say things you don't mean. Either of you. Words are powerful. You can't just sling them around and expect people to discern your intent."

There was a short silence.

Finally, Rob said, "That makes sense."

I smiled.

"It's so tough because you want things scheduled," Michelle said.

"Of course I want things scheduled," I said. "A) That's a personality trait of mine: I like having at least a tentative plan. B) Polyamory is worlds easier with scheduling. Every resource I've found says it's the key to maintaining a healthy balance."

"Well," Rob said, "Love is infinite, time is finite, energy is finite."

"Oh, good gravy," I said. "What you've been saying tonight is *not* that time is finite – because it's not like *I'm* asking you for time and not getting it. *You've* been asking for mine and not receiving it. And really not even that. You've been *hoping* for my time and not receiving it. You didn't even ask me until after I started to see someone else. The time has been there all along, yours for the taking, and you didn't ask for it. Michelle, you even rejected my offers to schedule. That tells me that what you're really saying is that your initiative was finite and now your patience is, and you should just own that."

Michelle said, "Yeah, I suppose that makes sense. But at the same turn, why can't you be patient with Justin and take your time there?"

"I've been patient for months," I said, "I'm still patient. The funny thing is: I've been *wanting* to go out with you. But I'm done making all the sacrifices, all the compromises, being the only patient one."

"It's just…" Rob said. "With you going out so much with Justin this week, it makes me really lose trust in our connection."

"So you're telling me that you had all this trust in me and our connection, and I was hard to reach for a week and a half, and now you have doubts," I said.

Rob nodded. "Yes."

"So the length of your trust is a week and a half. That is the half-life of your trust of me," I said.

Rob sighed. "I guess so."

I continued. "And I was mocked and called weak for asking for any sort of reassurance while you were 900 miles away

– all the while sending you the sporadic reassuring emails, etc."

"Yeah," Rob said.

I wasn't done. "I bet you understand me a little better now and the work I do to keep things stable and how shitty it feels when that work isn't done."

"I do," Rob said.

"And how shitty it must have felt to have been criticized for requesting a fraction of that same support," I finished.

Michelle started to cry again.

"Although," Rob said. "Well, let's put it this way: Would you rather build your relationship with me or your relationship with Justin?"

I frowned. "What a question! I'll tell you it's a bad sign, a red flag when someone makes you choose."

"I think I want to hold off on sex until you and I build our relationship better," Rob said.

I nodded. "I agree. That's a good idea."

"Really?" Rob said, clearly taken aback.

"Yes."

"Subject to change, of course," Rob added.

I rolled my eyes. "Well, Rob, *everything's* subject to change."

"But I might want to have sex with you again, I mean," Rob said.

"Then you'd need my consent, like anyone else. I'm not an automatic yes."

By Rob's reaction, it seemed to me in that moment that he was trying to use withholding sex as a bargaining tactic, a way of reinforcing his "it's me or Justin" ultimatum. It was a bad calculation on Rob's part as I was about to suggest holding off on sex as well.

"It's not only the problems between the three of us. With the strained dynamic with you two regarding sex, I feel really uncomfortable having sex with you right now, Rob. I think you guys need to work on things in that regard," I explained.

"Well, from my perspective," Michelle said, "I'd much rather that Rob have you as an outlet as it helps me not feel guilty for not providing that to him."

"Honestly, that makes me feel like a backup cunt, and I resent that," I said.

Rob and Michelle were quick to disagree, firing off no's in unison.

"Here's the thing," I said, "My sex life, my sexual connection, giving of myself physically is not something that you can just use as a handy resource completely on your terms without my consideration."

"Well, you have such a high libido," Michelle said.

"It doesn't mean that sex isn't highly personal, emotional, and raw for me," I said.

We thanked each other for the talk and then went our separate ways, of course. It occurred to me after the meeting that as upset they had been, they hadn't set any expectations with me. It really made me wonder if the whole point of the meeting had been to try to convince me to stop seeing Justin.

As upset as they were, I felt good about how I had approached it. I had given Rob and Michelle plenty of advance notice that I was interested in Justin. Even when I was questioning my relationship with Rob internally over that long winter in the basement apartment, I had struggled to give him the benefit of the doubt in what was essentially an emotional vacuum. I had tried so damn hard, and Rob didn't try at all. And I was the one being blamed. Under those conditions, it was becoming increasingly difficult to care.

As I wrote in my journal:

Declaration of Independence

I don't care if I'm right or wrong. Blame is an artificial subjective system and patently unproductive in my opinion, but I'll take the blame if it'll spare a few feelings.

The last month or so, I've been in the constant position of no matter what I'm doing, I'm making someone unhappy, disappointing someone, depriving someone of something.

Moving out here has been its own mind fuck. I am struggling for my own survival, emotionally, financially, and otherwise. I've also discovered that I require a great amount of freedom and privacy, maybe enough so that it makes me incompatible with certain people, even as friends.

Even if I could change this fact about myself, I don't think I'd want to, and I don't think I'd be happy if I did.

The great thing (and sometimes scary thing) about life is that no one is beholden to anyone. Life is a series of micro-choices, and I do not require anyone to accept me the way I am, but I will say now that I am not changing for anyone (unless it's what I truly desire), and I will continue my struggle to survive and treading water here no matter what it takes.

If you want to help me swim, it's up to you. If not, I'll endeavor to take it gracefully.

It didn't help that Rob and Michelle weren't my only source of stress. As supportive as Seth was of my relationship with Justin, financially supporting Seth was taking quite a toll on me.

My new job was going well enough, but I worked for production-based pay, and between the difficulty of the cases and the poor quality of the tools I was given to do the work at the new company, it was turning out to pay far less than I had thought when I took the position.

Little had changed with Seth and money problems. Seth loved to buy things and had never really cared on an emotional level what they cost. The sad part, too, was that the things he bought didn't even really make him happy past a point. Seth would forget he even had them.

I ended up feeling like a meal ticket, even if it wasn't how Seth felt. And whenever I expressed that we don't have the money, it was like I'd done something wrong.

At virtually every opportunity, a strange slippage would occur, where even when I would set limits on things, he'd push them.

When he let me know he was going out to the mall with some of his new friends, he asked me, "Can I buy a game?"

I said, "Let me see how much money is in there."

Seth added, "Nothing spendy like *Arkham Horror* – that's $60, nothing like that."

I told him how much money was in the account and said that sounded fine.

He came home with two games that cost $44. And while it's technically correct that he didn't spend $60, it did not seem to agree with the spirit of what we had discussed.

And he did this all the time. It was a bad situation. I hated being the one who said yes or no. It made me feel like a parent and not a lover – and he didn't even listen to me. Worst of both worlds.

Still, Seth was so great about Justin. Even when it felt crazy to say so, because it was too much, too soon, and I was clearly in the throes of NRE, I was able to tell Seth that I wanted to live with Justin.

"That's a big deal," Seth said. "But I'm on board for it as a long-term plan."

Seth always trusted my judgement. In a way, he had to because he never knew where I was coming from. He didn't understand me. Pretty much every interaction he had, he had to trust me. It had been that way our entire relationship but had grown even more obvious as we dated others.

The big talk with Rob and Michelle did little good. As Michelle's behavior continued to grow more controlling and strange, I avoided the house more and more. I started to carry my nightgown and birth control in my purse so I'd have the option to stay away any time I chose to.

Michelle grew more and more upset with me. One time when she and Rob went away for the weekend to work at another convention out of town, her first act upon returning home was to yell at me about dishes in the sink – typically normal roommate behavior, sure, but not when you consider that they were *her* dishes, a fact that she did not dispute. The fact that I hadn't picked them up for her (a habit of mine) signaled to her that I hadn't been home all weekend. And that made her livid.

I admit that avoiding her was probably not the best idea, but it was becoming the case that every time she did encounter me, she was hostile and unpleasant, further reinforcing my preference to stay in my room or go over to Justin's. As much as I loved Rob, this was getting a little hard to take.

It should not come as a great shock that my love story with Rob had no happy ending and that what I have learned from my initial foray into polyamory comes not from my successes, but my failures.

I felt really bad and conflicted in an ethical sense. Even if they were to become more reasonable and to ask for my time, I began to realize I didn't want to give it to them anymore. I was too hurt from how they'd acted. I'd seen sides of them that would be tough or impossible to un-see. And I wasn't convinced that I wouldn't continue to be the one to do most of the emotional labor.

They were so worried they were going to get replaced, and it kind of happened.

Not for the reasons they thought, but still I had moved on.

I had reached a point where I didn't even care if it was my own fault anymore that the relationships were ruined. I just wanted out.

I still cared for Rob a great deal, but pursuing a relationship with him in any serious terms was going to take a great deal more effort to fix and sustain (on both sides, really, what with his unemployment issues, the stress of being a father, and the strained dynamic with Michelle) than it was worth. I hadn't had sex with Rob since the night he'd suggested cooling things off sexually, though I was still living at their house for the time being and paying them rent. And I did care about Rob, though I was starting to think a relationship with him would have to be a secondary one, if anything, to endure. When Rob asked me to lunch to discuss the state of our relationship, I had the strong sense I was playing for a consolation prize. He was so different that day, so intense.

"What do you want from me?" I asked him. "What can I do to make you happy?"

"More time," Rob said. "I just want more time with you."

"I've been available," I said.

"I know."

"You want me to seek you out, you mean?" I asked.

"Yes."

"Okay," I said. "I can do that."

As we walked home from the Indian restaurant, Rob took my hand, not something he often did. I noticed then that his grip was lacking the warmth I'd feel from Seth or Justin – or even Tina. It felt like Rob was thousands of miles away, even as he touched me. Why hadn't I noticed this before? Had it not been there, or had I just missed it?

When we got home, Rob kissed me in the kitchen.

"Did you and Justin have sex?"

"Yes," I said.

"Well," he said, his voice dripping with sarcasm. "I hope it was everything you dreamed."

I ignored the bitter tone. "It was great."

Rob excused himself to go wait for a contractor who was going to do some work in the attic. After I had some time to absorb everything that had been said, I started to feel bad about the exchange in the kitchen. Rob was clearly hurt. I decided that the best way to make it up to him would be to honor the request he'd made at lunch, to seek him out to spend more time with him.

Once the contractor had left, I headed down to the basement to see Rob. I would be seeing Justin in the evening, but I had a good 3 or 4 hours to spare.

"You said you wanted more time," I said.

Rob's face lit up.

"Are you sure you were assaulted?"

I'm sure something went horribly wrong.

I remember thinking to myself "This is wrong. This is wrong. Why is he doing this?"

I remember saying no, rolling away, covering myself. His eyes growing reptilian, insistent, burning white hot, as if fueled by my resistance. How he tried to overcome my objections with circular logic, pressing the weight of his shoulder on top of me. Feeling trapped inside my body, watching a horrible movie play out, hoping he'd finally orgasm and stop trying to penetrate me.

We'd had a good lunch, a good talk, even a good cuddle. But this, this is not what I wanted.

It had started in a place where I was comfortable. He invited me to go lie down with him and talk. After a bit, he became aroused and asked if I minded if he masturbated. I didn't.

"You know what would really help me get off?" he said. "If I could see your body."

I got naked for him, continued to talk to him about where we were headed. It was absolutely fine up until that point.

But then it all took a downturn. His fingers slipped into the waistband of my panties before I moved his hand away. Then there was unwanted spanking, rapid fire cuing of my verbal triggers, imploring me to let him inside me. I finally was able to convince him that his wife wouldn't approve of what he was asking me to do.

"What a waste of cum," he said bitterly, before rolling over and finishing himself off.

I followed him numbly into the shower, kissed him in the steam, dazed from the experience, wanting everything to be okay, trying to convince myself that we were good, that what had just happened was A-OK, 100% fine.

It had deeply confused me. I hadn't wanted to have sex with him, but I cared for him still, and as he asked me over and over to have sex, there was a palpable desperation and vulnerability in his voice.

It was as though he felt like if he could fuck me that I would be his pet again, that everything would be okay.

"You're my pet, aren't you, Page?" he asked me.

"Of course, always," I said. But I felt like I was going to throw up. Everything felt terribly wrong. I couldn't stretch a smile far enough over it to cover it up, to make myself feel okay, as desperately as I wanted it to all make sense.

It was odd. Nothing quite cohered in my mind about it. He was both the monster with reptilian eyes and a lost little boy who just wanted me to love him again.

"What the hell was that?" Seth asked me as I climbed the stairs into the attic, the commotion downstairs having raised questions.

"I guess Rob and I are back together," I replied.

I felt terrible after it happened. Not violated, not victimized, but like I'd done something terribly wrong. After it happened, I posted a cheerful entry in my journal in a narrative voice quite unlike my own. Justin was instantly suspicious. Seth and I went over there to hang out with Justin and a few other friends, and after a few drinks and a bit of probing by Justin, who could tell something was up with me, the story spilled out.

Though I blamed myself for everything and apologized profusely for what had happened, my friends interrupted, told me that what had happened was totally unacceptable, that I had been sexually assaulted. Not only that, but Justin and Seth were categorically opposed to my returning to Rob and Michelle's house as they felt it was unsafe for Rob and me to be alone together. They felt so strongly, in fact, that both stated that they would break up with me if I returned to the house.

Our other friends started calling around and in the matter of a few hours managed to assemble an emergency moving crew to get Seth and I moved out the following day. We would live with Justin.

THE NEW HOUSE

I adapted to life at Justin's quickly. Seth, still wrestling with depression, struggled more with the change as though he still had his own room at Justin's, it was significantly less room than he'd had up in the attic at Rob and Michelle's. Not only that, but Seth blamed himself for what had happened between me and Rob. He knew how bad things had gotten, how much Michelle was harassing me. Seth felt he should have seen what was going on with Rob, stopped it somehow.

I was able to see a counselor for free, and I suggested to Seth that he come in and talk to someone, too, as he would be eligible as well. He was driving me to my appointments and sitting in the lobby. It would be a simple matter. Seth refused and when pressed further refused to provide an explanation.

When it came to getting help, I showed Seth the door and he refused to walk through it. Literally.

Moving in with Justin so soon after our relationship started (our physical relationship anyway, as we had been talking for months) should have sabotaged it, and I was warned by friends to that effect, but instead it flourished. Justin and I were extremely compatible with how we liked to live, our attitudes about work and money, our sleep schedules. Practically everything that came up, we found we meshed well, where Seth and I had never quite fallen in step with one another, even after all these years.

With all the upheaval I'd experienced with the bad break-up with Rob, I decided to put an indefinite hold on having new relationships:

NO VACANCY

I've had a rough week, the reasons for which will be something best addressed in future writings once I've had a chance to mentally and emotionally process a lot of the resultant inner turmoil resulting from the events which transpired. No matter. That is another essay indeed.

I am living day to day in the realm of the pragmatic. Through the course of a number of discussions with people, it became clear that I am running on much less than 100% in the wake of the total implosion of relationships I thought would endure anything and discovered would ultimately endure nothing, save sacrifices ones trusted to me advised me I never should make.

So I'm off the dating market. That is to say that while I'm maintaining my relationships with my current partners and am grateful every day that they exist and have found me a worthy object of their affections and attentions, I am absolutely closed to the idea of taking on new romantic or sexual partners right now.

Riding with Justin to pick up some sandwiches for dinner, I saw a couple strolling on the sidewalk and said, "There's something to be said for simplicity."

I don't know if this paradigm shift changes much. I still have more than one partner (two of which with whom I live), and they're both free and even encouraged to seek out other partners, so I wouldn't call myself "polyfidel-itous" or these relationships "closed," but my coquettish "maybe" has turned into a firm "absolutely not" for right now.

That said, I absolutely love meeting new people and am incredibly enthusiastic about making friends, setting down roots in my new home, and living life to its absolute fullest.

Seth had started seeing a few girls in Ohio, one in particular that he was spending a lot of time with and another that had invited him back to her place after one of our parties (though he'd refused at the time, not sure what to make of her offer) who had taken him around to get job applications and apply for work.

The next afternoon I found those same job applications in the trash.

Seth was sitting on the couch shooting zombies and seemed particularly stressed, so I came over and gave him a hug.

He pulled away from me. "Don't touch me. We don't have a relationship."

Not long after, Justin told me that he wasn't going to see other people. He just wanted me.

It was a mind fuck. With Justin's decision to date just me and Seth's pushing me away, I suddenly found myself essentially monogamous, without meaning to be.

Sure, I was married. And had been with Seth for 10 years, married for 6. But with recent developments, with his saying we didn't have a romantic relationship anymore, I felt monogamous. Seth and I were starting to feel more like friends. It didn't feel great, but we had been struggling for months. And I was happy that he had multiple girls interested in him.

Justin's desire to date only me, however, *that* came as a bigger surprise. I'd never really had that sort of sentiment come from a romantic partner. It left me a little overwhelmed but in a good way.

As unusual as it seemed, I reasoned out that Justin must be coming from a sincere place since we started out in an open relationship, and he consciously asked to close it.

Even so, the prospect that someone would *want* to be monogamous with me made head spin. With Seth, even though we were monogamous the first 8 years of our relationship, from day 1, he had wanted to have group sex, swinging, and later to open our relationship to full-fledged relationships, etc.

But Justin was different. And here I was. So I digested it. Let it sink in.

Seth's depression raged on.

I continued to go to counseling on my own, trying to make sense of the big changes that had transpired and adjust to life in Ohio.

And it was through that counseling that I discovered I wanted to end my relationship with Seth.

My therapist had given me a simple assignment: To figure out what I wanted – from our sessions together, from life, from anything. I had 2 weeks between appointments to consider.

One day it came to me: "I want experiences."

I realized that my unhappy marriage to Seth was a huge drain on me – financially, emotionally, and otherwise. We were extremely different people.

He was a homebody. I loved to travel.

He loved to buy things. I wanted security.

I was satisfied with very little. He would never have enough.

He walked slowly. I walked fast.

He wanted to relax. I liked to work hard.

He was certain he was right about most everything. I doubted my own opinions.

My sex drive could eat his for a snack.

I made a new friend every time I turned around. He took a while to warm up to people.

I was extremely physically affectionate. He liked his own space.

I liked to talk. He found most of what I said boring.

I loved romance. He found such things pointless.

I was kinky. He was vanilla.

"So I've been thinking, Seth," I said.

He looked up from his first-person shooter. "Just a minute, Page." A few minutes passed while he finished the round. "Okay," he said. "What's up?"

"Well, you know how you said you don't feel like we have a relationship anymore a few weeks ago?" I said.

"Yes," he replied. "And before you ask, I meant that."

I nodded.

"You're predictable," he said. "I know what you're gonna say before you say it half the time."

I hesitated, not knowing what to say.

"Was that it?" he asked. "Can I play my game in peace now?"

"No," I said.

"Jesus."

"That's not everything," I said.

"Well, c'mon, Page, spit it out."

"I've been talking to my therapist. And I think we should get separated," I said.

"Alright," Seth said. "Doesn't matter to me."

I was shocked by this. By how well he took it. So I kept on explaining, more for me, than for him. Justifying it to myself, pawing at some sense of closure. "Well, it's just that we've been talking about it for a while. Since this winter, really. None of the stuff that I wanted to happen has happened. And even *you* say there's not much of a relationship here anymore." I sigh. "So I think we should make it official."

"Page," he said. "You're going on and on. I get the fucking point. You know how I feel." He picked up the controller and began to play again.

"Good morning," the account rep said. "What can I do for you?"

"I'd like to open a checking account," I replied.

"Not a problem," she said. Opened a drawer. Slid a form to me across the desk.

For her it was a simple gesture. Just another normal day at the bank.

But for me? This was everything. A huge step towards independence.

I shook a bit as I filled out the paperwork. I didn't know how everything would turn out. What would happen. How Seth would react.

I feared he'd be hurt by the finality of the separation. Official matters often bring the reality of something home. But he had taken the news so well.

And besides, we'd agreed back in Maine that we'd separate out the finances once he got a job, regardless of whether or not we stayed together since being so financially interdependent was causing both of us so much stress.

And despite some false starts, like the applications in the trash, he had gotten that job.

"So when are you heading out tonight?" I asked Seth.

"Probably in about 20 minutes," Seth said. "Why?"

I sighed. It was best just to come out and say it. "I wanted to let you know I opened a checking account today," I said.

"Fuck you," Seth said.

I was stunned.

"You fucking go behind my back and do this!"

"I thought that—"

"No shut the fuck up. You're so selfish, Page," Seth said.

"But we're getting separated. Separate finances are part of that, and –"

"Fuck you!" Seth said, again. "That's what YOU'RE saying to ME, after all."

And it was at that point that Justin came into the living room. Since we all lived in the same house, Justin had been in a sort of hostage situation for weeks, watching the tension play out between Seth and me but unable to do anything about it. As Justin wrote in his journal:

> I hate watching her get hurt, and watching him
> continue to jab at her emotionally. He lashes
> out constantly, and can't even admit that he
> does it.

And as Seth continued to rant about what I had done, Justin finally couldn't stay out of it anymore. He cracked. Interjected.

"Oh, cry me a river," Justin said.

And like that, Seth began to back down. He got on his feet, gathered his stuff.

"We kind of need to talk about logistics," I said.

"No," Seth said. "Not now." Still on his feet. He said he was going to over to her house early, the new girl he was seeing. And then he was gone in our car. Less than a minute after Justin spoke.

Seth stayed incommunicado for days, hanging out at the girl's house, so I sent him an email, outlining the current state of the previously shared checking account, which was now his and still had money in it. And added:

> Also there are a myriad of logistics and pragmatic concerns about our possessions and living situation that still need to be hashed out and were not addressed the other day. I do not feel comfortable addressing those with you alone and would prefer to have mediation for that. I know you felt ganged up on the other day with Justin there. I also know that the girl you're seeing has mediation experience, and she might be able to facilitate advocating for you and being present during a discussion with us.
>
> Hope to see you soon. Much needs to be addressed.

It would seem that Seth reached out to Megan for emotional support because not long after that, she sent me this email:

> Ok, when you said you and Seth were in a slump, I didn't realize you meant you were going to give up on him all together. I almost feel like by telling me that he's got those other girls interested in him, you were trying to justify what you were about to do. That's not compersion, that's avoiding the issues that are coming between you.
>
> If you don't want to work it out, you don't have to work it out, but throwing away 6 years

of marriage is a very different thing from
whisking from one boyfriend to another. I know
it's none of my business, but I care about both
of you, and this seems like a really uncharacteristic thing for you to do. I've seen you
support each other for a very long time, and
you've always been completely dedicated to one
another, no matter what, even (especially) when
things were difficult.

I know you're going to do what you're going to
do, no one has ever been able to change your
mind once you've made it, but I really think
you would be wise to take a hard look at your
priorities and figure out why this is suddenly
ok. Is it because you've changed, or because
he has?

I didn't reply to this communication and unfriended her on Facebook. Not terribly mature, but Megan's timing was atrocious.

As news of our separation spread through social networks, others crawled out of the woodwork questioning the wisdom of the decision. Saying I was being hasty and that the separa- tion came out of nowhere.

I also was pretty offended by the way Megan had put every- thing, well meaning or not.

I wasn't doing very well. Initiating the separation was the hardest thing I'd ever done. I didn't have anywhere near the emotional resources to deal with reassuring her (or anyone else) that I knew what I was doing. Plus, the more I shared publicly about what had transpired between Seth and me, the more I jeopardized his ability to find social support. My emo- tions cried "amputate." And I did.

So of course Megan sent me this followup email:

> I'll keep this brief. We've been friends for 6
> years. I tried to let you know that I'm worried
> about you because you make the most life al-
> tering decision in all those years, seemingly
> out of the blue. You can't be bothered to give
> me an explanation, or even a "I'm fine, I know
> what I'm doing, please mind your own business"
> (which really would have been reasonable). In-
> stead you chose to unfriend me (and apparent-
> ly everyone else this side of the Appalachian
> trail) with absolutely no communication.
>
> Whether or not I agree with what you're doing
> is irrelevant, I'm sure you have your reasons,
> and you certainly have the right to do as you
> see fit. But to do it in this way? I feel like
> you've slapped me in the face. It was just
> plain rude.

And so I wrote a response back to her (edited because a lot of what I shared with her is in this book):

> A lot of the behaviors and financial problems
> that have caused problems between us have been
> going on for years. I never told anyone because
> I wanted things to get better, and I didn't
> feel like it was anyone's business, really. Why
> burden my friends with the stress within my
> marriage? …I'm sorry if it hurt you when I cut
> off communication in that way. Honestly, a lot
> of times when people get divorced, friends feel
> a need to side with one party or another, and
> for a variety of reasons, I'd much rather Seth
> have the love and support from all of you back
> home than if I have it. There are many reasons.
>
> Seth has always said that he has trouble mak-
> ing new friends, and he *really* needs friends

right now as it's a rough time for him (understandably), and there's the geographic distance
complicating everything – so it seemed preferable to cut off communication, make you all
upset with me, so that I could be "the bad guy"
so that you could support Seth 100% without
worrying about the shades of gray, the nuanc-
es, the fault that he and I both share for this
relationship ending.

Also I want Seth to have a clean break, to help
get over me, and mutual friends, social net-
working, etc, all have the potential to rip
up wounds anew as he reads the minutiae of my
life or it filters in through friends who have
done the same. We are also going to be divorcing so legally it's a safe course for Seth and
I to be as separate as possible and not talk to
one another.

This is all added to the fact that this is the
hardest thing I've ever had to do. It is much
harder breaking up than remaining married, and
I wouldn't be doing this unless I absolutely
felt like it was the best thing for us both. My
emotional and financial support has enabled Seth
to have no motivation to grow and learn and explore himself. I don't think I'm good for him.

I still love Seth, deeply. I don't think he's a
bad person any more than I'm a bad person. The
combination of the two of us is the trouble.

It is what it is. I don't expect you to agree
with what I'm doing or to even understand (as
it's taken me a long time to personally accept
it's what needs to be done – even being in the
center of things), but it is what it is.

Seth and I met the following week and divided up our possessions. Seth was accompanied by two girls he was dating, and
I had Justin present.A few weeks after I opened that separate
checking account, Seth moved back to Maine to live with
his parents. I filed for divorce 3 months later as state laws
required I be a resident of Ohio for 6 months prior to filing.
Another 6 months after that, we were divorced.

POLY SIGNPOST #10: HOMING PIGEON PRIMARY

❝ You can't lose a homing pigeon. If your homing pigeon doesn't come back, then what you've lost is a pigeon."

–Sara Pascoe, writer and stand-up comic

"So I know you've been asking for an open relationship for an awfully long time," I said to Seth.

"I have," he replied. "And it's okay because I've given up on it. I know it's never going to happen."

"Well, that's the thing," I said.

He cocked his head.

"The reason I said no is because I was sure it wouldn't work."

He nodded. "And you've never been one to change your mind."

"Well, not without a good reason," I said. "But I see Megan and Pete, and… well, they're making polyamory work." Friends of ours. Mainstream. Like Barbie had married GI Joe. Two kids. Good jobs. Nothing like the hot messes of my youth – when I swung from bedpost to bedpost, chasing the next high.

"They are," Seth said, looking excited, liking where this was going.

"But it's more than that," I said. "I've decided that I can accept our breaking up."

Seth's expression instantly changed. "Page, what the fuck? Don't say things like that."

"I'm sure it sounds terrible, but it makes sense to me," I said. "I realized that's what was making me afraid."

"Breaking up? Well, if you're afraid of it, then why are you even thinking about it?"

"Because if I can accept it, I won't be afraid of it anymore," I said.

"That doesn't make any sense," Seth replied. "But I'm glad you're open to poly."

"I am," I said. "It occurred to me that the reason I worry about losing you is because what we have means everything to me. But you know, if we're really meant to be together, if it's as good as I think it is? Nothing will be able to break us up."

He smiled. "Nothing will."

"And, if it does? It'll mean I was wrong about us. And isn't it better to find that out now than another 10 years down the road?"

"I still don't like that line of reasoning. But you've always been weird. Guess I'll take the 'yes' and roll with it," he said.

Finding a Homing Pigeon

It's been 8 years since Seth and I agreed to open our marriage.

We are divorced. Live in separate states.

We are both happy — happier than we were together.

We write to each other on occasion. And laugh now that we were ever primaries.

I'm amazed sometimes we lasted as long as we did, I wrote.

Me, too, Seth wrote back. *Fear can go a long ways. I'm in an infinitely better place now.*

I'm so glad to hear it. Me, too.

If you had told me 8 years ago that I would live halfway across the country married to another man, I don't know that I would have believed it. I certainly wouldn't have been able to predict the path I took here.

But I believe now, more than ever, that things that are meant to last are really, really hard to fuck up. And that there are relationships that are really, really easy to fuck up and will end, without emotional martyrdom from everyone involved. The kind that, incontrovertibly, should end.

And then there are many, like my marriage to Seth, that are somewhere in between. And it's hard to tell which side it's closer to, will never end versus should end.

Which begs the question: How are we supposed to know the difference?

Simple. You let the pigeon go. If it flies away and never comes back, you lost a bird.

If they come back, well, you know you really have something. A homing pigeon primary. Someone who always comes back to you of their own volition, no matter what temporarily separates you.

Not Restricting Their Choices, Even When They Lead Away From You

It's taken me all these years to understand the popular saying (attributed to educator Jess Lair): "If you want something very, very badly, let it go free. If it comes back to you, it's yours forever. If it doesn't, it was never yours to begin with."

I used to grumble and get really hung up on the idea of setting someone free. What that could mean. It didn't sound loving or fair at all. I envisioned abandonment. A test where you leave the room and see if they come check on you.

But I've grown to realize that letting someone be free isn't about abandoning them. Walking away. Hiding.

It's about not restricting the choices in their life. Even when those choices lead away from you.

It's about finding the homing pigeon hidden among other birds.

PRESSING PAUSE

Justin and I went on to marry. It was a small celebration at our house, surrounded by our families. And kinkster friends.

I wrote the ceremony. My best friend officiated.

It was important to us to celebrate our bond without making that bond contingent upon monogamy. We suspected we might one day reopen and a number of our friends (and wedding guests) were themselves polyamorous.

The vows were carefully worded to signal commitment without exclusiveness.

Prior to the ceremony, Justin and I had cut a variety of ribbons to convenient tying length. One by one, our friends came forward and tied our hands together. It was a beautiful way for people in our life to show their support for our relationship, and the visual effect was quite pretty.

It was a take on pagan handfasting, but instead of just one connection, it emphasized that we had many, that we were joined together by all the people (and things) that we held in common.

Plus, being tied together is extra meaningful to kinksters.

Justin and I took a hiatus from establishing new connections, preferring to work on self-improvement. I went back to school and started a new career. We paid a lot of bills.

And as for practicing polyamory again? Having multiple partners? We agreed that all it would take is one conversation to reopen.

Follow the continuing journey

Join us on the web at
https://poly.land

ABOUT THE AUTHOR

Page Turner is Godzilla in stilettos. She is a clever mix of 5-year-old and viking who doesn't mind if you round her up to lesbian. She loves statistics, unagi rolls, and the way the air smells after it rains.

Her alter-ego is an award-winning poet and playwright who works as a relationship coach in the poly and kink communities. No matter what she's doing, she draws upon her professional background in psychological research as well as her unapologetically random sense of humor.

Prior to her days as a coach, she worked as a jazz musician, editor, newspaper reporter, medical transcriptionist, and organizational development consultant. She lives in the Cleveland suburbs with her husband Justin, her two cats Ratface and Bela, and her two birds Buddy and Galileo.